The hunt for the
60's RIPPER

ROBIN JAROSSI

Published by Mirror Books,
an imprint of Trinity Mirror plc,
1 Canada Square,
London E14 5AP, England

www.mirrorbooks.com
twitter.com/themirrorbooks

Executive Editor: Jo Sollis

ISBN 978-1-907324-65-9

First paperback edition

Printed and bound in Great Britain
by CPI Group (UK) Ltd, Croydon, CR0 4YY

Every effort has been made to fulfil requirements with regard to
reproducing copyright material. The author and publisher will be
glad to rectify any omissions at the earliest opportunity.

Front cover image: Trevillion

CONTENTS

For Heidi, Joey, Luca and Doris –
one of the women, written about in these
pages, who experienced the stigma of single
motherhood in the 1960s, in order to raise me

Introduction

In February 1965 John du Rose was desperate for a holiday. Despite sunny foreign breaks becoming increasingly popular in the post-war years, holidays were still modest affairs for many people – even one of Scotland Yard's Big Five detectives. So, on 16 February, Detective Chief Superintendent du Rose and his wife, Constance, were eagerly looking forward to a much-needed bungalow break in St Mary's Bay, Kent.

Du Rose was the top man in the Criminal Investigation Department at the Yard, overseeing murder probes along with inquiries into other criminal activities involving forgery, drugs, industrial spying and illegal immigrants. He had spent an exhausting year looking into the activities of a violent Metropolitan Police detective sergeant called Harold 'Tanky' Challenor, a former SAS soldier who had won the Military Medal, but whose police career included planting evidence and punching suspects. Du Rose had been tasked with conducting a thorough investigation of the sergeant and his team. By the time Challenor was sent to a psychiatric hospital to be treated for paranoid schizophrenia and his aides imprisoned, du Rose was badly in need of some time off.

However, the cherished holiday was to be snatched away

from him before it had even started. During the drive down to Kent, he and Constance heard a BBC news report on their car radio. 'Another nude woman was found dead in the alleyway close to the Central Line Tube at Acton this morning…' Years later, in his autobiography, du Rose still seemed disgruntled by his recall. 'I was furious because my holiday was long overdue and my wife, particularly, had been looking forward to a break. But I had no choice. I returned to London – and started work during the early hours of the morning.'

Bridget 'Bridie' O'Hara, aged 27, had been discovered by the side of a storage shed on the Heron Trading Estate near Westfields Road, Acton, that very day. She was the sixth – possibly seventh – young woman to become a victim of the Nude Killer.

The previous 12 months had seen an unprecedented murder spree in west London that sent shivers of dread through the capital's streetwalkers and made international headlines. Someone, possibly the driver of a grey Hillman Husky van, had been picking up prostitutes in the street, killing them and leaving their unclothed bodies either in the Thames or at various public locations. O'Hara's death suggested the campaign of murder would now plague 1965 as well.

No one had witnessed the kerb-crawling stalker actually picking up one of his victims, and so far he had been exceedingly cunning in leaving virtually no evidence behind.

He was methodical in targeting a certain type of woman. All of the victims were diminutive, averaging around 5 feet 2 inches in height. They were aged between 21 and 30 years old and had moved to London from other parts of the UK and Eire. They were heavy drinkers, often passing their evenings in a pub until closing time before hitting the streets. Drugs were also frequently part of their lives, particularly pep pills, or amphetamines, stimulants that would have fuelled nights out with their punters. They worked the Bayswater, Notting Hill and Shepherd's Bush areas, and the police believed their clients were mostly car-driving professionals, 'either company directors or wealthy businessmen'. The killer seemed to avoid operating at the weekends, the victims apparently being picked up either on weekdays or in the early hours of Saturday mornings at the latest.

Strangely, another factor linking them was that they were all missing several teeth. The last four victims – Helen Barthelemy, Mary Fleming, Frances Brown (also known as Margaret McGowan) and Bridie O'Hara – had been asphyxiated. The first two killed in 1964, Hannah Tailford and Irene Lockwood, were thought to have drowned in the Thames, but detectives later speculated that they too might have been asphyxiated, owing to slight bruising on their faces similar to those on the following four bodies.

Detectives also saw similarities between these killings and Elizabeth Figg, who in 1959 was discovered partially clothed and lying by a tree at a secluded Thames bankside spot in Dukes Meadows, Chiswick. At the post-mortem she was found to have been strangled. Senior officers accepted that, despite a five-year gap between her murder and the six that followed in 1964–65, she might still have encountered the same killer.

The women showed no signs of sexual violence, but detectives were considering a bizarre theory that they may have been victims of murder by oral masturbation, or asphyxiated while giving oral sex.

The lurid elements of this rapacious reign of murder certainly fired up the press. Addicted to a snappy headline, they called the mystery killer Jack the Stripper, referring of course to the Whitechapel serial killer who, 77 years before, had brutally murdered five or possibly six women, and was never identified.

'Giant hunt for maniac sex killer' was the *Daily Mirror*'s front-page splash on Saturday, 25 April 1964, following the discovery of 'former striptease girl' Helen Barthelemy in Brentford. 'Last night,' the story read, 'top Scotland Yard detectives leading the hunt were looking for a man with a lust to kill – a mass murderer like John Christie, who was hanged in 1953.'

Later that month the *Mirror* reported that Scotland Yard had launched its 'biggest ever probe into London's world of vice', believing that criminal bosses running a prostitution ring might be behind the murders.

The case made headlines in the United States, too. On 18 February 1965, as an air of crisis was engulfing the investigation, the *Chicago Tribune* said London was being 'combed for a man with a round face'. The article also reported a police source. 'The man may be a henpecked husband taking vicarious revenge, or a morality maniac.' Such attitudes were not only hopelessly sexist but also revealed how little understanding there was of psychopaths and serial killers, among the police and the public.

Time magazine was more interested in the female officers who had been disguised as street prostitutes to gather information on kerb-crawlers. It reported on 8 May 1964 that, 'In the sleazy lower reaches of Soho and Notting Hill, scores of rouged recruits have joined London's army of prostitutes. In hip-tight skirts and needle heels, [they] wiggle from drinking club to strip joint brazenly soliciting customers.' The report managed to trivialise what was a delicate and sometimes hazardous attempt to unmask a highly dangerous predator.

The reality flashed up by these theories about vice rings, hen-pecked husbands and a man with a round face, however, was that Scotland Yard's enormous investigation involving hundreds of officers was in trouble. Despite all the hours and hard work that had gone into gathering data and interviewing witnesses, detectives had still not uncovered one truly compelling suspect after six murders in 12 months. It was time to inject a new perspective into the operation.

So John du Rose may have been disappointed but he was not surprised when, five hours after arriving at his bungalow in Kent, a uniformed sergeant from Dymchurch police station knocked on his door. 'Would you please ring the Yard, sir?' Du Rose could no doubt guess what was coming. The assistant commissioner was giving him the job of taking over murder HQ at Shepherd's Bush and leading the investigation.

Up to this point, the individual murders had been investigated by leading divisional detectives before being coordinated from Shepherd's Bush police station. Playing a leading role in the inquiry at the time were seasoned detective superintendents Maurice Osborn, Bill Marchant and Bill Baldock.

However, the investigation had stalled. Du Rose was a detective with a big reputation and a public profile. He had been nicknamed Four-Day Johnny by a reporter for the speed with which he solved cases. If ever one needed a fast resolution it was this case, before the death toll became even more horrific.

Cheroot-puffing du Rose had notched up major successes, as he would later recount in his 1971 autobiography *Murder Was My Business*. He had featured in the capture of serial killer John George Haigh, played a part in the break-up of the

Messina prostitution network, and went on to become part of the team that brought down the sixties' most notorious London gangs – the Richardsons and the Krays.

London's *Evening News* greeted his appointment to the Nude Murders case with the headline, 'The trap to catch a killer' on 17 February 1965, while a couple of days later the *Daily Mirror* was more bullish, 'Scotland Yard's top murder detective was certain last night that London's phantom sex killer will soon be hunted down. Detective Chief Superintendent John du Rose – who broke his holiday to lead the hunt – expects the final link in the puzzle to fall into place in the next 24 hours.'

This referred to a four-hour search of a west London house by du Rose and four senior detectives the day before. On returning to Shepherd's Bush they were followed by detectives carrying bundles of women's clothing.

'Detectives were convinced that the killer – a pervert – is building up a "Black Museum" of his victims' clothes and jewellery, somewhere in the murder area,' the front-page lead story revealed. However, the dingy flat in Hammersmith, again suspected to be connected to a vice ring, proved to be another dead end.

While du Rose was furious at having his holiday ruined, 'Thank heavens we're away at last,' he had said to Constance, before his recall – there was no doubt that he threw himself into getting to grips with the enormous case file confronting him. He started work in the early morning and spent 52 hours familiarising himself with the notes and scene-of-crime photos for Bridie O'Hara's case and those of the other victims.

Writing in 1971 about the case, du Rose said, 'The story of the man who became known as Jack the Stripper is certain to have as prominent a place in the annals of crime as that of Jack the Ripper or the Boston Strangler.'

Of the killer he concluded, 'One thing is certain, the girls died extremely quickly and another certainty is that some time or other they had all suffered from venereal disease. It would have been easy to assume that the man we were hunting was a man carrying out a personal vendetta against prostitutes because he had caught the disease. That was never my view. Early in the inquiry I became convinced that the killer was a man in his forties with extremely strong sexual urges which, perhaps because of his age, were not easily satisfied normally. It was probably this physical difficulty that took him away from his wife and into the twilight world of the prostitutes. He knew these women set no limits to the sexual acts in which they would allow their clients to indulge.'

Despite his four-day legend, du Rose found it was taking a long while to see if his theories were correct. Progress in the inquiry was painstakingly slow and du Rose was soon keenly aware of its unique problems.

There was a huge amount of data to contend with in those pre-computerised days, during what had become the biggest police manhunt in British criminal history. Night observations were conducted from points around a 24-square-mile area to spot suspicious drivers, particularly kerb-crawlers. Hundreds of these men had to be questioned, often delicately in the presence of their wives. House-to-house inquiries across 648 streets meant that approximately 120,000 people were seen. Dust samples from 500 storage facilities were taken and tested. More than 7,000 current and past employees on the Heron Trading Estate were also interviewed. This is to say nothing of the problems of trying to extract reliable information from a night-time sex trade in which many participants were either secretive, drunk or on drugs.

In addition, this was an era when the understanding of

psychopaths and serial killers was not as advanced or well studied as it has become in the decades since. Hence, the focus at the time on perverts, sugar daddies and vice kings. The term 'serial killer' was not current in the 1960s and the explosion of scientific research into psychopathic personalities only came later. Everyone had heard of Jack the Ripper or the more recent case of Rillington Place killer John Christie, but there were few insights into what compelled such 'monsters' to hunt other humans.

Meanwhile, for du Rose in the spring of 1965, the clock was ticking. Around the time a new murder seemed overdue (assuming a roughly three-month interval between murders after Bridie O'Hara), du Rose told the *Daily Express*, 'There are hundreds of police involved in this inquiry… more than any inquiry ever before. We'll get him. Oh yes. We'll get him. You can be sure of that.'

They never did. The killer got away, and could still be alive today.

How strange and sobering that this extraordinary case is now largely forgotten. TV dramas and books still appear about the likes of John Christie, Peter Sutcliffe and Peter Manuel. Whereas, apart from a trickle of books (some very poor) and the odd newspaper feature in the 1970s, the Nude Murders started to recede from public consciousness as the investigation was wound down in January 1966.

Part of the explanation for this is clearly that no killer was unmasked, so there is no bogeyman to appal us and grab our attention. It is a sad fact that killers usually emerge as the star of their crimes along, to a lesser extent, with the police officers who hunt them. The victims are generally far down the cast list.

Introduction

The Nude Murders made headlines galore at the time, with mentions of good-time girls, stripteasers, vice rings and prostitutes found 'naked and strangled'. But there was a detachment in the coverage. It was a titillating glimpse into a sordid and alien world for many readers. You need to look hard at the reports to find compassion expressed for the women whose lives had been taken. But read closely and you will locate the odd mention that a victim had children, a partner or was married. Away from the public glare, they were mourned and missed.

Mainstream society's desire to keep a cool distance between itself and heartfelt concern for the victims is seen frequently during this investigation. While I do use the terms prostitute and prostitution in this historical narrative, I am aware of the stigma attached to these terms and do not want to denigrate or judge the victims. A term such as sex worker is more common these days, but I have stuck with prostitute because it is the term used in this context.

The general indifference to the victims is probably down to the fact that they were engaged in a lifestyle that was disapproved of, and activities such as soliciting were illegal. The Street Offences Act 1959 was a recent attempt to clear soliciting prostitutes from the pavements by introducing a scale of rising penalties, with imprisonment as the punishment for habitual offenders. The Wolfenden report of 1957 outlined the strategy to remove public soliciting and this aspect of it was popular. A *Daily Mirror* poll found that thousands of readers overwhelmingly approved of its proposal to clear prostitutes from the streets (the proposal to decriminalise homosexuality was not so well received). Ironically, while the Act did initially remove many soliciting prostitutes, the women soon congregated instead at off-street venues – bars, clubs, even launderettes – that were harder to police. Another unseen result was the rise in kerb-crawling, which became the method of entrapment used by the Nude Killer.

This book will include the victims' stories alongside a look at the investigation itself. The Nude Murders inquiry was unprecedented in scope. When John du Rose became involved, he said he wanted to flood the whole of the West End with police officers and he was given the resources to do just that. But the killer evaded the huge hunt, and there were tensions within the senior ranks when du Rose arrived to take over from the men previously in charge. While the Met undoubtedly threw everything it could at catching the murderer, it was operating within the wisdom and techniques of the time. Today, detectives would take a different approach to narrowing the search for a serial criminal. In the following pages, questions will be asked: How would modern officers and profilers approach such a case today? How close did du Rose's squad come to exposing the killer? What kind of man was he and how did he manage to elude and frustrate Scotland Yard's finest detectives?

The Nude Murders crossed paths with notorious scandals and infamous figures, from the Profumo affair to the Kray twins. The following chapters expose the flip-side of London in the Swinging Sixties. The dazzling, daring fashions and singing sensations that gave the capital its much-admired vibrancy at the time, co-existed with slum housing, racial tensions, Second World War veterans sleeping along Bayswater Road and the prevalence of a street prostitution trade that is hard to picture today.

And what of John du Rose? His involvement with the Nude Murders continued with his claim in 1971 that, despite there being no arrest, he had actually known all along who committed the murders. In *Murder Was My Business* he wrote, 'I know the identity of Jack the Stripper – but he cheated me of an arrest by committing suicide.' This was a striking claim, but was it true? Or was du Rose covering for a major failure on his record by pinning the crime on a dead man?

Finally, the large gallery of potential suspects who were looked at by the police at the time and by several authors since will be reviewed. Detectives followed up a huge number of tips and leads on various 'kinky sex hounds', professionals, foreigners, violent offenders and loners. Into the void of speculation, authors have since pitched a celebrity boxer and a convicted child killer as potential culprits.

However, despite du Rose's claim to know the killer's identity, there was a strong suspicion in the murder squad in 1965 that someone with a police background was behind the killings. And though they could never prove it against the man they suspected, it remains the most intriguing, and chilling, possibility to this day.

PART 1

THE VICTIMS

Chapter 1

Thameside – The Killings Begin

Dukes Meadows is on the north-side bend of the Thames at Chiswick. It is something of a hidden London jewel, not that well known outside its immediate locality. A beautiful stretch of dense meadowland with views across the water, today it is occupied by sports clubs, playing fields and tracks used by cyclists and joggers. It was only in 1923 that the local council bought the area from the Duke of Devonshire, and turned it over to public use.

Always popular with courting couples in the evenings, its seclusion eventually attracted a new clientele – west London prostitutes who needed somewhere discreet to take their kerb-crawling customers. Today's detectives will tell you that the vice trade is all about a speedy turnaround, but in the 1950s time was taken to drive to a quiet spot for the transaction. The drive from, say, Bayswater to Dukes Meadows is a distance of 6 miles, which would take up to 30 minutes. A lift back to the West End for the woman was usually part of the deal.

June 1959 was a sunny, dry month. Liberace was playing twice nightly at the Chiswick Empire, and after his final performance the old place was to be demolished and replaced by offices. Horseracing fans were flocking out of town for Royal Ascot – 22 miles further west – and Dukes Meadows was a pleasant and popular spot during the hot days and evenings. In fact, Pathé news would describe the weather that greeted Royal Ascot on 16 June as 'a blaze of perfect glory'. The next day the papers would also note that the young queen and Prince Philip had discarded the traditional coach-and-four ride and opted for a motorcade. However, the front-page headlines in the tabloids would puncture such summer froth with more chilling news.

Police car Foxtrot 4, based at Chiswick police station, had been patrolling the nearby main roads, watching the traffic from Ascot gradually dwindle as racegoers returned to town in the early hours of 17 June. At around 4.30am they left the main roads to check out the riverside between Barnes and Chiswick bridges. PC Mills was behind the wheel and PC Sparke and acting team sergeant Baker were with him.

It was the officers' second scouting of the area that morning, the first having been at 12.45am. This time, however, Mills spotted something in the early daylight – a woman's bare legs protruding from behind a willow tree. She was facing the river with her back to Dukes Meadows. A drunk? A vagrant?

When they got out of their car for a closer look, the police officers found she was neither. The woman's eyes and mouth were open, but she was frozen in that expression. Her blue and white striped dress was torn and undone, her breasts exposed. She had scratches on her throat. Mills said later, 'She was quite cold and obviously dead.' She wore no make-up or jewellery and had no shoes. The officers could find no handbag or other belongings. PC Sparke radioed the duty officer.

An Inspector Edwards arrived to view the body for himself. Then the Criminal Investigation Department team was called in; the area between Chiswick and Barnes bridges was closed and a tarpaulin shelter was put up around the body.

At 7.30am Dr Donald Teare arrived at the scene. He was one of the three senior pathologists who dealt with all suspicious deaths in the London area. Among the high-profile investigations he had dealt with previously were the murders in 1949 of Beryl Evans and her daughter, Geraldine, at 10 Rillington Place, Notting Hill, home of serial killer John Christie (whose name will haunt this story). Teare would go on to perform the autopsies on Jimi Hendrix (1970) and Bruce Lee (1973), before retiring in 1975. On making a preliminary examination of the body by the tree, Dr Teare noted the markings on her throat and the beginnings of rigor mortis in her arms and legs. He would later estimate that she had died between midnight and 2am.

Modern-day investigating officers would be horrified to learn that only three photographs were taken of the body at the scene and none were taken at the mortuary. There was also some confusion over whether the body had been moved. The patrol car officers were said to have found her lying on the grass beneath the willow tree, but Detective Constable Arthur Phillips said that when he arrived she was sitting against the tree, facing The Ship pub on the opposite bank of the river. If the crime scene had been disturbed it is not clear who might have done it, though Dr Teare would have probably been the only person with the authority to do so.

The body was taken to Acton mortuary at 9.45am, where Dr Teare performed the post-mortem. She was found to be 5 feet 5 inches, weighing 8½ stone. She had dirty feet and abrasions on her legs and throat. Several teeth were missing. The woman may have suffered a miscarriage at some point in her life. Dr Teare noted that blood on her anus may 'have been caused by a fingernail'. She had recently had sexual intercourse. The pathologist settled on manual strangulation as the cause of death, no later than 2am.

So, who was she? Her fingerprints were taken but she was not on police records. An alert was put out to all stations:

Dead body of woman found on bank of Thames at Chiswick at 5am today, 17.6.59. Age about 25, height 5 feet 2 inches [they got that wrong], slim build, hair dark brown, teeth discoloured, tooth on left upper jaw recently extracted, two teeth on right side upper jaw missing. Small circular scar below knees on each leg. Faint scar on right knee... Please have missing persons register searched to identify.

That afternoon at the mortuary a couple of detectives had the tricky job of taking a fourth photo of the victim. To keep her eyes open they used matchstick pieces to prise her eyelids apart. The picture was given to the press in an appeal for information about her.

In the meantime, the murder squad looked into a report from the landlord of The Ship pub across the river. He and his wife reported seeing a car's lights going out on Dukes Meadows at the murder scene. The car had come down Great Chertsey Road at Chiswick Bridge, stopping at the foreshore car park. The car lights went off – then there was a piercing scream that stopped abruptly. 'Choked-off' was the witnesses' description. This was around midnight. The area was searched by uniformed officers, with help from council employees and the River Police, including the river bed, nearby tennis courts, allotments and playing fields. Nothing was found that could help the investigation. Courting couples at Dukes Meadows were interviewed the following evening, but all said they had not been there the previous night. It later turned out that the scream could not have come from the victim.

The photograph of the woman was in the papers on 18 June. It was the lead in *The Star*. 'Murdered girl: Yard issue picture' was the headline, with the subheading, 'Do you know this Miss X?'

Someone did. Elsie King and her husband, George, turned up at Chiswick police station two days after the body was found. It was late at night, but they were taken to Acton mortuary, arriving around midnight. There, Elsie identified her daughter, Elizabeth, with whom she had had a distant, unloving relationship.

Elizabeth Figg was 21 years old. She had not been working long as a prostitute and had no police record.

Born on 24 March 1938, she had a childhood that saw her parents' marriage break up and various upheavals in her home life. Her father, James Figg, had been a commercial traveller, but during his wartime RAF service his wife, Elsie, had an affair and James divorced her. Elizabeth and her sister, Patricia, were left with James's mother in Bebington, Cheshire, while James was posted to Canada. After the war, he married Florence and took Elizabeth and Patricia to live with him in Rhyl, North Wales. In 1950, James left his wife and took his daughters to live with another woman, only to return six weeks later. By 1953, the household was in near chaos, with the family being evicted from their home and James receiving a conviction for assaulting a county court bailiff. As if that were not enough for Elizabeth, her father had also developed a strong dislike for her. Her stepmother, Florence, is quoted in David Seabrook's 2006 book on the case, *Jack of Jumps*, as saying James called Elizabeth a 'filthy slut, just like her mother'. His ex-wife's infidelity apparently still riled James, and he seems to have taken some of this out on Elizabeth. Father and daughter grew to detest each other, but she stood up to him. He frequently told her to leave home.

Eventually, she did - and in 1954 began an itinerant life, getting by in poorly paid jobs, first stopping in Colwyn Bay to work in a hotel. In August 1955 she traced her mother Elsie to a south London address. Elsie was now Elsie King, having married a George King. Elizabeth had not seen her in 11 years. She stayed with Elsie for around four months, getting a job in a grocery shop. But this period of apparent stability did not last. Soon mother and daughter were arguing, and once again Elizabeth was sent packing.

She spent a little more time with her stepmother Florence, did another stint of hotel work and fell in and out of various relationships with men. In 1956 she was back in the capital, scraping by in casual jobs and dodging rent-seeking landlords. The year 1958, however, was relatively settled for Elizabeth, when she lived rent-free by babysitting for a woman in Kennington. But March 1959 saw a major change for her. On the Tube she met Fenwick 'Baby' Ward, who was from Trinidad and Tobago. The nickname might have been ironic, because 'Baby' weighed 15 stone and was an accomplished heavyweight boxer, though he had lost his last pro-fight in February. Elizabeth wrote to Florence in March seeking approval for the new man in her life, who was 'coloured', a 'nice chap, clean and all that', and revealing that her friends had been talking about her. This was a little more than a decade since the first Caribbean migrants arrived on the *Empire Windrush;* racial prejudice was raw thanks to housing shortages and the failure of the authorities to facilitate any kind of integration for the new arrivals. The first Race Relations Act banning some forms of discrimination was only passed in 1965, following vicious race riots in Notting Hill in 1958 and the stabbing to death of Antiguan Kelso Cochrane the following year. Commonwealth migrants also experienced prejudice when seeking employment or a place to live. Elizabeth's relationship with a Trinidadian was a bold one in this climate, which makes her writing for Florence's blessing understandable. It seems she wanted an escape from babysitting six nights a week and hoped Ward was it. He arranged for her to move into her last flat, at 97 Duncombe Road, Archway. The dynamic of their relationship, however, is impossible to know from today's vantage point, and somehow around this time Elizabeth ended up working as a prostitute.

She covered the busy kerb-crawling streets of Bayswater and Holland Park, where she became friends with Pauline Mills, a 19-year-old streetwalker who already had a formidable record of 33 convictions for soliciting. Elizabeth found the Irish navvy punters she encountered in Finsbury Park – many of whom were working on the new Victoria Line – to be drunk and abusive. So she and Pauline, known as 'Big Pauline', often worked the Harringay area before midnight and Holland Park later on. The pair never took punters home to Duncombe Road, which they ended up sharing; they always had sex in their clients' cars.

On the last night of her life, Elizabeth went to see a seamstress in Durley Road, Stoke Newington, at around 9.30pm. She was wearing a blue and white striped dress that Ward gave her. She had no make-up, stockings or jewellery on, and was wearing black stilettos. At 11.45pm she met a man cruising in his Morris Ten along Endymion Road, Finsbury Park. He was a 34-year-old self-employed builder called Ernest

Patrick Forrest. She directed him to drive to a quiet spot by some garages on Mount View Road, Hornsey. They had sex on the back seat for 30 shillings, about £30 in today's value.

Forrest then drove Elizabeth to Holland Park. He wanted to spend the night with her but she told him she had to be in west London at 2am, giving no reason. When she said she was getting a cab there he offered her a lift, and they arranged to meet in Holland Park later and she would spend the night with him for £4 (£85 today). He dropped her at Holland Park Tube at 1.10am – so it could not have been her screaming at midnight on Dukes Meadows. She said she would be a couple of hours and would meet him at the Tube station. Elizabeth was never seen again and was probably dead within the hour.

Her companion drove around the West End, returning to Holland Park Avenue at around 3.10am. He said, 'She was not there and I walked out to the junction of Lansdowne Road and Holland Park to see if I could see her and I could not.' Two beat officers, PC Nash and PC Dalton, approached him at 3.20am and asked what he was doing. He said he was having a smoke. They told him to finish it and move on. He waited for Elizabeth until 3.45am and then drove home.

Forrest had an odd sense of morality. He turned himself in three days after Elizabeth was found, following a police appeal. He was Catholic, he told the police, and had con-sulted his priest. At the same time, he had a steady girlfriend whom he would visit in the evenings, before going kerb-crawl-ing. But his story checked out and he made his Morris Ten and rented room in Hackney available for examination, with nothing incriminating being found. It was hard to confirm his whereabouts between 1am and 2am, when Elizabeth must have met her attacker, but detectives found nothing to con-nect him to the crime.

During the summer of 1959, the police made a huge effort to gain traction with the investigation. Finsbury Park, Endymion Road, Mount View Road, Holland Park Avenue – they made house-to-house inquiries, they interviewed cab drivers and prostitutes, and checked on cars stolen or drivers behaving suspiciously. They also worked tirelessly to trace Elizabeth's missing property – her shoes, underwear and bag. Descriptions of these items were sent to every police force in Britain, but nothing was found.

The murder was a puzzling one. There was little doubt that Elizabeth had been driven to Dukes Meadows. Was she dead on arrival? There was no way of knowing. Detective Superintendent James Mitchell told the inquest at Ealing Coroner's Court on 13 August, 'It could have been that she kicked off her shoes, that she removed her own garments, and that her clothing and handbag were in the back of the car and remained in the car after the body was taken to where it was found.' Her missing underwear implied that she had been partially re-dressed, her stripy dress being ripped at some point. There seemed to be no clear motive (robbery seemed unlikely). And once Ernest Forrest was discounted, there were no suspects.

'Baby' Ward showed a copy of *The Star* to Pauline Mills back at Duncombe Road. She said she had to go to the police, and Ward told her not to mention that he had been poncing off Elizabeth. He said, 'I never murdered her. You know that, don't you? But a coloured man has got no chance in this country.' He need not have worried because he was never treated as a strong suspect. Mills identified Elizabeth's body at 9.45pm at Acton mortuary on 18 June.

Elizabeth's estranged mother also identified her the

following day, but Elsie King didn't bother with the funeral. In fact, there was no family interest or financial support for Elizabeth's burial. Instead, the council had to take charge and, as was customary in such sad circumstances, placed the deceased in a common grave. Elizabeth was the second of five deceased persons interred in plot 85 J at Chiswick New Cemetery. The burial took place on 4 September 1959, costing the council just £3.10s (around £74 at today's prices). A detective inspector who worked on the case said, 'It was just me and the undertakers. The vicar thanked me for coming. I felt sorry for her.'

She had only worked as a prostitute for probably two or three months, but that was long enough for her to meet her killer. Was it the shame of such a lifestyle that led her mother and father to abandon her so totally by the end of her life? This was an era when even women having children out of wedlock attracted a tremendous stigma, so working as a prostitute would have placed Elizabeth well outside respectable society. However, it seems that her parents turned their backs on Elizabeth long before her brief career providing sexual services. Unloved, with a tempestuous upbringing, she drifted through her short life to a brutal end.

The inquiry went cold. Almost five years would pass before it came under serious scrutiny again. By then, west London would be in the grip of a one-man killing spree, and detectives would realise that Elizabeth's murder bore enough similarities to the later cases to suggest she was the first victim of the Nude Killer.

Chapter 2

Four Years On – Gwynneth Rees

What a difference five years made. In 1963 alone, events abroad and at home – the Cuban missile crisis, the assassination of President John F Kennedy, the Profumo scandal and Great Train Robbery – helped to shake Britain out of its fifties' complacency. The scandal-rocked Tory government would be replaced by Harold Wilson's first administration in the autumn of 1964. London was getting into its sixties' swing for a decade of cultural revolution. The permissive society and youth culture were causing increasing outrage from elders and betters. However, some things did not change and sectors of British society still got by with a huge dollop of hypocrisy and prejudice.

While British fashion, movies and photography had a new 'poptastic' vibe and UK bands were causing hysteria internationally, the reality of life on the capital's streets was more shocking and seedy. Today a playground of the rich, large parts of Notting Hill back then were slums, with notoriously rundown areas from Portland Road to Southam Street. Colin MacInnes's novel *Absolute Beginners*, featuring the summer of racial tension in 1958, was set there. He wrote of north

Kensington as a 'rotting slum of sharp, horrible vivacity'. It had hideous, overcrowded housing and racial friction that fostered an ugly mood, reaching boiling point in the race riots of 1958. This was a series of disturbances lasting for five days from the end of August, involving white youths and black residents, with Oswald Mosley's Union Movement stirring trouble with its campaign to Keep Britain White. The police arrested 140 people for offences including affray, having offensive weapons and grievous bodily harm. Lettings notices were allowed to proclaim, 'Room for rent – no coloureds'. Several property-owning sharks (the most notorious being slum landlord Peter Rachman) were able to cash in on such prejudice and make a fortune by exploiting the new arrivals from the West Indies. A tactic of this type of operator was to intimidate secure tenants into leaving their rent-controlled accommodation. Large Notting Hill properties would then be subdivided into flats and rooms, with Rachman exploiting the West Indians he moved in. Many of his subdivided rooms were used for prostitution. As one former police officer from that era, Chris 'Frank' Gibbings, told me, 'Back then, Notting Hill was really rough and tough. No one wanted to admit to living in Battersea, Fulham or Notting Hill.' A new arrival from Trinidad would describe terraces of drab, crumbling stonework, smashed windows, doors with peeling paint, while the streets were strewn with rubbish and abandoned cars. Every few doors along there was an empty house with corrugated iron on the windows, and grubby kids swarmed around playing outside. 'A total slum,' was how *Tribune* journalist Mervyn Jones described the area. 'I'm talking rats as big as cats.'

The prevalence of street prostitution around nearby Bayswater and Queensway would be shocking to anyone today. In the mid-1950s prostitutes were a common sight on many street corners from Marble Arch to Shepherd's Bush. During one evening in November 1958, between 10pm and 10.30pm, 73 prostitutes were seen by the police soliciting between Notting Hill and Shepherd's Bush. By the 1960s, and despite the 1959 Street Offences Act, which aimed to clear the streets of the trade by outlawing public soliciting, the west London area was still a thriving extension of the Soho vice world.

Hyde Park, further along from Bayswater Road, was virtually a sexual theme park, humming with people having sex on the grass or in the bushes. It had the greatest post-war increase in prostitutes and arrests, and attracted women without rooms, of all ages, as well as housewives who went out in the afternoons to go with customers in cars. In 1950 the assistant commander of A Division stated, 'Charges [in Hyde Park] are preferred against not just a few regulars but hundreds of different women from all parts of London.' Dr Alfred Kinsey, the American author of the Kinsey reports on human sexuality in the 1940s and 1950s, visited London in 1955 and said he had never seen so much blatant sexual activity out in the open. He even claimed to have counted 1,000 prostitutes in the West End on one Saturday night, which gives some idea of how prevalent street prostitution was at this time. While in town, Kinsey reported to the Wolfenden committee on prostitution and homosexuality, which was set up in 1954. His graphic account confirmed the view of several committee members that there should be a crackdown on the touting of sexual services in public; Kinsey's intention was probably to shift them away from overly involving criminal law in private sexual activities. Nevertheless, the committee decided that prostitution was 'an evil of which any society which claims to be civilised should seek to rid itself'. The resulting 1959 Street Offences Act did attempt to make neighbourhoods decent for 'respectable' residents by penalising soliciting prostitutes. Men could still take to their cars in increasing numbers to cruise for sex. Kerb-crawling and the persistent soliciting of women would not be dealt with until the Sexual Offences Act of 1985.

The focus on prostitution during the 1950s gives the impression that there had been a major growth in the trade at this time, but was that the case? The Wolfenden report acknowledged that there were no reliable figures to show a significant rise in prostitutes during recent years. There was a steady increase in convictions from 10,300 in 1952 to 11,800 in 1955, when the Wolfenden committee was meeting. However, a moral fuss in the media and political circles certainly projected prostitution as a big issue. Newspapers started to fret over the visibility of the street trade in the run-up to Queen Elizabeth II's coronation in 1953. What would tourists say if confronted by London's sex trade? *Reynolds News*, for example, reported that 7,000 'good-time girls' would converge on London for the royal event. Other newspaper campaigns were also run against the influence of foreign gangs such as the Messina brothers and their prostitution racket. Away from the media, in 1951 the Paddington Moral Reform Council urged the government to tighten the solicitation laws. Prostitution was a prominent talking point in the Paddington area – which abuts Bayswater and Hyde Park – throughout the decade. Many houses had been subdivided into flats occupied by single women, who were said to be working as prostitutes. Alderman Walter Goss called for them to be evicted and for new anti-soliciting legislation. Whether there was a major post-war surge in streetwalkers or not, prostitution was certainly highly visible in newspaper headlines and on the political agenda.

Frank Gibbings, now in his seventies and living in Paignton, was a young CID officer in Kensington during the 1960s. He said, 'Street prostitution wasn't just concentrated at Queensway and Bayswater, it was all over the place. The underpass in Fulham was also a regular beat. There were a lot of street girls, a lot of them. At Kensington there was a small group of plainclothes officers whose job it was to try to keep the street girls under control. If you went to West London Magistrates' Court every single morning, there were prostitutes up for walking the streets and importuning and god knows what else. They'd just plead guilty – it was like paying tax. Then they wouldn't be disturbed again until it came round to being their turn.'

However, the law could be exceptionally blind on occasion. 'I was in court one morning,' Giddings recalled, 'and there was a brand new magistrate. This Tom [prostitute] pleaded not guilty and everyone said, "What?" Gross indecency, I think she was charged with.' The arresting officer testified that he found the woman having sex with a client while standing in a doorway. 'But the magistrate dismissed the case on the basis that it wasn't possible to have sex standing up in a doorway.'

In 1958, the year before the Street Offences Act, there were nearly 17,000 arrests for prostitution involving around 2,000 women in the capital. It was estimated, however, that there were in the region of 5,000 prostitutes in London. The conviction rate for soliciting was reported by the *Sunday Times* to have immediately dropped by 90 per cent in London following the new law. Although it succeeded in curtailing street soliciting – call-girl agencies and hostess clubs sprang up

– many streetwalkers were still not deterred, using multiple aliases to avoid the mounting fines for repeat offences, or moving to different neighbourhoods. The Nude Murders case confirmed to senior detectives how rife the trade still was. During the night surveillance operation to monitor cruising motorists in a bid to trap the killer, they noted that kerb-crawlers kept the street trade thriving, with men constantly driving around the block or queuing to speak about 'business' with soliciting women.

A little known feature of this era was the number of homeless former Second World War soldiers who were sleeping rough. 'You had a lot of ex-soldiers dossing on the street,' said Gibbings. 'Many would lie on the benches in Kensington Park. I know this was the sixties, 20 years after the war, but many of them had no life. You look at it now and would say many had post-traumatic stress, but in those days they came back from the war and would just be told to get a job and get on with it. We had to disturb them and ask them to move on. A lot of them had their medals on their chest under their army greatcoats. They would pull back their coats and show us their medals, and we would say, "All right, mate, go to sleep, you'll be all right."'

Streets were full of squalor and desperation – the ideal environment in which the Nude Murderer could re-emerge to stalk new victims.

Detectives would eventually number the victims at six, possibly seven if Elizabeth Figg was included (and she did have a qualified inclusion in the murder team's final 1965 report on the killings). However, there was another murder, which occurred in 1963, and, though tenuously linked, it is sometimes considered alongside the others. In this book it is not included as one of the linked murders because the cause of death was so difficult to determine. It was also impossible for the police to work out whether she had fallen victim to a back-street abortionist, one of the many criminals who abused her or a serial killer.

A 10-minute stroll from where Elizabeth Figg was discovered in 1959, just west along the river and across Chiswick Bridge, there is now a recycling centre on Townmead Road. In 1963 it was a dump, a refuse-transfer depot used by Richmond and Barnes councils. A digger driver, 23-year-old Patrick Dineen, made a grisly discovery on the afternoon of 8 November while loading a lorry with clinker, the waste material from industrial processes. At first he thought it was a dead animal.

'I was driving over it and didn't take a lot of notice, although I did notice a horrible smell,' he said. With the digger's scoop he shovelled it up. 'I saw two legs hanging out of the shovel. There was a stocking on one of them and I stopped my machine and shouted to the foreman, "There's a body there."'

Richmond police attended the scene, with Detective Chief Superintendent Jack Mannings and Detective Superintendent Frederick Chadburn in charge. The body was buried two feet under rubbish and was badly beaten up. The head, with several teeth missing, was separated from the body, which was decomposed and naked except for the nylon stocking rolled around the ankle. The pathologist, Professor Arthur Mant, wrapped the corpse in plastic and had it taken to Kingston mortuary. While he did a post-mortem, the police sifted through tons of trash for a murder weapon or clues. Mant's job was not easy as internally much of the torso had putrefied and the body was in an advanced state of decomposition. He estimated that death had occurred four to eight weeks previously. Concerning the cause of death, he consulted a colleague at Guy's Hospital, where the skeleton was kept, and said the hyoid bone had been broken at the time of death, or shortly after. This is the small semi-circular bone in the throat that is nearly always cracked during strangulation. While the breakage of the right-hand fork could have occurred at the dump, Mant decided it was highly likely the woman had been strangled, but it could not be determined conclusively. The other stocking was found at the site, but none of the body's other belongings were uncovered.

There were few clues to her identity. Police dredged their missing persons reports from all over the UK and turned up 144 women unaccounted for. A description of the dead woman – aged 20–25, 5 feet 3 inches tall – was circulated in search of a match. Her particulars were also publicised on radio and in the press. Hundreds of concerned families contacted Richmond police looking for women who were missing, many never previously reported. Details of 483 came in, 85 of whom were found, 258 were ruled out for dental, age or height specifics, and 140 cases remained open.

But, remarkably, despite the body's decomposed state, the police were able to secure one vital clue from the remains – a thumbprint. This was frozen and x-rayed. It was a match for Gwynneth Rees, aged 22, who had 13 convictions, one for theft and 12 for soliciting under the name of Tina Smart.

Like Elizabeth Figg, Gwynneth had a difficult early life. She was born on 6 August 1941, in Barry, Glamorgan, to Gwilym Rees, a labourer, and his wife, Amelia. After leaving school at 15 she worked as a machinist in a lingerie factory. Her mother died in 1957 of a blood clot on her brain. Gwilym wanted Gwynneth to stay at home and look after her three younger sisters (she also had an elder brother and sister). She resented this and began staying out late. To escape her premature drudgery she went to live with her older married sister, Joan Oxley, on Canvey Island, Essex. But they ended up rowing about her going out, and Joan suspected her sister was pregnant, which Gwynneth denied. She returned to live with an aunt in Barry and found herself a job in a rope factory.

However, she did become pregnant and went back to Joan's. In August 1958 Gwynneth's daughter was born. The father, apparently, was a labourer she had met. Gwynneth returned to work and Joan looked after her baby. The sisters' relationship became more and more strained and finally snapped when Gwynneth started to bring boyfriends home. One night in February 1959 Joan found her at 3am with a man she had brought back. Joan refused to let him stay. Gwynneth left with the man and that was that: Joan would bring up the baby. It is almost impossible to imagine today the shame and stigma attached to single motherhood half a century ago. Lone women with children – even in cases of rape – were often seen as little better than prostitutes. The social pressure on teenagers or unmarried women of low income to give up their babies for adoption, or even have an abortion, which was illegal at this time, was inescapable. Pregnant single women were often cajoled into mother-and-baby homes to hide their condition by scandalised families, social workers or doctors. There were 172 such homes in 1968, run by the Salvation Army or church bodies, in which mothers would have various degrees of pressure put on them to hand their newborns to childless married couples. That same year also saw an all-time peak in adoption orders in England – 16,000 – and many were against the will of the mothers. For those who resisted pressure to give up their babies, it was common to enlist the help of family members in raising their children. It is impossible to know what Gwynneth's reasons were for leaving her daughter with Joan. Without a steady job or place to live, it could be that she simply thought the baby would have a better life with a sister she trusted.

Instead of returning to Barry, Gwynneth went to London, when, in March 1959, she was stopped and questioned by the police in Backchurch Lane, Stepney, apparently for soliciting. When taken to Leman Street police station she said she was using the name Tina Smart because she rejected her father's name. She told them he used to beat her and her mother, and that she had attempted to kill herself when her mother died. Joan would later acknowledge that her sister had suffered a terrible home life. However, by trying to escape the misery of her family, Gwynneth fell in with a rough, brutal crowd. Joan began to suspect the truth about how her sister was living. Gwynneth visited her and the baby frequently; she was usually given a lift by a different man. Then there was the fact that she slept during the day and was out during the nights. 'I knew she wasn't working and I had a good idea how she was getting a living,' Joan said.

Gwynneth had 28 known London addresses, lived with various prostitute friends and used many aliases – Georgette Rees, Tina Wales, Tina Rees. Giving fake names was a tactic used by frequently arrested prostitutes to avoid being correctly identified and liable for mounting fines under the 1959 Street Offences Act. However, it made investigating her rather complicated for Superintendent Chadburn's team. They found that she solicited in the East End most frequently, but also Battersea, the West End and the Angel, Islington.

Her best friend was another Welsh prostitute, Peggy James, who lived in Oban Street, Poplar, and with whom she stayed after spending three months in Holloway Prison, apparently for soliciting. She probably needed a bit of support and sympathy – she was pregnant again. Her son was born on 27 December 1962.

The father was 20-year-old Micky Calvey, and here events turned sinister. Calvey went to prison for theft and had summoned her to visit him. He was in some sort of scrape, but she didn't go to see him. Men started calling on Gwynneth, demanding money. She was threatened with an axe. Later she disappeared for three days and returned covered in blood, saying the gang had beaten her. Calvey's right-hand thug was a man called George Kitchener Dixon. He was an associate of Ron and Reggie Kray, and may have been attempting to raise money for Calvey's defence. Following Gwynneth's death, detectives would question the feared East End twins, but Reggie would refuse to look at the photo of Gwynneth that they showed him and their solicitor advised them to say nothing.

Gwynneth's grim existence continued. In June 1963 she was in Poplar Hospital, having been dragged along the road by a car whose driver she had got into an argument with; she had abrasions on her legs and feet. She was also pregnant again, and suffering from a venereal disease. This was a regular hazard for women working the street. All the victims of the Nude Killer caught sexually transmitted diseases at some time, suggesting that if they did carry condoms they often did not use them – often under pressure from their customers. Before long Gwynneth became involved with Cornelius Whitehead, another friend of the Krays, who would eventually be jailed alongside them in 1969 as an accessory to the murder of Jack 'The Hat' McVitie in 1967. Whitehead pimped off her and gave her black eyes and a broken nose when she worked for another pimp, Victor Hatt. Sadly, she told Ann Bari, owner of the Quatus Cafe, 'It was my own fault. I asked for it.' Malnourished and battered, she was now fuelled by cigarettes and purple hearts, the street name for the stimulant Drinamyl.

Gwynneth was last seen when out working with her friend Brenda Meah, on 29 September 1963. She got into a two-tone Consul or Zodiac on the junction of Commercial Road and New Road. She was wearing a speckled coat, white jumper, black skirt, tan stockings and high heels.

What had been her fate? Gwynneth had apparently twice tried to self-abort her pregnancies, in 1960 and 1961. Now five months pregnant, had she attempted this again, with disastrous results? Abortion wasn't legalised in the UK until 1967, and having an illegal abortion cost money. So had it been a backstreet abortion this time that went wrong? Had one of the East End thugs who used her ended up killing her? Or had she crossed paths with a serial killer?

The police interviewed Whitehead and Hatt, among 1,135 other persons connected to the case. Superintendent Chadburn and his men could never establish whether she had died as the result of an abortion or at the hands of a man she encountered on her last night. The pathologist thought strangulation was a strong possibility; Chadburn leaned towards an abortion gone wrong, while Kingston Coroner's Court recorded an open verdict on the death.

Detectives would not include her among the victims in the sequence of Nude Murder cases. So much was unknown about her brutal life and death, but with her body being found so close to Elizabeth Figg's in south-west London and that of the next two victims, and the fact that she was unclothed, there remains the very real possibility that she was victim number two.

Chapter 3

Murder Year 1964 - Hannah Tailford

Allan 'Jock' Lynch arrived home at the top flat of 37 Thurlby Road, West Norwood, on the evening of Friday, 24 January 1964. His partner, Hannah 'Terry' Tailford, was playing with their little girl. Hannah cooked dinner, changed and went out at 9pm. As she was leaving she made a comment to their toddler that perturbed Allan. 'How would you like a new mother?' He said, 'Don't talk like that.' She was wearing a dark blue coat, flame-coloured nylon blouse, black cardigan and skirt, and a light blue pixie hat. She also wore a wristwatch and a plain wedding ring. It was the last time Lynch saw Hannah alive.

As the ensuing investigation unfolded, it became difficult for detectives to know what exactly was in Hannah's mind when she asked her two-year-old if she would prefer a new mother. Was she depressed? Was she walking out on her partner, Lynch? Whatever the answer, the unintended result of her departure would be to cross paths with the Nude Killer.

That Friday night, Lynch watched television till it went off air, then retired to bed. The following day he went downstairs and called on his neighbour, Theresa Eyles. According to her, he said, 'The cow's left me with the kid.' Staying out late was not unusual for Hannah, so initially Lynch was not too concerned. By Sunday afternoon, though, he was calling at local pubs and cafes looking for her. By Monday he was desperate. 'I couldn't go to work as I had the baby to look after,' he said, speaking of his billiard hall job. He was leaving their little girl with various babysitters, including Hannah's friend Jean Bishop. 'He said he ought to have realised there was something wrong because [Hannah] kept asking [their daughter] if she would like a new mummy,' Bishop said later. 'He seemed very worried about Terry because she would not have left the child.'

By Tuesday Lynch was still trawling the West End. He later tracked down Thomas Trice, Hannah's 69-year-old friend who lived in Kent and took nude photos of her, keeping a set for himself and giving her some copies. Trice told Lynch, who was virtually in tears, that Hannah was planning to marry someone called Don or Dennis. Trice would later say, 'She was very keen to get married. I thought she wanted to break away from the life she had been living.' Was all this marriage talk just wishful thinking? Whatever it was, it made Lynch decide their eight-year relationship was over. The following Saturday after his partner's disappearance, Lynch told Theresa Eyles he was quitting the flat. He gave her three shillings to pay the milkman for him. She asked if he had found Hannah. 'He said he hadn't found her and wasn't going to bother any more to look for her.' Lynch took all of their child's toys and clothing to Amy Higgs in Battersea, one of his daughter's regular babysitters, and gave Trice all Hannah's clothes. Trice, a retired foreman carpenter, had a colourful alternative life – he liked to dress in women's clothes and be called Auntie Gwen. However, he kept the box of Hannah's clothes aside 'in case Hannah might want it back. I did not know anything had happened to her.'

Lynch told the police he got drunk for three days over the following weekend. Then, 'Last night, Tuesday 4th [February], I bought an *Evening News*, which I put in my pocket. Later in the evening I was having a few drinks when I pulled out the newspaper and read about Hannah being found in the Thames.' He does not reveal how upset this made him, but he did go straight to Lavender Hill police station.

She had been found two days earlier on the Thames foreshore, the part of the shore between the high- and the low-water marks, near the landing stage of the Corinthian Sailing Club, Upper Mall, Hammersmith. It's a lovely spot, offering expansive views east towards Hammersmith Bridge, and west towards Chiswick Eyot, a small uninhabited island in the Thames. Brothers Douglas and George Capon, aged 23 and 20, were on the foreshore below the clubhouse preparing a rescue dinghy for a race later that afternoon. They saw her lying face down, caught under the landing-stage pontoon. She was covered in driftwood, including a discarded Christmas tree, feet pointing towards Hammersmith Bridge. She was naked, though her nylon stockings were caught round her ankles. Douglas stood guard while George telephoned the police.

Area car F1 arrived, along with other officers and a police inspector. He pulled Hannah out and turned her over so that divisional surgeon Joshua Stein could examine her. Divisional surgeons were called out to pronounce life extinct. The inspector with Stein at the Thames crime scene said, 'I then saw that she had an item of clothing stuffed in her mouth.' These were her semen-stained knickers. Stein could see no clear injuries, but did note that her eyes were red, her hands were sodden and semi-closed, her skin was livid in parts and her abdomen was blue. His impression: she had been in the water for some days. The tide was rising so permission was given to remove the body. At 3.30pm, nearly two hours after the discovery, she was taken to Hammersmith mortuary.

Pathologist Donald Teare went to work again. He found she was 5 feet 2 inches tall, with brown hair and eyes. She had a scar from an old caesarean operation, several missing teeth and a one-and-a-half-inch wound on the back of her right calf that had occurred after death. Teare also found bruising on her lower jaw caused before death, perhaps by punches. In her stomach was a fairly large meal. The body was sodden, suggesting immersion in water for between two to seven days.

Hannah Tailford was identified by her fingerprints. Her sister, Mrs Elsie Youngman, a civil servant who lived in Newcastle-Upon-Tyne, went to the mortuary for the grim duty of confirming who the body was. Detectives were now faced with another painstaking investigation, unpicking a complex web of friendships, punters, sex parties, late-night coffee stalls and acquaintances with multiple names.

An incident room was set up at Shepherd's Bush police station. Detective Chief Inspector Ben Devonald of Scotland Yard headed the investigation. During the war Devonald had served with the Special Investigation Branch of the Military Police. In peace time he had climbed the ranks and served with the Flying Squad. The inquest at Hammersmith Coroner's Court on 28 April would show a snapshot of Tailford's fractured family background and her scramble for survival on London's streets. In an unsympathetic assessment, Devonald told the court and coroner Dr Gavin Thurston, 'Miss Tailford was a sexual pervert. She was known to have attended parties at which sexual orgies took place.' Devonald, perhaps showing a distaste for Hannah's lifestyle that would have chimed with many in the court, seems to have decided Hannah was a pervert because she went to orgies, for which she was presumably paid. He also said she often used purple hearts – no doubt to stay alert and awake on work nights – and had three convictions for prostitution, the last occurring in January 1963. 'She used to frequent cafes and coffee stalls in the Charing Cross, Victoria, Shepherd's Bush and Finsbury Park areas. She would go with clients and was prone to discard her clothing.'

Elsie Youngman said she had last seen her sister alive in Newcastle in 1960. 'She was with a "Jock Lynch", who I believed was her husband.' Elsie first met Jock in 1958 when he and Hannah visited their mother, staying about a month after finding rooms in the Jesmond area of Newcastle. They went back to London early in 1959. 'I did not hear from her again until spring 1962 when she was in hospital,' Elsie said. Hannah had called to say she had given birth to a baby boy the previous day, and revealed she had a baby girl aged 13 months. 'I have not heard anything from her since.' Hannah gave the boy up for adoption at the hospital when he was born. Lynch would later tell her inquest that Hannah had four children, including another boy before he met her. 'I don't know what became of this child.'

So, Hannah parted with three of her children, while keeping her little girl. Why did she hand over her boys to new parents? It is possible she had been worried or scared about the prospect of single motherhood. In addition, the pressure on her as a young unmarried mother to have the child adopted would have been considerable. As noted in chapter 2, the shame and impending hardship of bringing up a child alone were daunting, and this could have been why Hannah gave up her first child in 1957. Jock Lynch denied knowledge of this boy but was certainly her partner when she later gave birth to two boys and a girl, and all three were registered in the name of Lynch. But interestingly, under police interrogation Jock Lynch denied paternity of the two boys. This may be why she handed over the boys to new parents if Lynch did not consider them his own.

Brian Collett was 79 years old when I spoke to him in 2017. At the time of the Nude Murders he was a young reporter at the *Acton Gazette*. He recalled when he first heard Hannah Tailford had been found. 'I went to court one morning in February 1964 and a copper I knew said, "You'll never guess what they found? A woman floating near Hammersmith Bridge, stark naked, strangled." That was the first I knew of the case. We did a smallish piece on it, because we didn't know there was a series of killings coming.' The *Gazette*, which had its offices on King Street, specialised in covering crime stories. 'It was a violent sort of place,' Brian said. 'We were so used to grisly things in Acton, Shepherd's Bush and Hammersmith that this didn't look like the start of something big.'

There was no clear pattern so far, so no one could suspect that a mass killer was on the loose. The police studied the Thames' tides and currents and initially concluded that Hannah's body, which they thought might have been alive when it went into the water, had probably been thrown in the river at Chelsea or Fulham. But later Devonald also considered the most likely spot to be Dukes Meadows, where Elizabeth Figg was found in 1959 and which was used by many prostitutes. However, the police would eventually settle on the Chiswick Church Street slipway as the place where she was put into the water, 680 yards to the west.

Hannah Tailford – like Elizabeth Figg and Gwynneth Rees – was a young woman who fled from her family, lost touch with her relatives and lived a lonely existence of lies, sex with strangers and quiet desperation.

She was born on 19 August 1933, in Heddon-on-the-Wall, Northumberland, the second girl of John Tailford, a miner, and his wife, Elsie. By the age of 15 she was sent to an approved school for having been caught stealing and was identified as a youngster who needed care and protection. Her parents were apparently struggling to manage her, though details of her teenage life at home are scarce. Her older sister (also called Elsie) would later explain, 'She used to stay out late and go with men.' The thieving continued the following year when Hannah, then living with a man in South Shields, was arrested for stealing clothes from him.

Elsie said, 'We refused to have her home as my mother by this time was on the verge of a nervous breakdown.' Her sister's words outline the events but give no insight into Hannah's personality or motivations. Instead, we learn that Hannah was sent to an approved school in South Norwood, but deserted the establishment. Rearrested, she was placed in another approved school, this time in Addiscombe, Surrey. She absconded again. Soliciting caused her next scrape with the law. In 1954 she was arrested near Hyde Park and fined 40 shillings. Sent to borstal, she went on the run again. The cycle continued: another arrest for soliciting, borstal. She was released in 1956, arrested again for soliciting, went to borstal and was let out in 1957.

In the first book written about this case, 1974's *Found Naked and Dead* by journalist Brian McConnell, there is an account of some of the weirdos and degenerates she encountered when she tried to make her way in London. There was the white-haired ex-army officer she met at King's Cross station, who offered her a cleaning job, generous pay and a room. When she discovered she was also required to wear a scanty maid's uniform and perform bizarre sexual services for her employer, she fled.

These and other degrading experiences must have taken a toll on Hannah that is hard to imagine. By 1959 she was 25 and her life was a sad and chaotic scrabble. Then she hit the headlines. She put an ad in a newsagent's shop. 'Young mother to be (25) offers unborn baby for sale to good home. Due end of April.' Such trading of a child for money could result in criminal proceedings under the Adoption Act 1958, which was a response to the 1954 Hurst Committee's call for greater involvement of local authorities in adoption. This was an attempt to better regulate a situation in which adoptions could be fairly informal arrangements between friends and acquaintances, or professionals such as doctors or matrons. Hannah's advert was picked up by reporter James Cameron of the *Sunday Pictorial*, which ran the headline 'She wanted to sell her baby'. She is quoted under the name Theresa Foster. 'I know it is wicked and shameful of me, but I was forced to make this terrible offer to attract attention to my plight.' She said she had no savings and her husband had run off. She eventually gave birth to a boy in May, the second of her four children, and sold him for £20 to a Staffordshire couple who had seen the article. In the event, the London County Council took no action against Hannah or the couple involved.

Three years before this she met Allan Lynch. They lived together for the rest of her short life. Hannah occasionally wrote to her sister and sometime around late 1957 she told Elsie about her new man, but exaggerated the news, perhaps for appearance's sake. 'I had a letter from Hannah saying she was married to a "Jock Lynch" and she was very happy.' However, Hannah and Jock never married. Embellishing the facts of her life was a tendency Hannah slipped into frequently. It would create confusion later when the police came to investigate her movements and associates.

She and Jock moved between various south London furnished rooms prior to visiting her parents in Newcastle in the autumn of 1959. They stayed for a few weeks before finding rented rooms. The new decade saw her in Newcastle working as a domestic servant – but she was caught stealing from her employers, being conditionally discharged with 15 shillings costs and £5 compensation for her victims. Back in London living at 75 Highbury New Park, Islington, she ended up in court again for forging a cheque. She was sentenced to three months in prison.

Lynch and Hannah swapped dingy lodgings around town, leaving behind debts and unpaid bills; Thurlby Road became the latest of them. Lynch told the inquest that Hannah would leave the house every night at 9.30pm and return at 6am. He claimed he thought she worked as a cashier at an all-night restaurant on Southwark Bridge Road. However, he knew more about her lifestyle than he told the inquest, perhaps to avoid suspicion of living off her earnings. When questioned by the police he was more forthcoming during four long interrogations. These started after he entered Lavender Hill police station in a 'distressed state'. He told officers about the names he'd seen in her diary, which she had left with. The *News of the World* called this diary 'dynamite' – it could name her killer but also 'in the wrong hands could spell shame for many family men'. From memory, one name Lynch gave detectives was that of a man she visited at his sub-Post Office in

Harringay every Wednesday afternoon, but officers could not locate him. One married shopkeeper they did trace admitted to being her customer, but said he had not seen her since November the previous year.

Piercing the wall of deceit and men with fake names and vague addresses was a headache for detectives. They tried but could not find André, supposedly a French diplomat Hannah visited for orgies at Dolphin Square. Detectives did, however, find a married shopkeeper Hannah met regularly for sex in his car. But time and again the officers ran into a brick wall of unsubstantiated allegations about orgies at addresses that did not exist or an elusive waitress who was Hannah's contact for kinky parties. This was a circle of characters who lived on half-truths and nearly always used pseudonyms to avoid being charged for soliciting or to keep some other aspect of their shady lives hidden. Hannah, another mistress of the phoney name (Anne Taylor, Anne Lynch, Hannah Lynch, Theresa Bell), also spun quite a few stories. She told Tommy Trice a vague story about marrying someone called Don or Dennis. She told another friend, Jean Bishop, that a man called Del wanted to marry her. On the day she was last seen at home by Allan Lynch, she said to her friend Jean Bishop that this Del was taking her to see *The Black and White Minstrel Show*.

There were various sightings of her. A caterer, David Bateman, who knew Hannah, claimed to have seen her at the Kenilworth Cafe on Warwick Way, SW1, on 25 January. Another who knew her, Charing Cross coffee stall manager Frederick George saw her there on 27 January. Shirley Woolley, unemployed, had known Hannah for four years. She spotted her on 27 January at Victoria Station, wearing a blue coat. On 28 January salesman Robert Boyd, who had seen a picture of Hannah on *Police 5*, also said he knew her and saw her at the Charing Cross coffee stall. Off licence owner Donald Brodie said she called at his shop on Churton Street near Victoria on 27 or 28 January. It was the Charing Cross coffee stall again on 30 January, when a Joyce Todd saw her at around 4am.

Hannah was at the same stall when she met Arnold Henry Downton, a 44-year-old railway shunter, and his partner Elizabeth Ritchie-Downton, 27, who both knew her, on 31 January. Elizabeth told the police, 'I was at the stall with Arnold Downton and we saw Doll [as they called Hannah] and she was starving, so we took her to the Florence Cafe and bought her a meal. She was miserable and had been crying. She said she was so fed up she felt like doing away with herself. When she left she said she was going to meet someone at the coffee stall, but did not say who it was. I have not seen her since that time.' Arthur gave her five shillings when they left her. It sounds like a depressing and painful encounter, but unfortunately gives no clue to why Hannah was wandering around in such a distressed state.

Perhaps the final sighting was on 1 February by window cleaner Frederick Townend, 21. Again, he knew Hannah, and saw her around the coffee stalls, bars and clubs of the West End. Between midnight and 2am he spotted her at the Charing Cross coffee stall, stating that she was 'high as a kite' on amphetamines. 'She was always on purple hearts.' He had first met her at the Nucleus Club on Monmouth Street. He gave the police the full benefit of his opinion. 'I'm inclined to think she was done in by two or three blokes. I've seen her in a temper and she gave me the impression she could really handle herself. I've seen her go with two or three men on a number of occasions. She was silly in that respect and didn't care who she went with – with her it was business.'

On 19 February her blue coat would be recovered from the Thames, wrapped round a police-boat propeller.

There were so many dead ends and dud trails. Neighbour Theresa Eyles supplied a tantalising detail – every evening around midnight a car would pull up outside 37 Thurlby Road and collect Hannah. Eyles told the police she thought it was taking her to her job at a canteen in Victoria. She had never looked out to view the car. She said this had been the case on Hannah's last night at home. But Lynch said she left at 9.30pm. Why the discrepancy? Who was picking Hannah up? Where had she lived in the nine days after she walked out on Lynch? Who had been her final customer?

Chief Inspector Devonald summed up his evidence to the inquest on 28 April by saying his team had spent the previous three months dredging through all the lies and secrecies of Hannah's circle, interviewing 700 people in the process. Detectives visited the cafes and hangouts, and checked the addresses given by prostitutes of clients who were physically abusive or who had a thing for strangling them during sex. However, with her remarks about ending it all and, 'How would you like a new mother?', suicide seemed a possibility. Or had she simply intended to walk out on Lynch and their daughter? The inquest eventually played down the likelihood of suicide. Dr Donald Teare gave evidence regarding the knickers in her mouth, saying he had heard of a case in which a suicide put something in their mouth to stop their own screams being heard in the event that they lost their nerve. Dr Teare reported the bruising on both sides of her jaw, perhaps from a fist, or a fall. The inquest also heard that Hannah had a last meal of bacon, eggs and cheese shortly before her death. The pathologist said it was rare for someone planning suicide to eat a large meal beforehand. Suicide could not be discounted, the coroner Dr Gavin Thurston said, but it was 'wildly improbable'. The jury returned an open verdict.

The police had devoted a lot of resources to discovering what had happened to Hannah in the final days of her life. They ended up with many more questions than answers. But they would soon become sure of one fact – Hannah Tailford met the same killer that five more women would encounter in a terrifying murder campaign over the next 12 months.

The question that still taunts us today is: who was Hannah Tailford? We can see that for some reason she left home for a bleak existence of petty crime and prostitution. She had children, met a lot of people, many of whom used her badly, and she told a lot of stories. But the facts do not reveal what the pain at the centre of her life was. Even her sister Elsie is inscrutable in her account of Hannah, her final words in her police statement of 5 February 1964 being, 'Today I attended the mortuary at Hammersmith where I identified the body of my sister.' This matter-of-fact statement coupled with Jock Lynch's speedy severing of ties with his missing partner make Hannah's last days sound all the lonelier.

Chapter 4

Murder and Confession – Irene Lockwood

It was the Thames again. Near Corney Reach steps, Chiswick. She was beached amid the refuse as the tide went out. Naked.

On 8 April 1964, Sergeant Robert Powell of the River Police was patrolling when he saw her. He came onto the foreshore and examined her, seeing a 6–8-inch wound above her right breast. *Acton Gazette* reporter Brian Collett saw police photos of the victim and recalled, 'The pictures of her that I saw were gruesome because the blade of a passing boat caught her and caused a huge gash across her torso. It was awful. We started to think there was something happening here.'

Corney Reach is a little under two miles downstream from where Elizabeth Figg was found on Dukes Meadows, beneath the willow tree, five years earlier. It is also just 300 yards upstream of where Hannah Tailford was found in the river. In addition, it would turn out that this latest victim, like the first two, was also a prostitute, unclothed, with missing teeth. Fingerprints and a tattoo – 'In memory, John' – led to her being identified as Irene Lockwood. Her landlady, Pamela Edwards, would confirm this at Acton mortuary. Edwards had known her as Sandra Russell, one of several aliases (others were Barbara Norton, Sandra Lockwood, Barbara Lockwood). She lived at 16 Denbigh Road, Notting Hill. Another detail Lockwood had in common with the previous victim was that semen was found on both her vaginal and oral swabs. This suggested they may have had sex with their killer or perhaps another customer prior to their death. No positive semen samples being found – as was the case with the next victim, Helen Barthelemy – did not prove the victim had not had sex, however, as they could obviously have used a condom.

Sergeant Powell called his find in and searched the fore-shore. Irene Lockwood had been wearing a check coat, black skirt and 'kinky boots'. None was found, nor any items to help the police. She was 25 years old, 5 feet tall with bottle-blonde hair. Her body was covered in dirt – pathologist Dr Donald Teare described it as 'recently acquired', suggesting it perhaps came from the riverbed.

Detective Chief Inspector Ben Devonald was still heavily involved in the Hannah Tailford investigation. Shepherd's Bush police station now had to make room for another team to dig into this latest death. Detective Superintendent Frank 'Jeepers' Davies took charge (the nickname apparently referring to his preference for suede shoes). Davies, aged 48, had Flying Squad experience and was a highly commended officer. His immediate priority was clearly to learn all he could about the victim.

Divisional surgeon Joshua Stein had pronounced her dead. During the post-mortem at Acton mortuary Dr Teare discovered that Irene Lockwood was 14–18 weeks pregnant. Her flatmate, Maureen Gallagher, said later, '[She] told me she only did business with "rubbers" so she didn't think it was a client.' This would suggest the father was a man she was seeing socially who was not using condoms. Nearly all of the victims had unplanned pregnancies in addition to contracting venereal diseases, so while they may have carried condoms for work, it seems likely that many of their street customers would often insist on not wearing them. While the Pill had been introduced on the NHS in 1961, it is unlikely the Nude Killer's victims were early users of it. Until 1967 it could only be prescribed to married women and initially it was mainly given to older women who already had children and did not want more.

During the mortuary examination, it was felt that the wound on Irene's breast happened in the water, perhaps by a propeller, and that she was unconscious when she went into the river. It was decided she had been in the water for no more than 48 hours. Drowning was given as cause of death. Because she was naked and had not been in the river that long (so it was unlikely her clothes could have been washed away), Davies believed she had been murdered.

The police made a public appeal for details of her final movements. They stated that she was often found at Kensington Church Street and Charing Cross Station. Her favourite outfit was a fake leopard skin coat, three-quarter-length boots and a tight skirt. However, the appeal resulted in no breakthrough news about the victim's fate.

Like the previous victims, Irene had come to London from elsewhere in the British Isles, in this case Walkeringham, Nottinghamshire. She was born illegitimately to Minnie Lockwood on 29 September 1938; she left school at 15 and went to work on a farm run by her grandfather. When she was 19 she gave birth to a son, who was taken into care. Again like Tailford, she was prodigious at incurring convictions, 14 in all, including five for soliciting, a couple for insulting behaviour and one for indecent behaviour.

She fell in with another prostitute, Vicky Pender, and together they fleeced punters by posing for indecent photos with the men and then blackmailing them afterwards. Pender was found murdered in an Islington flat a year before Irene's murder. The police suspected a former paratrooper called Colin Welt Fisher, who possessed 500 pornographic photos of women. He told detectives at the time of Pender's murder that he been at a hotel with a Sandra Lockwood – one of Irene's aliases. Irene denied it, and Fisher was later convicted of killing Pender.

Another scam was run at her Denbigh Road flat. Irene and her flatmate Maureen Gallagher would bring pick-ups back there and ask them to undress in the front room, then follow them into the bedroom. While engaged in sex, one of Irene's two unsavoury parasitic 'friends' – or pimps – Ray or Simon, would creep out from behind a kitchen curtain and help themselves to a portion of the client's money, perhaps to make the loss less noticeable. Maureen explained, 'They would only take some of the client's money – say, if he had £10, only £2.' Irene also occasionally conducted business in clients' cars. The two women needed to keep working hard because they had the circling sharks Ray and Simon demanding money and 'loans' from them, along with an extravagant weekly rent of £12 10s. (This is equivalent to about £230 today, which is less than London's contemporary average rent, but still very hefty for the 1960s.)

At this point it becomes easy to understand how bleak the lives of the two young women were. To escape her pimps, Irene asked an old friend to try to find her another flat. Easter weekend 1964, she and Margaret parted company. Margaret, who was seven years younger than 25-year-old Irene, ended up drifting around Paddington, staying a night with a man she met at a club, before attempting to kill herself by cutting her wrists in the Ladies at Bayswater Tube station. Fortunately, she was found and taken to St Mary's Hospital, Paddington.

Meanwhile, the landlady at Denbigh Road, Pamela Edwards, was sniffing around for her rent, which was over-due. She let herself into the flat on the Saturday after Easter, 4 April, and found no one in, just the electric fire and a light on. Mrs Edwards said later, 'Dirty crockery was left in the flat and I was of the opinion that she had run off without paying her rent.'

Irene was last seen at 8pm on 7 April, the day before her body was found. She was at the Windmill pub, Chiswick High Road. The pub was three-quarters-of-a-mile from where she was found.

Then the case took a bizarre twist.

Aged 54, tubby and deaf, Kenneth Archibald was a care-taker at the Holland Park Tennis Club, Addison Road, West Kensington. He bumbled into Notting Hill police station on 27 April 1964, just over a couple of weeks after Irene's body was found. He had been drinking and was a mess; he said he wanted to confess. He was talking to DC Stan Moorehead, who asked Archibald if he was referring to a break-in at the tennis club that he had reported to the police earlier that same day. 'No,' Archibald replied. 'I pushed the girl in the river. You know the blonde, Lockwood, at Chiswick.' A result for the detectives? Not quite. For a start, he was confessing to Irene Lockwood but said he had nothing to do with Hannah Tailford's killing, and police were convinced the two were committed by the same man. So what was going on?

Archibald was born in Sunderland, served in the army and was a former merchant seaman. In middle age he was back on dry land, doing a variety of deadbeat jobs. Eventually, he ended up as caretaker at the tennis club, a position that offered him 30 shillings a week and a free flat on the premises. He received a weekly service pension of £1 18s and a disability pension of £2 8s (a manual worker could earn around £15 a week). But he also had a secret income that came from the club's dodgy caretaker, Joe Cannon. He paid Archibald a whopping £30 a week to allow him to run an illegal after-hours drinking den at the tennis club. Boozers, punters and prostitutes, including Irene Lockwood, were among the clientele.

On the day after Irene Lockwood's body was discovered, DC David Bretton interviewed Archibald to follow up on a card being found in Irene's handbag back at her flat. This carried a telephone number, PARK 7157, for the phone box outside Archibald's flat, with 'Kenny' scrawled on the back. Bretton showed a photo of Irene to Archibald, who said he had never seen her, an apparent lie because Joe Cannon said she was a regular at the drinking den. He was taken to Shepherd's Bush police station to make a statement, the first of several visits. Before he turned up to confess on 27 April, Archibald had already seen the police earlier that day to report the tennis club break-in. This report had prompted DC Moorehead to search Archibald's flat for the stolen goods, Moorehead, perhaps, being suspicious of the caretaker. It was an eventful day for Archibald. Later that same morning, he was in Marlborough Street Magistrates' Court charged with another matter – the theft of a hearing aid. Pleading not guilty, he was due back in court the following day. In the meantime, he went to the pub, the Colville in Notting Hill, where a friend said he was tearful and maudlin. He announced that he was going back to the police station.

It was in this frame of mind that the sad man made his confession. He said after work at the tennis club on 7 April he had gone on a pub crawl, ending up at the Windmill on Chiswick High Street shortly before closing time. He chatted to 'the girl standing at the bar' and bought her a gin and tonic. In his statement Archibald said, 'She asked if I fancied going for a short time with her. I said, "Yes." We left the pub and arrived at the river sometime about 11pm. There were no people about and she asked for £4 (£70 at today's prices) and said she wanted some money first... I must have lost my temper because I had my hand around her throat.' When she collapsed, he decided to undress her, having some vague idea that if she were found clothed witnesses at the pub may have remembered him as her companion. He said he rolled her into the river, bundled up her clothes and walked home, burning her things the following day.

Apart from Archibald's denial that he had also killed Hannah Tailford, there were other problems with this confession. John Ranklin, the landlord of the Windmill – a cheerless pub that looked like a prefab and finally closed down in 2005 – stated that he saw Irene that night, but could not recall anyone with her. However, pathologist Dr Teare said that he could see nothing in Archibald's statement to contradict his findings. And yet, as usual, nothing was straightforward with this case. The business card with 'Kenny' and the tennis club number on it could be seen as suspicious. But then in Irene's diary, which had the same Park 7157 phone number in it, was a mention that, 'Kenny is coming April 2nd or 1st. He is young and handsome.' Kenny Archibald? Was she talking about another Kenny – or was Irene having a giggle about tubby Kenny? It was probably another Kenny because her flatmate Maureen Gallagher described him as having sunken cheeks and dark hair 'like Adam Faith's'. Another contradictory factor was Archibald's claim that he had never met Irene before the fatal night, and yet Joe Cannon said Irene came to the tennis club booze nights. He also claimed Archibald had paid her for sex.

Superintendent Davies was under pressure with a tricky decision to make. According to author Dick Kirby, he was apparently told by Deputy Commander Ernest Millen to 'make sure you've got the right fucking bloke'. Archibald was charged on 30 April. The next day the *Daily Mirror* plastered its front page with the headline: 'Nude in river – murder charge'. The story led with the charge against Archibald for Irene Lockwood's murder, and continued, 'Last night, detectives investigating the deaths of three other women, whose naked bodies were found in or near the Thames, stepped up their inquiries... The detectives are working in three separate squads.' The three other cases were Gwynneth Rees, who at this stage was included as one of the Nude Killer's victims, Hannah Tailford and the latest – Helen Barthelemy, found in Brentford on 24 April.

Magistrate Major Charles Fisher decided on 22 May that there was enough evidence for the case to proceed. Archibald appeared at the Old Bailey on 19 June 1964, by which time he changed his story. He pleaded not guilty before Mr Justice Nield. EJP Cussen presented the prosecution case during the five-day trial, during which Archibald said he made up his confession because he was depressed. It took the jury 55 minutes to accept this and set him free. In the *Daily Mirror* on 24 June Archibald gave his embarrassed explanation. 'It was silly to let my imagination run riot... I just hope everybody will let me forget it. Now all I want to do is find a new home, preferably out of London.' With that, he faded back into the fabric of the city, apparently never escaping it after all. He died from a heart condition at his flat in Coleman Road, Southwark, just eight years later on 20 October 1972.

In the meantime, on 8 May, Ealing Coroner's Court returned a 'drowning' verdict on Irene Lockwood, largely because there was little other evidence to go on. Irene would stand out from all the eventual victims in one respect – her body showed no underwear marks after death, suggesting she was one woman the killer did not have to undress. However, her murder marked the end of the Thames phase of the killings. All the remaining bodies would be found in parts of west London away from the river. Detectives would later speculate that, despite Lockwood and previous victim Hannah Tailford having been found to have drowned at their inquests, perhaps they too were asphyxiated as was clear with the later killings. The drowning verdicts were based on river water combined with air in their lungs, but investigators later wondered if the women's diaphragms could have been manipulated by the churning tides to pull in some water after they had been asphyxiated. In that case, and considering that the women had similar facial bruising to subsequent victims, asphyxiation could link all of the murders.

Frustration among detectives was already leaving one or two of them short-tempered. One pair found themselves at the end of a long drive leading to a mansion outside London. The occupant was a man whose pseudonym and three telephone numbers were found in Irene Lockwood's diary. These were for telephone boxes near the mansion, and by talking to other prostitutes the police discovered that the man would be called to arrange to pick up the women in his car and take them to a quiet spot. The police also found a telegram in Irene's belongings with a telephone number on it that led them to the man's mansion.

When the detectives knocked at his door, the man's wife answered. The officers gave her a story about wanting to speak to her husband because they thought he might have witnessed a traffic accident. They then had an embarrassing wait with the wife and the man's aunt until he returned home. When he did he then eased his wife and aunt out of the way, saying, 'I think I better talk to the officers alone – it was rather a nasty affair.' Once alone with the officers the man did not deny knowing Irene and the other women. They asked, 'Can you account for your movements on the night she disappeared, and also on the night Hannah Tailford vanished?' Having been given time to remember, the man later he went to the police station to give a detailed explanation of his movements.

The man then said, 'I wish to thank both of you for the discreet way you handled this inquiry. I never realised just how humane a policeman could be.'

To which the senior detective, a sergeant, was reported to have replied, 'No, a dirty bastard like you wouldn't know, would you?'

With the false confession and lack of a breakthrough, it certainly may have felt as though the investigation was getting nowhere. The Irene Lockwood investigators could not find 'young and handsome Kenny' referred to in Irene's diary and Superintendent Davies's team could unearth no compelling suspect. Several detectives felt Archibald was a fantasist and had been a waste of their time. Again, a great deal of police work went into tracing Irene's associates and movements. In the days leading up to her last sighting by the Windmill's landlord she was seen near Queensway Tube station, at the Wimpy Bar on Queensway, on Bishop's Bridge Road and on

Kensington Church Street, usually drunk or soliciting. Where she had been picked up and by whom was never established. No sooner was Archibald cleared than the press revealed that a new hunt for the killer was under way. But reading the press reports reveals that in reality Archibald had been nothing but a distraction. The *Daily Mirror* said in its 24 June report that detectives working on the killings of Gwynneth Rees, Hannah Tailford, Irene Lockwood and now Helen Barthelemy 'have always believed that the killings were linked'. The story continued. 'In recent weeks they have had a mass of new information from people who knew the victims, but who until recently have been frightened to talk. Many of these people, involved in London vice rings, feared the vengeance of their bosses.' In the previous two months, 200 prostitutes had spoken to officers and 100 men who knew the victims had made statements. 'Last April senior Scotland Yard detectives considered that the four murders had a pattern of violence which pointed to a vice ring,' the *Mirror* stated. 'The new information has confirmed this view.'

Irene Lockwood was buried in a pauper's grave, a basic burial paid for by the local authority, at Chiswick New Cemetery on 9 July 1964. She, like the previous victims, left a mess of questions for the squad investigating her murder.

Chapter 5

A Ticking Clock – Helen Barthelemy

The killer changed his method with Helen Barthelemy. This time he avoided the Thames and left the naked body of the 22-year-old Scot in an alleyway at the rear of Boston Manor Road, Brentford. She was the third murdered woman found since February and the second one in April. London had a murder spree on its streets and some of the press headlines were now shouting about the 'Maniac sex killer'. Elsewhere, coverage was still fairly restrained and speculative. The *Evening Standard*'s headline on page 16, for example, was, 'Tattooed nude may be fourth victim of river killer'. Throughout the entire investigation there would be reports of fears caused by the killings among women working the west London streets. However, the press coverage revealed no discernible panic among local women not involved in the sex trade. Brian Collett, an *Acton Gazette* reporter at the time, confirmed this on a local level to me, too. He said what panic there was only affected streetwalkers, who, for example, would eventually abandon their well-known spots on Horn Lane. The general mood as the police hunt grew seemed to remain constant – the murderer only inhabited the world of vice.

The big guns of Scotland Yard descended on the latest murder scene. Commander George Hatherill was a very big gun indeed, standing at 6 feet 6 inches and the man in charge of Scotland Yard's CID. He was there along with Deputy Commander Ernest Millen. With them was Detective Superintendent Maurice Osborn, who would lead the investigation into Helen Barthelemy's murder. Chief Superintendent Jack Mannings, who had worked on the Gwynneth Rees case, was in attendance. But the key figure was Detective Superintendent Bill Baldock. Tall, black hair slicked back with a trim moustache, Baldock headed the local CID and he would take overall direction of the murder hunt once the bigwigs had departed. Baldock was a man with presence and he was popular with many officers. The war had interrupted his police career, when he had been posted to the Special Investigation Branch of the Military Police. Afterwards he went on to serve with Special Branch and built a terrific reputation for his work resulting in the capture of several armed and violent men. He would remain heavily involved in the Nude Murders investigation right to the end.

Daily Mirror photographers took photos of detectives peering over a tarpaulin curtain in the puddle-strewn alley, which connects Swyncombe Avenue and The Ride. By contemporary standards, the trilby-and-raincoat brigade, along with a few uniforms, would seem to be trampling all over potential evidence as they inspected the body-deposition site. Another picture shows Det Supt Osborn waving the cameras away. Tetchiness was understandable as pressure was growing to find the killer, and this latest discovery would prove vital in several areas – not least in the first potential sighting of the killer.

Helen Catherine Barthelemy was found at 7.15am on 24 April 1964, by local resident Clark May. Going out the back of 199 Boston Manor Road to get rid of some ashes, he found her body by some rubbish. This was a quiet service road, with the backs of Boston Manor Road's houses to one side and playing fields to the other. It's a solidly residential area, roughly a mile from the Thames, on the flight path to Heathrow. Mr May, a 42-year-old horticulturalist, said, 'I went to the back gate at my address, which leads to a service road... I opened the rear gate and I saw a naked body lying just outside the gate. I did not touch anything but immediately returned to my house and telephoned the police at Brentford. I cannot remember how the body was lying. I was very shocked at finding it there.'

Again the pathologist Dr Donald Teare was called in for the post-mortem at Acton mortuary. The young woman had been dead for between 20 hours and two or three days. The body was covered in dirt. Hypostasis – blood or fluid accumulating in lower parts of the body – revealed that she had lain on her back after death. Pallid outlines on her skin showed the markings left by her bra and pants. She had been on her back for up to eight hours and her underclothing removed after death.

Asphyxia was the cause of death, inflicted via pressure on the woman's neck. Dr Teare felt this was probably done by pulling some of her clothing round her neck and tightening it. In common with all the victims, Helen had abrasions on her neck, probably caused by her attempt to ease the pressure there. Unusually in this case, there was swelling on her left cheekbone and the bridge of her nose. She had probably been punched. Only Hannah Tailford's body showed similar signs of violence, in the form of bruising on both sides of her jaw – but these could have been caused by a fist or a fall. Helen, on the other hand, appeared to have definitely put up a fight, and was beaten into submission. It was not clear whether there had been sexual contact. Unlike Hannah Tailford and Irene Lockwood, the anal, vaginal and oral swabs taken were negative, though a condom might have been used.

Four of her teeth were missing, removed after death. A fragment of tooth was also found lodged in her throat. While all the six confirmed victims of 1964–65 had poor and missing teeth, she was the only one that seems to have lost teeth around the time of her death. Dr Teare reported that such injury would be caused by a blow or upward pressure, rather than a horizontal blow to the mouth. There was no bruising on the lips or mouth. 'It is possible they were knocked out immediately after death,' he stated in his report, but he also thought it possible the teeth were removed just before death while Helen was unconscious. Or perhaps a legitimate dentist removed them a short time before her murder? Hospitals and dentists in X, T, V and F police divisions were all checked with negative results. Detectives even considered the possibility that Helen had bitten the killer's penis and been murdered in a fit of rage. Again, inquiries at hospitals to see if any men had called for treatment to such an injury drew a blank. The question of the missing teeth would never be resolved by the investigation.

Finally, her clothes and belongings were not discovered at the scene.

The conclusion was that Helen had been punched, strangled and laid on her back somewhere dirty. Her teeth were extracted and after some eight hours her clothes were removed. Later, she was taken in a vehicle to the alleyway. But there was a breakthrough. When the dirt on her body was analysed, coal dust and paint particles were found. When further scrutinised, the coloured paint material was shown to have come from a spray-gun nozzle, with a preponderance of the colour black. Garages that sprayed cars were a possibility to look into.

Up until this point the killer had been incredibly careful and elusive. No one had seen him picking up his victims or disposing of their bodies. But with the deposition of Helen Barthelemy he seemed to have got flustered and almost made a disastrous blunder. At 5.50am on the morning Helen was found, a farmer, Alfred Harrow from Buckinghamshire, was driving in his Bedford van along Boston Manor Road on his way to Brentford Market. Reaching the junction with Swyncombe Avenue he had to violently swerve and jam on the brakes to avoid a grey Hillman Husky, or Hillman Estate-type vehicle. The Hillman raced out of Swyncombe Avenue into his path, turning left towards the Great West Road. Mr Harrow came to a stop, but the Husky driver ignored him and accelerated away. The junction was 40 yards from where Helen was found just over an hour later.

Mr Harrow did not get the Hillman's registration number in all the drama, but he was sure it was a Husky-type model, that the colour was grey and it had been driven by a man. When that evening he read newspaper reports about the body, he immediately thought of his near miss in the morning and contacted the police. Detectives leading the inquiry seemed impressed by Mr Harrow, who ran a thriving business as a smallholder in Buckinghamshire, was a leading member of the council and looked solidly reliable to them. He used the same route several times a week and – perhaps this is an indication of how much less heavy London traffic was then – he often saw the same vehicles on these roads, but had not spotted the grey Husky before, or ever again after the near crash with it. Detectives concluded that the Husky driver was not there on any routine business. The long search for the grey Hillman Husky began.

Meanwhile, the questions for investigators started to pile up again. Why had the killer left the body in such a well-populated area? Why do so just before 6am on a spring day – it was virtually daylight? Was that him driving like a maniac? Having been so meticulous before, why was he taking such risks now? Detectives wondered about his desperate, anxious mindset on this spring day.

A murder pattern was becoming obvious and the press immediately devoted a lot of space to the investigation. On 24 April the *Evening Standard* ran the story on its front and back pages, complete with a map of where the previous four women had been found. 'Lovers' walk death starts massive new hunt by Yard.' They followed this up with another big front-page lead the next day. '50 detectives on trail of the strangler.' This story quoted her landlord, Earl Burton, who said, 'We let the room to Helen some months ago. She said she worked in a club and I think she went out at night. But I have no idea of her last movements.'

The next day the *Daily Herald*'s front-page lead story was, 'Yard warn women'. This piece outlined two police theories. 'The killer could be a man who hates women of the streets. Or he could be a new monster like [John Reginald] Christie, who was hanged in 1953 for killing seven women at his home in Notting Hill.'

The *Daily Mail* called it a 'Giant Murder Hunt'. Inside it ran a feature with a map detailing all five murders so far (including Gwynneth Rees). The paper also pointed to a police suspicion that 'one man, a sexual pervert with a hatred for prostitutes, may be responsible for the five murders'.

That weekend the *News of the World* also went big on the story: 'Yard ace hunts strip killer', it said, referring to Commander George Hatherill of Scotland Yard. Its splash upped the ante in luridness. 'Fear stalked the mean streets of London's viceland last night. Fear of the silent killer who strikes in the darkness and vanishes by dawn. Fear that has not been so widespread since the days of Jack the Ripper.' It quoted a 'small, sad-faced' prostitute in Westbourne Grove. 'This goon has frightened away most of the girls. I'll have nothing to do with strangers.' Another woman, Gloria from Stoke Newington, said, 'Some girls have given up because of this maniac. And I won't take a lift in a car.' The article, written by a reporter called Charles Sandell, concluded, 'As I drove back through the ill-lit Brentford streets into the bright lights of London's West End, I wondered if the legend of Jack the Ripper had risen from the gas-light era of 60 years ago.'

'Dramatic new clues' had been uncovered by the murder squad, according to the *Daily Mirror*. This was the paper's lead story, which explained that 120 vice girls had been interviewed and given detectives the names and addresses of men they dealt with, adding, 'And they have told of the demands the men made.' The *Daily Mail*'s angle on Monday, 27 April, was how the police were 'combing out' the West End's 2,000 clubs to find the killer. It seems fanciful to imagine that 2,000 clubs could even be squeezed into the West End, but the report took no half measures in emphasising what a huge effort this was for the murder squad. 'Scores of detectives are involved in the operation, which matches the big hunt for deserters in the West End in 1946.' Two days later the *Mail*'s theme was the widespread panic and fear in the capital. It reported that 'Girls in fear' had responded in 'staggering'

numbers to an appeal from Commander Hatherill for prostitutes to come forward in secret to help the police, particularly
if they had been made to strip and been assaulted by a client.

With the discovery of Helen Barthelemy's naked body in
that Brentford alley, this blood-chilling murder campaign
was becoming a huge source of dread for the authorities and
women working the streets.

The preliminary hearing at Ealing Coroners' Court on 27
April offered another sad look into the life of a young woman
who left home as a youngster and ended up in prostitution.

Helen was born on 9 June 1941, in Ormiston, East Lothian.
Her mother, Mrs Mary Thomson, who had left her father when
Helen was aged four, told the hearing she had last seen her
daughter about four years previously. After she left her husband,
Maurice Barthelemy, a steward with the Free French Navy, she
took Helen and lived with her parents in Ormiston, before
moving to Troon, Ayrshire. It was here that she married Albert
Thomson. What the bald facts don't tell us is how and why
Mary lost her connection with her daughter.

At the age of 16, Helen left home and was living near
Blackpool, having found work as a housemaid in a boarding
house. Mary's account to the police of what followed makes
painful reading. 'After about 12 months she left that employment and I lost touch with her. Then about four years ago I
saw her in Blackpool where she was working in a side-show in
striptease. Mr Thomson and I tried very hard to persuade her
to come home with us but she would not. Since we last saw her
four years ago we have had no letters from her. In fact, I did
not know she was in London.' The next time Mary – who by
1964 was a widow – saw her daughter was at Acton
mortuary.

Helen became pregnant and gave birth to a son on 7 October 1960, the father being a man called Kenneth Ferguson, a cotton feeder. The baby was given up for adoption.

A couple of years later Helen, still living in Blackpool but of no fixed address, got into serious trouble. On 8 October 1962, she was in Liverpool assizes (assizes were periodic courts in England and Wales set up to try more serious crimes) charged with robbing with aggravation a holidaymaker by the name of Friend Taylor. Apparently, she had got to know the 22-year-old Taylor and gone with him onto the dunes at Squires Gate. Taylor was then beaten up by three men who slashed his face with a knife or razor. Taylor said Helen at one point shouted, 'Stop it, Jock, he's had enough.' The thugs stole Taylor's wallet with about £22 in it and he was taken to hospital by a passer-by. He received 18 stitches in his face. The prosecution said Helen knew the robbers. She denied she was even there, or that she had ever met Taylor, claiming she had been at the Rendezvous Cinema on Bond Street, Blackpool, watching Charlton Heston and Sophia Loren in the movie El Cid. Two prosecution witnesses, however, said they saw her with Taylor on the day of the alleged robbery, and the cinema manager denied seeing her on the relevant evening, but had seen her the day before. When asked what she had done after the film, Helen said she 'went on business' to Stanley Park, going with three 'clients'. Police inquiries would later reveal that she had worked as a prostitute in Blackpool, Liverpool and Rochdale from the age of 16. The official reports give no clue to whether something in her home life propelled Helen to cut herself off from her mother at such a young age and take up the risky lifestyle she did. In Blackpool, however, a harsh reality hit her – she was eventually found guilty of robbery with aggravation and sentenced to four years in prison. On hearing the sentence, she fainted.

However, a few months later on 4 February 1963, Helen was back in court, this time at the Court of Criminal Appeal in London to challenge her conviction. Here it was revealed that Friend Taylor was not the upstanding citizen Liverpool assizes had been led to believe. He had in fact appeared in court several times for dishonesty and in 1961 was jailed for 12 months for housebreaking. Helen's conviction was quashed, but the trial demonstrated that by the age of 20 she was working in the vice trade. It also came out earlier at Liverpool assizes that she had been fined £20 in March 1962 for helping to run a brothel. Now she was free, though her subsequent move to London would end in the grimmest way.

Helen moved to the capital six months after the appeal hearing. She immediately seemed to be at ease in the racially mixed neighbourhood of Notting Hill, which was home to many new arrivals from the Caribbean and Africa, often living in overcrowded houses. The first friends she made were young black men, the three men whom she probably looked upon as boyfriends were Jamaicans, and she was well known in venues such as the Jazz Club at 207 Westbourne Park Road and Wragg's Cafe on All Saints Road. These were not pick-up joints for her. They were night venues where Helen met acquaintances, went dancing, and could smoke a joint in the Ladies or grab a meal in the early hours. If anything, they were havens for her to take a break between clients during the night or once she was finished working. To those who knew her she was often 'Teddy' or 'Helen Paul'.

Her favoured neighbourhoods for soliciting were nearby Bayswater and Queensway. These were natural areas for prostitutes to gravitate to because the trade was well established there. The police estimated that between Bayswater, Shepherd's Bush and Chiswick there were 600 resident prostitutes, while sex workers from other parts of London also visited looking for customers. Helen occasionally also worked the West End, Cricklewood Broadway and Shoot Up Hill. Kerb-crawlers were her clientele and she would point them in the direction of suitably secluded spots, Dukes Meadows being one.

She did not have many friends who were prostitutes, but there was one, a 25-year-old called Jean, who had known Helen in Glasgow and Blackpool. They bumped into each other again in the Wimpy Bar on Queensway at the end of 1963. Jean's comments about Helen give the impression of a young woman hardened by the sex trade, but who was a good friend. 'Teddy was very kind-hearted and if anybody was in trouble she would help them.' However, when it came to sex work, Jean was alarmed by Helen's behaviour. She described going with Helen and a client called Bill to the Hilton Hotel, Park Lane. Helen warned Jean that Bill was 'kinky'. Jean said, 'What does he want? I'm a business girl. I'm not doing anything but intercourse. He was real kinky and did everything in the book with Teddy... I felt sick and wanted to get out... She used to go in cars with clients and never worried.'

Helen was living at 34 Talbot Road in Willesden. The house was crammed with occupants. On the first floor there were two young couples with a single child each, both families living in one room. On the ground floor, Helen was in one room, there was another couple in the rear room with their child, while the last room, at the front, was occupied by a 53-year-old Jamaican nurse, Nellie Manhertz. The kitchen and toilet were shared.

Nellie became Helen's closest ally in the house. They got to know each other when Helen came home from hospital after a car accident in March 1964 – her boyfriend, Von Barrington Adams, was badly injured in the same crash. Nellie saw that the younger woman was having trouble walking and had a plaster on her face. She bathed her leg and put Helen to bed, fetching her own water bottle for her to use. She fed Helen in subsequent days and called a doctor for her. Nellie told the police, 'Helen said she had a mother in Blackpool and when she was sick, I asked her for her phone number so I could phone her, but she said she would write to her.' It is perhaps typical of this bedsit-land, transient existence that while Helen was only on nodding terms with her neighbours, it took her to be unwell before she got close to someone in the next room. Even then, however, she was not entirely forthcoming with Nellie. 'I remember Helen telling me that she was married and had a little boy four years old,' Nellie told the police. 'She said her husband had been killed in a car accident. I never noticed her wearing a wedding ring.'

Detectives tracked down Helen's boyfriends, the most regular for a time being the 23-year-old Von Barrington Adams, who came from Jamaica in 1957. Helen was not his only partner, however. He actually lived with another woman, with whom he had two children, only visiting Helen a couple of times a week. He spent his evenings DJing at the Roaring Twenties at 50 Carnaby Street, which was where they met. Another boyfriend spoken to by the police was a British Rail fitter, while the third, with whom she spent her final weeks, was thought to have lived off her earnings. However, all three said they were unaware she was being paid for sex with other men. 'I did not know she was a prostitute as she told me she worked at a clip club in the West End,' Adams said, probably referring to a hostess nightspot of the kind that Soho specialised in.

Another favourite haunt of Helen's was the Flamingo Club at 33–37 Wardour Street. While this venue was popular with gangsters and other shady types, it also won a reputation as a music spot. Stars such as Ella Fitzgerald and Billie Holiday performed in the 1950s, while musicians like Georgie Fame and Eric Clapton appeared there in the 1960s.

It was the Jazz Club, however, that featured most heavily in the final weeks of Helen's life. Its owner was 37-year-old Peter Aboro, who was born in Nigeria and came to England in 1947 after serving in the RAF. He ran the club with help from Lee Otty, 29, a fellow Nigerian who described himself to the police as a relative of Aboro's. 'That means he belongs to the same tribe as myself, the Ibo tribe.' Aboro told the police about his club's membership, 'There are about 200 members, mostly coloured people but about 50 of them are white girls. There are also about 12 white male members.' This would be interpreted in the police report on the case like this, 'Most of the [club's] frequenters are coloured men but there are numerous white girls of dubious morals who also frequent the club to associate with the coloured members.' Otty would say of the venue, 'The club sells Coca-Cola, orange, shandy and hamburgers. There is a record player and members sometimes dance.' Other more intoxicating substances were also undoubtedly traded there, however, and several witnesses spoke of drugs being consumed or bought. Otty said of Helen, 'To my knowledge she came about twice a week, about 11pm by herself, sign the book, never brought in guests and usually talked to other members of the club, men and women. She was a quiet girl who never caused any trouble. I have never seen her leave the club with a man, white or coloured.' It was in the Jazz Club that Helen would leave her handbag around the time she disappeared. This was important because it had her front door key in it, so detectives suspected this may have been her last night. But which night did she leave it? Once again all the witnesses gave conflicting accounts to the police.

Helen's last confirmed sighting was at Talbot Road. She was seen by another tenant, Purgy Dennis, on Tuesday, 21 April. 'I think the last time I saw her was early in the week around Tuesday evening as I was going out about 8.30pm. She opened her door and looked out. I think she was going to the kitchen.' Nellie saw her for the last time on the Monday. 'This was between 6.30pm and 6.45pm when she borrowed some paraffin,' she said. She called on Helen on Wednesday or Thursday and, finding she was not in, Nellie said, 'I locked her door for safety.' As ever, she was looking out for her young neighbour.

Peter Aboro told the police that Helen had given him her handbag to look after at the Jazz Club a couple of days later. 'To the best of my memory the last time I saw Helen Paul was at about 2am on Thursday, 23 April. I remember I was playing records when she came up to me and asked me to look after her handbag. She was on her own.' He thought she was wearing a grey skirt and black jumper. The confusion began when police spoke to Aboro's customers. One woman said she remembered sharing a spliff with Helen in the Ladies, while the four people with her could not agree on what happened that night. Meanwhile, Lee Otty said he saw the handbag at the club on 21 or 22 April, a day or two before Aboro said she left it...

Handel Cascoe, who worked at Wragg's Cafe, said he saw Helen several times on the night of 21 April, when she dropped in for tea and then a meal. He later saw her outside the Jazz Club after leaving the cafe at 5.20am. He invited her for a drink, but she said she was going with a couple of friends to

Ealing and had, anyway, left her handbag in the club. Cascoe's boss, Harold Williams, also claimed Helen was in his cafe – but on the following night, Wednesday, 22 April. Williams told the police, 'She appeared to be worried and depressed. This was unusual as she generally appeared cheerful.' He said she left the cafe at 4.15am and told him a similar story to the one Cascoe mentioned, of having to meet a married couple at the Jazz Club at 5am. 'She told me,' Williams said, 'she was half-minded to go home as she hadn't been there for two days.' So, while Helen's last confirmed sighting was at home on the Tuesday, confusion reigned over her precise subsequent movements. Witnesses were also not clear about what she had been wearing, what she had eaten or even what colour her purse was. And there were other intriguing questions. Why was she depressed? And why had she not been home?

Frustration mixed with racism in Det Supt Maurice Osborn's summary of the investigation. Commenting on Cascoe and Williams's statements, he said, 'Although these two men are trying to be helpful and sincere, I am of the opinion that they cannot be relied upon as to the actual day they last saw Barthelemy. As is typical with most coloureds, they usually cannot remember one day from another.'

Detectives tracked down a white couple who were casual friends of Helen, but they said they had no arrangement to meet her at all. The police checked her friends and acquaintances without any breakthroughs. Members of the Jazz Club were traced, but could offer little assistance. Boyfriend Von Barrington Adams was still badly injured from the crash at the time of the murder, no forensic evidence against Handel Cascoe could be found where he lived, while another friend of Helen's, Horace Bellafonte, had no driving licence or access to a family car. He was watched for several weeks to see if he did secretly use a car or had a place where he could have hidden a body, but again the police found nothing.

When did Helen meet her killer? Pathologist Dr Donald Teare told the inquest into her death on 2 November 1964 at Ealing Town Hall, 'The naked body of the girl was very dirty and had been dead for about two days.' Det Supt Osborn believed that after her last confirmed sighting at Talbot Road on Tuesday, 21 April, Helen may have been killed on Tuesday or Wednesday before her discovery on Friday. His testimony to the inquest revealed how much difficulty the investigation was still in a year since the discovery of Gwynneth Rees. 'We haven't discovered who the assailant was or when the girl died… We could find none of her clothing, only a handbag at a jazz club.' He said most of her clients were white men, but she socialised with 'coloured people' a lot, 'probably drug addicts'. The coroner, Dr Harold Broadbridge, summed the case up perfectly for the jury. 'The police are up against a brick wall. They have done everything possible to trace the people responsible but without success.' The verdict was 'murder by a person or persons unknown'.

So, after a spate of four, possibly five, prostitute deaths in west London the murder teams were still unable to latch onto a convincing suspect. Even piecing together the twilight lives of the victims was proving to be a considerable headache. While press reports suggested that detectives were focusing on vice rings and their violent bosses as the culprits, following Barthelemy's killing there seemed to be a shift in that approach. Kerb-crawling punters were the danger that street women should beware of, Scotland Yard warned. An appeal was issued at the end of April to the sex trade. 'All the dead women usually picked up clients from the streets or clubs in the central and west London area and often went with them in vehicles.' It went on to state that murder investigators had come across instances in which women in cars had been forced to strip, with one man brandishing a knife and other men becoming violent. They asked women to come forward and report such encounters before another prostitute could be killed. 'This appeal is urgently directed to all those women whose means of livelihood place them in danger of meeting the same fate.'

How much use was such a warning? It's unlikely that women getting into cars with strangers had not encountered violent or threatening customers before. The man women needed to be wary of was one who did not use much violence, who seemed able to lure them into a situation in which he could overwhelm them quickly. But as detectives were desperate for concrete leads, the appeal was certainly needed.

Were the police floundering at this point? In David Seabrook's 2006 book on the case, *Jack of Jumps*, he quotes an unnamed police cadet as saying, 'It was around this time, at a progress meeting in the murder room at Shepherd's Bush, that Maurice Osborn said, "If anybody's got any suggestions, I'd like to hear them – and that includes you, lad. Because I haven't got a clue. It could be witchcraft, voodoo, for all I know."'

What detectives did know for sure was that Helen Barthelemy had been picked up, asphyxiated, undressed, stored in a place where airborne globules of paint found her body, and then recklessly dumped in a Brentford alley. On 16 September 1964, Helen was buried in the same common grave at Chiswick Cemetery as Irene Lockwood.

For some reason she had wanted to leave home as a 16-year-old and never returned. She had instead endured a soul-grinding life as a prostitute. There is something almost heroic in the way she tried, with limited education and prospects, to make some life for herself on her own in London, immersing herself in the alternative culture of Notting Hill and making a few friends. One of these was Horace Bellafonte, a 24-year-old cook from Jamaica. He had met her at the Roaring Twenties and used to spend time with her, finally sharing a chip dinner and coffee in her room a few days before her murder. 'I have never had sex with Teddy, I just liked her because she was jocular and was easy for coloured boys to talk to,' he told the police.

When he saw her photo in the *Daily Mirror* he rushed to Talbot Road, not believing it was the same woman. 'I went to Talbot Road and saw the coloured woman from the front room [Nellie Manhertz] and asked for Teddy. She said, "Haven't you seen the paper, Teddy's murdered." I said, "Yes, but I just can't believe it."'

A common grave was a melancholy end for Teddy, but in her short, harsh life she had at least begun to win the kindness of new friends.

Chapter 6

Panic in the Streets – Mary Fleming

Another body in west London; another close call for the killer.

It was the early hours of the morning, 14 July 1964. William Kirwan, Patrick Beads and John Boyle were pulling an all-nighter, decorating the ABC restaurant on Chiswick High Road, part of a once-popular chain of tea shops. They were on the ground floor working on the staff room at the back of the building. Kirwan was painting the windowpanes over-looking the car park and Acton Lane.

'I saw a vehicle drive up the service road and reverse towards the pedestrian passageway, stopping and reversing for about eight or ten feet,' Kirwan said later. He thought it was a small van. This was at around 2.20am. The van's appearance was certainly unusual enough at that hour to make Kirwan stop and call Boyle over to look, particularly as the van had its lights switched off.

A man got out of the driver's seat and walked round to the rear of the van. He was aged 25–35, 5 feet 10 inches tall, medium build and clean shaven. He wore a suit. Kirwan decided to wind the stranger up. 'While the man was walking round the vehicle he was looking all around him as if looking to see if the coast was clear before doing something.' The man's strange behaviour prompted Kirwan to shout through the open part of the window, 'Who dat out dere?' The stranger saw the decorators watching, rushed back to get in the van and sped off. Kirwan and Boyle could not give a make or number plate, but confirmed it was a grey estate-type vehicle with no rear windows. It sounded like the vehicle farmer Alfred Harrow nearly collided with when Helen Barthelemy was found.

This was about 12 weeks after the discovery of Helen Barthelemy. A short distance further along Acton Lane, less than five minutes by car at that hour, a vehicle was heard hurtling in reverse down Berrymede Road. Residents remembered it revving at around the same time that Kirwan later said he saw the van. It was not much of a stretch for detectives to conclude that the Nude Killer was about to unload his latest victim at the back of the ABC when he was scared off by the night-shift decorators. He then sped off to quiet Berrymede Road and threw her out into the street. This was a cul-de-sac, which was why he was thrashing the car in reverse. It was two-and-a-half miles from where Helen Barthelemy had been dumped in the alley. The killer seemed to know these streets well.

It made a macabre start to the day for George Heard, a 34-year-old chauffeur living at number 52. He happened to be up at 4.45am because he had to drive his daughter to Acton, where she was joining a trip to France. 'I looked out of the window to see what sort of a day it was and I noticed what I thought was a tailor's dummy lying in the entrance to the garage of number 48 Berrymede Road,' he said. 'I went over there and found it was the body of a woman. She was naked. She was sort of cross-legged with arms folded and her head slumped forward.' Her clothes were nowhere to be seen. Heard saw marks on her that he guessed had been made in the boot of a car. He phoned 999. He also reported that he had been woken between 2am and 3am by a car reversing. 'I didn't take any notice because cars often come down here not knowing it's a blocked-up road.' Other residents also heard it some time after 1am.

An extraordinary incident connected with this crime was told to *Acton Gazette* reporter Brian Collett by a police contact with whom he was friendly at the time. 'The strange thing is that neighbours heard the car coming, reversing and then flying away. It turned into Acton Lane towards Turnham Green and a police car happened to be coming along Acton Lane in the opposite direction, heading north, but didn't think anything of this car coming out rather fast and shooting off up Acton Lane. If they had been coming the other way [so they would have been behind the car] they might have given chase and stopped him.' If this is an accurate account, it means the killer was almost exposed twice within a short period of this night, once by the decorators and then again by a passing police car. A night of two such heart-stopping close calls for the killer might explain why the biggest gap between 1964–65's murders – about 15 weeks – then followed. Once again the killer had been in a hurry to rid himself of a body, and once again he had nearly been exposed in his haste.

Forensic tests then revealed that dust and paint particles on this latest victim matched those on Helen Barthelemy, making it clear the body had been stored in the same place.

News of another nude body must have made hearts sink at Scotland Yard. First on the scene at 5.20am were a couple of constables from Shepherd's Bush police station. Then came, among others, Detective Chief Superintendent John

Mannings and Detective Superintendent Maurice Osborn (murder squad). Next were two detectives of the Metropolitan Police Laboratory. Detective Superintendent Bill Marchant was reported to be leading the murder hunt with Osborn. At 8.30am the pathologist Dr Donald Teare was on the scene.

The body was in a strange position, head and torso tipped forward over her right knee. Dr Teare found a corpse that once again was dirty, with hypostasis on the back, indicating that she had been kept somewhere on her back. Blanching marks indicated the outline of where her underwear had been, again suggesting she had been undressed after death. At 11.40am Dr Teare did the post-mortem at Hammersmith mortuary. Asphyxia due to strangulation was again the method of death. The body had abrasions below the chin, where perhaps she had grasped at the ligature round her neck. There were also linear marks around the sides and front of the neck in horizontal and parallel patterns, probably caused by the woman's clothing being used to strangle her. Had she, like Helen Barthelemy, put up a fight? There was a bruise above her coccyx, possibly inflicted during a struggle. The more violent wound was on her chest. This was a large bruise, caused by a particularly powerful punch. A swollen left eyelid and other abrasions also suggested a struggle. The victim was just under 5 feet 1½ inches tall, weighing around 8 stone. They took her fingerprints for identification.

She was Mary Fleming, born Mary Theresa Cuthbertson Betty in Clydebank, Scotland, on 16 September 1933. Her parents, coal salesman Richard Betty and Helen moved to Barrow-in-Furness in 1937. She left school at 17 and joined the Women's Royal Army Corps, serving as a cook until 1952. She then became a factory hand until August 1953 when, six months pregnant, she wed James Fleming, a private in the Royal Army Medical Corps. James returned to his posting in Germany and Mary lived with her parents. Her son was born on 15 November 1953. However, all was not rosy at home. In October 1954 Mary's mother seems to have made it clear she did not like the people Mary was mixing with. Mary then walked out and never saw her parents or son again. We do not know the details of this breakdown in relations, or what company it was that Mary's mother disapproved of. What is known is that on his discharge from the army, James Fleming went to live with Mary's parents. He was still there with his son at the time of her death. In view of the pressures on single pregnant women at this time to do the 'respectable' thing and marry their child's father, it could be that Mary felt trapped into a marriage she did not want. Whatever the truth, she left her parents, husband and son for good, writing home only occasionally. Husband James received one of Mary's letters. After her death he told the police, 'About 18 months ago I received a letter from her saying she was sorry about leaving home but have heard nothing since.'

Her life became a chaotic cycle of moving, prostitution, thieving and more children. She landed in Newcastle and met a seaman called Owen Hardie. They headed to London in 1955 and wound up in Dalston. Mary gave birth to a second boy in February 1956, by which time Hardie had gone. Norwich was next, where her child was put into the care of Norwich City Council. Back in London, Mary was arrested for soliciting in October 1956 on the Commercial Road. The next month she was charged with the same offence. In 1957 she was fined twice for soliciting and once for an act of indecency with another person. Perhaps she got sick of the sex work, because the following year she stole property valued at

£65 from her landlord in Hornsey and fled to Scotland. There she stole money from her relatives' gas meters. She was eventually arrested back in London for the theft against her landlord and given a conditional discharge for 12 months. However, the law came down hard on her in 1959 when she stole gas meter money at her East End digs. She was imprisoned for three months.

The early sixties found her living with Michael Turner, a former Coldstream Guard, in a flat in Powis Gardens, Notting Hill. In 1961 Mary was five months pregnant when she was picked up for soliciting, for which she got 12 months' probation. In April 1962 she gave birth to a girl. Michael left her, saying he realised she was on the 'game', but still returned to spend nights with her until February 1963. Then, on visiting the Powis Gardens flat in March he found their little girl, nearly a year old now, on her own. He stormed round to the Jazz Club on Westbourne Park Road, which was also frequented by Helen Barthelemy, and found Mary dancing with 'coloured men'. A fight erupted between one of the men, Michael and Mary. In April 1964 she was living at 25 Geraldine Road, Chiswick, with her daughter and her fourth child, a boy, born in 1963. In May 1964 she scarpered from Geraldine Road leaving unpaid bills and found her final flat, a single room, at 44 Lancaster Road, Notting Hill. This was a big terraced house with rooms occupied by several families, black and white.

Mary had the ground-floor front room. It was a squalid existence, the room full of dirty nappies, used milk bottles, with one bed and a cot on the floor for Mary's unemployed boyfriend, Patrick Craig. A woman who was acquainted with her said, 'I felt sorry for her because I knew she had nothing.' She was still getting by as a prostitute, working the same neighbourhoods as Helen Barthelemy – Queensway and Bayswater. The police report commented, 'Despite her unsavoury mode of life, she would always return home to the children in the early hours of the morning to make sure they were all right.' Fuelled by cigarettes, amphetamines and alcohol, her favourite haunts were a couple of rough boozers in the Notting Hill area, the Warwick Castle and the Kensington Park Hotel.

She was last seen on the night of 10 July 1964, soliciting on Queensway. Earlier that evening she had changed into a green-grey blouse with matching light green woollen jacket and skirt, and white plastic slingbacks. She left her children with a babysitter and went out with a friend, Elizabeth Heywood. It was near closing time so they went to the Wimpy Bar on Portobello Road. A friend who saw her there, Harry Greenwood, said, 'I was impressed by the fact that Mary was looking very smart. I was also surprised that she hadn't had a drink, whereas at that time of night she had usually had a few drinks and was noisy.' She and Elizabeth separated and Mary went out to work after midnight.

Mary met a prostitute she knew on Porchester Gardens. Maria Newman said, 'I asked whether she had any rubbers which I could have. She told me she only had two and she couldn't give me any.' Mary said to a couple of other streetwalkers that she might see them at the Jazz Club later. Outside Whiteleys department store on Queensway, Mary met two more prostitutes, Mabel Goulding and Pamela De'ak. They discussed how poor business was that night. De'ak then saw Mary walk off with a man. Later, around 2.45am, a PC Andrew Ferguson of the British Transport Police spotted a red Volkswagen on the Bayswater Road near the junction with Leinster Terrace. The driver was talking to a woman on the pavement. PC Ferguson flashed his headlights at them. The woman strolled off quickly and turned into Leinster Terrace. The officer said, 'Passing Leinster Terrace, I glanced into the turning and saw the female walking away along the road. I now recognise this female as Mrs Mary Fleming.'

They said she carried a knife, someone claimed it was a 10-inch kitchen knife. She knew transactions could turn violent because she had been attacked at a flat in Porchester Gardens, Queensway, by a man who tried to throttle her. She fought him off that time. But if she had the blade on her that night, it – along with all her belongings – were not found. And one further mystery: her teeth. Fleming had previously had her front teeth removed and in all she had 12 missing teeth. Dentures were common in the 1960s, with millions of people in their 20s and 30s wearing them; an estimated 37 per cent of Britons needed false teeth. Mary had never had individual dentures fitted, but if she had been wearing a dental plate of some kind, it was never recovered. Had the killer taken it?

What seems certain is that night spent cruising for business around Queensway was her last. The pathologist found the partially digested Wimpy burger in her stomach. It seems she met her killer in the early hours of Saturday, 11 July, soon after leaving the man in the red VW. Three days later, the killer threw her onto the garage forecourt in Berrymede Road and sped off.

'Nude No 5 – river killer hunted' was the front-page lead in the *Daily Mirror* on Wednesday, July 15 1964 (they were at this stage including Gwynneth Rees but not Elizabeth Figg). Scotland Yard had launched one of its biggest manhunts to find the 'sex-crazed killer who has murdered five women in eight months.' The report pointed out the similarities in the two most recent murders, of Helen Barthelemy and Mary Fleming, stating that, 'Both girls had been strangled. And both had been killed away from the spots where they were found. And Scotland Yard detectives think that both girls were dumped from the same car.' It finished with a call to action that the Yard was making. 'This vicious killer must be found quickly – before he strikes again.'

The *Daily Herald* screamed, 'The Strangler again!' Once more the comparison was with that other most recent and notorious mass killer from this manor – at Rillington Place. The story stated, 'Scotland Yard believed last night that the man they are seeking for the murder of street-girl Mary Fleming may be the most dangerous sex maniac since John Christie.' The *Mail* reported that plain clothes officers, men and women, were deployed throughout Bayswater, Queensway, Holland Park and Paddington to interview women working the streets.

The discovery of Mary Fleming's body also made headlines across the USA, where newspapers from the *Oshkosh Daily Northwestern* in Wisconsin to the *Eureka Humboldt Standard* in California carried a report from the United Press International news agency about Scotland Yard hunting 'Jack the Stripper'. Associated Press also circulated the story, with newspapers carrying its report, including the theory from one unnamed detective that the 'killer delights in dressing up in his victims' clothing. This would explain why none of the clothes is ever found.'

The most overwrought coverage came back in London a few days later on 19 July. The *News of the World*, the Sunday paper that closed following the hacking scandal in 2011, carried an open letter to the killer written by reporter Ron Mount, 'who has been on his trail'. This urged the Nude

Killer to call Detective Superintendent Maurice Osborn and give himself up.

'Perhaps you can't help yourself when, in the midst of your obscenities with a cheap, bought woman, the red mist comes down and your hands tighten and tighten and tighten,' the story read. 'Perhaps, when you are caught, they will save you from the searing rope because you are ill, sick in your mind. And there is no doubt at all, if you ignore my advice, you will be caught. You cannot win…

'You are a murderer. A multi-murderer. A modern Jack the Ripper who has caused a wave of terror among the street girls of London.

'It is certain you have the deaths of two women on your hands. You may be responsible for four. And there is even a chance that your grim total of sex-crazed killings could be as high as six [he included Elizabeth Figg in 1959], which brings you into line with that other monster Christie [John Reginald Halliday Christie, the aforementioned Notting Hill serial killer, who killed at least six women – though he is generally credited with eight victims – and was hanged in 1953].

'I have roamed in the early hours through the "patch" where you find your victims, that sprawling, teeming, vice-ridden jungle from Shaftesbury Avenue down west to Queensway. I have sat in the bars, the clubs and the coffee bars where your victims were well known and where, nightly, detectives are now mingling with customers.

'I know the type of women you favour. All your victims have been scrubbers, cheap little tarts, pepped up by 50 purple heart tablets a day to perform unspeakable perversions with any man who pulls up in a car and has £1 in his pocket. You like small, petite women, don't you? All your victims have been slim-built and between only 5 feet and 5 feet 3 inches tall. Not very strong were they? Not much of a struggle for you?'

A piece that sneered at the victims while almost salivating over the murders, but also a snapshot of the more gaudy tabloid coverage the crimes were receiving. That a columnist in a mainstream Sunday newspaper could feel free to refer to the victims as 'scrubbers, cheap little tarts' reveals how little sympathy many people felt towards women working the streets. Even the police, as we have seen, viewed their lives as unsavoury. This is not to say that Scotland Yard was not sincere and rigorous in its investigation. The problem was that the criminalisation of activities such as soliciting and general prejudice against prostitutes isolated the women, and made investigating crimes against them more difficult.

The dust (coke dust, coal, red and black paint particles, minute specks of blue paint) found on Helen Barthelemy and Mary Fleming was the murder squad's one solid piece of forensic evidence. It became the focus of a huge amount of dogged detective work, sucking in enormous police resources.

The plan: find the premises where the bodies had been stored. The mix of dust and paint particles would help to pinpoint it. The globular paint particles had come from a spray nozzle, not a brush, so boatyards and garages were the main target, particularly those run by small outfits, perhaps one-man operations. Assistant Commissioner Sir Ranulph Bacon agreed that additional officers could be drafted in from other divisions to assist the investigation. The CID called in 105 aids to check residences, boatyards, garages, warehouses, lock-ups, sheds. A six-square-mile area stretching across the deposition sites of the two women, from Brentford to Acton and down to the Thames, was canvassed. Some 150 properties were visited and dust collected from many. Sixty staff were deployed at the Metropolitan Police Forensic Laboratory as the samples came in. However, none had the same combination of particles as that on the bodies.

Detectives spoke to hundreds of people who mixed in the same rough environment as the victims – prostitutes, punters, boyfriends, hangers-on. All-night observations were set up around Queensway for officers to note down registration numbers of cars opening their doors to streetwalkers. Times, dates, places, too. A similar watch was kept up at Dukes Meadows.

And yet, Det Supt Marchant, head of the team investigating Mary Fleming's murder, was as bogged down in misinformation as were the other investigations. Did Mary really have another boyfriend, an estate agent, as she told one of her pals? If so, Marchant's officers could not find him. And what of the purported strangler who attacked her in Porchester Gardens? Again, nowhere to be found. Tips came in – a weirdo psychiatrist, a transvestite cabbie who hated prostitutes, and many more. But not one convincing suspect was unearthed.

The inquest into Mary's death was held alongside Helen Barthelemy's at Ealing Coroners' Court on 2 November 1964. The *Mirror* reported the jury being told that police had interviewed thousands of people in connection with these murders. The jury's verdict was the same for Mary Fleming as it was for Barthelemy. 'Murder by a person or persons unknown'.

Chapter 7

Low Morals in High Places – Frances Brown

Chris 'Frank' Gibbings was a young constable in 1964, when he was ordered to go to Hornton Street in Kensington. A body had been found.

'I was a 19-year-old copper at Kensington,' he recalls. 'I was ordered to go up to this site and stand there because I was told the press were evil people and would use any excuse to get on the site. I had to make sure nobody got near it until the investigating officer arrived.'

This time the victim had been left under a bin lid in a car park just off Kensington High Street. Assistant civil defence officer Dennis Sutton got a shock when he lifted the lid on Wednesday, 25 November, at around 1.30pm.

Gibbings told me, 'Two guys turn up in a car and one said, I'm the superintendent. I said, Could I see your warrant card? He fumbled in his wallet and said, Oh, for goodness sake, I haven't got it. He said to the other guy, Sergeant, show him yours – and he hadn't got it either. So, I said, Well, you're not getting near the crime scene. Then they came back with a uniformed inspector, the duty officer. I thought, Oh, I'm in the shit now. I was a probationary PC. Anyway, the superintendent shook me by the hand and said, Well done.'

Once this confusion was over, investigators were greeted by a distressing sight. It was the body of a naked woman, which had been covered with the bin lid and other debris – wood, leaves – and crawling with maggots. The corpse was badly decomposed. Dr Donald Teare's post-mortem at Hammersmith mortuary on the afternoon of its discovery confirmed similarities that placed the victim as the latest of the Nude Killer. His examination had to be quite painstaking because of the condition of the body, but he was able to detect abrasions on the neck and linear marks near the larynx. Asphyxia caused by pressure on the neck was his verdict. As had been the case with Helen Barthelemy and Mary Fleming, the abrasions were possibly caused by the victim clawing at her ligatures; the linear indents again the result of that ligature. She seemed to have had venereal disease at some time, as was true of all the victims. Another blanched line on the left side of her belly suggested she had been stripped after death. She had three teeth missing from her lower jaw, though how and for what reason they were taken was not clear. Strangely, there was some plain paper placed in her vagina. But vitally, there were the same paint particles on her that had been found on Barthelemy and Fleming.

Identifying her was not straightforward. Her nose, eyes and much of her face had rotted away. But again she was petite, 5 feet 1 inch tall, weighing around 7 stone. On her left forearm was a tattoo: flowers with 'Helen' and 'Mum and Dad'. She was one of four victims of the Nude Killer to have tattoos. By the 1950s skin art was beginning to live down its association with sailors or criminality, and tattoos were becoming a trend for more daring women, popularised in part by celebrated female tattooist Jessie Knight. It was the victim's fingerprints, however, that eventually confirmed her identity, though there was still confusion over whether she was Margaret McGowan – as she was identified in the newspapers – or Frances Brown. McGowan could have been the name she gave, which ended up on her final charge sheet, one of many aliases she used (Nuala Rowlands, Anne Sutherland, Frances Quinn…).

How long had she been in the car park, a chaotic jumble of Minis, Bentleys, Oxford Morrises and other top models of the fifties and sixties? She was last seen on 23 October, but it was difficult to say when the killer deposited her in Kensington. Dennis Sutton thought the bin lid had been missing for up to six weeks until he spotted it covering the body. So, it was very likely that Frances Brown had lain there for a long time – which was lucky for the killer because the body evidence had degraded despite being in a public car park. It was at the back of Kensington Central Library, which included the civil defence office in its basement, where Dennis Sutton worked.

Following his near blunders in rushing the disposal of his previous two victims – when it seems he was seen by the farmer in Brentford and the two decorators in Chiswick – the killer had a cooling-off period of more than three months before committing his next murder. He then hid the body and switched to an entirely new drop site. Hornton Street meets the major shopping area of Kensington High Street, diagonally opposite where the Barkers department store used to be before it closed in 2006. It's a long way from the seclusion of Dukes Meadows. In some ways this was a daring move, leaving the body so close to a major, busy high street bustling with people. The car park itself was also surrounded and overlooked by houses. However, while this was an audacious place to choose, it did give him the cover he needed. The car park was dark at night and surrounded by high walls. House-to-house visits on Hornton Street and Campden Hill Road, which ran parallel, failed to find anyone who had seen suspicious activity in the car park. A search of it for evidence also drew a blank.

The *Daily Mirror* hailed the 'Murder drama of tattooed call girl' with a front-page splash revealing that 23-year-old 'Margaret McGowan' had been a witness in the Stephen Ward trial of 1963. Ward was the osteopath and artist caught up in the Profumo scandal. He was accused of living off immoral earnings and committed suicide before a guilty verdict was announced. The Nude Murders case is extraordinary for the intriguing links it had between the hidden world of street prostitution, the era's most notorious gang, the Krays (via 1963 victim Gwynneth Rees), and Profumo, the decade's most momentous political scandal. The Nude Killer's sixth victim offers a sobering insight into vice in high places as well as on the street.

Frances Brown was born on 3 January 1943 in Glasgow. Dad Francis was a railway worker, mother Helen McGowan had been a tailor's machinist. At the age of 11 she appeared in juvenile court and was found guilty of theft by finding. She was put on probation for two years. She left school at 15 and worked in various shops. Her mother could not control her and was in despair. Her mother would say later, 'I had a terrible time with her. She was staying out all night and I'd no idea where she was.' In 1958 she made her second appearance in juvenile court and was sent to an approved school until 1960. Even when she was returned home on licence, she went back to staying out all hours. By the time she was sent back to approved school, she was pregnant by a local man, who left her. Her daughter was born in April 1961. After a final stint in approved school, Frances was released. She went off to London, leaving her baby with her mum. Her first conviction for soliciting came quickly in October 1961. There were many more.

The man who became her partner had also had several run-ins with the law. Dublin-born scaffolder Paul Quinn had convictions for theft and break-ins, and had served time in prison. They lived together in Shepherd's Bush. She gave birth to her second child, a boy, at Queen Charlotte's Hospital in March 1963. An episode of depression followed the birth.

We get glimpses of the toll that prostitution took on these victims. The image of Hannah Tailford hanging round Charing Cross and starving, having walked out on her partner and little girl days before – 'How would you like a new mother?' The sightings of Irene Lockwood in the days before her death, soliciting or drunk in the streets of Kensington or Queensway. The cafe employee recalling Helen Barthelemy in her final days being in low spirits. No doubt the drinking and partying at spots like the Jazz Club were escapes, while amphetamines fuelled the street hustle. But the harsh reality of their lives was venereal disease, unwanted pregnancies, sometimes brutal clients and the unceasing pressure to keep earning.

In Frances Brown's case it is impossible to say what her state of mind was, but clearly her pregnancy triggered a breakdown. Hysterical and suffering from depression, she entered Springfield mental hospital on 23 May 1963. She told her carers that she had tried to kill herself during and after the pregnancy. She was kept as a compulsory patient under the Mental Health Act until 5 June, before being prescribed tranquillisers and sleeping pills, and discharged. She moved to

Smethwick, near Birmingham, to recover. At this time her new son was placed in care. Smethwick County Council saw that he was adopted.

Charges for attempting to steal a car and child neglect followed. Paul Quinn paid the fine for the first conviction, but she was imprisoned for three months for the second.

Frances eventually signed over custody of her daughter to her parents. But having not been able to take responsibility for her first two children, she still ended up with a third. Her second son was born in May 1964 in East Dunbartonshire. Frances, Quinn and the baby lived with her parents in Glasgow for a while after the birth, before returning to London in August 1964, and a flat at 16a Southerton Road, Hammersmith.

She wrote to her mother, 'Paul and I have a great flat, 1 kitchen, 1 living room, 1 bedroom, 1 big lobby and it has a garden back and front.' She reported that Paul Quinn had a job and worked late nearly every night. 'Oh, Mammy we have a television and hope to get a radiogram this week.'

It was a happy domestic picture. But, however much Quinn was earning and however many mod-cons they had, it did not mean that Frances stopped soliciting. A couple of months later, she would meet her killer.

When her mother, Helen, saw coverage of her testimony in the Stephen Ward trial the previous summer, in July 1963, she must have realised her daughter was making her living as a prostitute. 'When she came to visit to me I asked her about this and she said that it wasn't her and was quite indignant about it all,' Helen Brown said. Frances claimed it was someone who looked just like her, and was frequently mistaken for her sister. How upsetting her mother found this is not known, but perhaps knowing the daughter with whom she had had such a 'terrible' time when younger, Helen felt it best to let the matter go.

However, she was clearly right about her girl. Frances was a prostitute and had played a small role in the Profumo affair, which led to the charges against Ward. Featuring sex, prostitutes, a spy and a government minister, it became a scandal that convulsed the political and legal establishment.

Ward was a 50-year-old osteopath with a high-society clientele, including such notables as Winston Churchill, the US ambassador to Britain, Averell Harriman, Sir Malcolm Sargent and Paul Getty, along with superstars Frank Sinatra, Ava Gardner and Danny Kaye. One patient who became a great friend of Ward's was Lord William 'Bill' Astor, who inherited the stately home Cliveden, the setting for the affair's initial encounters. Ward's practice was at 38 Devonshire Street, near Regent's Park. In his spare time, he was also a talented and in-demand portrait artist.

Christine Keeler, a 21-year-old model and girl about town, had struck up a platonic friendship with Ward. She lived at Ward's Wimpole Mews flat and often spent weekends with him at Cliveden. There they would mix with another pal of Ward's, Captain Yevgeny Ivanov, a Russian spy working undercover as a naval attaché. The infamous encounter in the affair occurred on the weekend of 8–9 July 1961. Astor had invited several high-powered guests to Cliveden, including Lord Mountbatten, President of Pakistan Field Marshal Ayub Khan, and the Minister of War, John Profumo, along with his actress wife, Valerie Hobson. This select gathering took place at the main house, while in the cottage on the grounds, Ward was entertaining Keeler, his girlfriend Sally Norie and a girl they had just met. Around the time that Ward's guests were frolicking in the pool, Astor and Profumo, in dinner dress, stumbled upon Keeler, wearing just a towel. It was Ward who soon did the introductions to the President of Pakistan, Valerie Hobson and others, and he clearly carried it off with charm and aplomb, because he and his attractive female friends were invited up to the big house the following day. To the ensuing pool party Ward also invited Ivanov. The Russian later drove Keeler back to Wimpole Mews, while Profumo wasted no time asking Ward for her telephone number.

Whether Keeler had sex with Ivanov is a moot point, but Profumo did have a liaison with her for several months. Also in part of Ward's circle was Keeler's younger (by two years) friend Mandy Rice-Davies. She had been crooked landlord Peter Rachman's mistress until his death in November 1962. She lived for a while with Ward and Keeler in Wimpole Mews.

Events began to career out of control. Away from the Cliveden set, Keeler had two violent men competing for her – Johnny Edgecombe and Aloysius 'Lucky' Gordon. They confronted each other at the Flamingo Club in Soho and Edgecombe, a former merchant seaman from Antigua, slashed Gordon's face with a knife. Keeler subsequently finished her relationship with the domineering Edgecombe. However, perhaps the moment that triggered the whole crisis came on 14 December 1962 when Edgecombe turned up again, this time at Wimpole Mews carrying a pistol, believing that Keeler had dumped him for Gordon. Keeler and Mandy Rice-Davies refused to let him in, and he fired shots into the door lock. He was arrested and sentenced to seven years for possessing a firearm with intent to endanger life. However, when Keeler failed to turn up as a witness having fled to Spain, the press – already hyper on rumours of her illicit triangle with Profumo and Ivanov – assumed someone influential had paid to get her out of the way. Gordon, who arrived in England from Jamaica in 1948, was vital to the scandal in another way, too. Keeler falsely told the police that he had assaulted her. (In fact, on this occasion, she had been punched and kicked after a row with John Hamilton-Marshall, brother of her friend, Paula.) At the Old Bailey she perjured herself by repeating the accusation. Gordon got three years in prison.

In the meantime, rumours continued to swirl and in March 1963, *Private Eye* dropped hints about the model, the spy and the minister. That such a ménage had the potential for Britain's top secrets to leak during pillow talk was the slightly far-fetched conclusion latched onto by excitable politicians and the media. And that is to say nothing of the minister's reputation as a respectable married man. To save that reputation, Profumo then lied to the House of Commons in a statement drafted by the Tory government. This stated that his 'friendly terms' with Miss Keeler did not include sexual intercourse. Anyone living in the real world could see it involved little else, but this was the pose struck by the government. In this way the stakes were raised in that the reputation of Harold Macmillan's government were now tied to a lie.

Ward initially kept quiet about Profumo's affair, and for a couple of months the minister continued to be portrayed in the press as a clean-living government stalwart, even being photographed with the Queen Mother. Tragedy overtook Ward when Home Secretary Henry Brooke decided to go after him, perhaps feeling that the louche-living osteopath had somehow caused the mess. However, by scapegoating Ward, the home secretary blew open the whole scandal again.

The police watched Ward's home and office 24 hours a

day, and his phone was tapped. They interviewed his friends, such as Lord Astor, and asked patients leaving his consulting room whether anything improper had occurred. Ward attempted to fend off this inquisition by telling the prime minister's private secretary that he would tell all he knew if the police did not stop persecuting him. He wrote to the home secretary and newspaper editors complaining of his treatment. He even wrote to Leader of the Opposition Harold Wilson that Profumo had lied to the House of Commons – a transgression that if true would be politically fatal to any politician. Ward's letters to the press and political pressure finally led Profumo to tell his wife the truth. He resigned on 4 June 1963.

Ward was now wide open to the full vengeance of the establishment. He eventually faced five charges of living off immoral earnings and procuring. While nearly all of Ward's influential friends were scared off from testifying on his behalf at the Old Bailey, one of the few witnesses who did give credence to his integrity was Frances Brown. She refuted testimony given by a woman called Vickie Barrett, who had told the court that Ward was her pimp, and that regularly at his mews flat over a couple of months she would horsewhip or thrash customers with a cane, while dressed in high heels and underwear, or have sex with them. The price was £1 a stroke or £5 for intercourse. Ward, Barrett claimed, took the punters' money and promised to get her a flat later on.

Writer and broadcaster Ludovic Kennedy was at the trial and wrote in his book *The Trial of Stephen Ward*, 'A small bird-like woman with a pale face and a fringe teetered down the court and into the witness box. She was wearing a dark blue dress with a white bow.' This was Frances Brown. Kennedy describes a courtroom hushed in expectation of new revelations. Frances was not easy to hear, but confident in her answers. She testified that she and Barrett solicited regularly together and they were twice picked up by Ward on Oxford Street. She also confirmed that they visited Ward's flat on two occasions. Kennedy reports her testimony in court:

'When was that?' asked prosecuting counsel Mervyn Griffith-Jones.

'Between the middle of March and the week the Pope died [Pope John XXIII died on 3 June 1963].'

'And what happened when you were there?'

'Well, the first time Vickie did the business with Dr Ward.'

'And what did you do?'

'I looked on.'

'And the second time?'

'We just had coffee.'

This and other responses she gave failed to corroborate parts of Barrett's evidence. Frances told the court that her reason for wanting to testify was that she had read Barrett's evidence in the papers and wanted to put her side of the story.

Some authors have found it hard to believe that Frances stepped forward to do the right thing for Ward. Journalist Brian McConnell, for example, wrote in his 1974 book on the case, *Found Naked and Dead*, 'Still the inevitable scrubber, she perhaps thought it would attract even more high-class clientele.' Such sneering disregard of prostitutes was still common into the 1980s and beyond. A glaring example of this prejudice would even surface during Yorkshire Ripper Peter Sutcliffe's trial in 1981, when Attorney General Sir Michael Havers felt justified in saying of the victims, 'Some women were prostitutes, but perhaps the saddest part of these cases is that some were not. The last six attacks were on totally respectable women.' Even today there are authors who assert that the prostitutes who testified at the Ward trial did so simply to get their photos in the newspaper. This conveniently ignores the fact that one witness, Ronna Ricardo, said she had been severely pressured by the police to make false statements against Ward. She bravely withdrew her evidence at the trial despite her dread of the police. In addition, and as we have seen, by coming forward with her testimony, Frances ended up revealing to her family the embarrassing fact that she was a prostitute. However, the assumption with some authorities and commentators is that the motivations of a woman involved in prostitution must always be self-serving and dishonest.

Maybe she just thought Ward was a decent man who was being shafted with a lot of lies. She apparently had some sketches of herself that Ward had done and was perhaps grateful that such a posh, accomplished acquaintance had taken an interest in her. In any case, her testimony probably helped to ensure that Ward was acquitted of the third count of living off immoral earnings.

However, after hearing Judge Sir Archie Marshall's hostile summing-up, Ward could see what was coming and took an overdose of sleeping pills. He was subsequently found guilty on two counts of living off the immoral earnings of Christine Keeler and Mandy Rice-Davies (who had denied that they were prostitutes) on 30 July 1963. Ward did not regain consciousness and died without hearing the verdict on 3 August. It was later reported that Frances had turned up at St Stephen's Hospital, Fulham, with flowers for Ward as he lay in a coma. She was turned away.

Several renowned authorities have since highlighted how the law was abused so that Ward could be made an example of. Human rights barrister Geoffrey Robertson has recently called for the verdict against Ward to be overturned on the grounds that he was innocent and did not get a fair trial. Robertson highlights the fact that Christine Keeler, whose testimony harmed Ward, had perjured herself at Lucky Gordon's trial and repeated that perjury during the Ward trial, which was not disclosed to Ward's defence team (she was later sentenced to nine months for perjury). The judge misdirected the jury by telling them they could infer Ward's guilt because he could call on no character witnesses. There was insufficient evidence that any money Keeler/Rice-Davies gave Ward came from prostitution; and they were not prostitutes 'selling their bodies indiscriminately for profit'.

The whole affair saw private sexual habits crash head-on with public sanctimony. While during the Ward trial the public was goggle-eyed at the tales of orgies and sexual improprieties in high places, the crowds outside the Old Bailey booed Mandy Rice-Davies and Ward, who was portrayed in court as a corrupter. It was easy for the authorities to capitalise on this mood to ensure virtue triumphed over loose morals with the Ward case. However, once the political scandal had been swept under the carpet with Ward's death, Frances Brown and Vickie Barrett could disappear back to their shadowy lives of selling sex to company directors, doctors and clergymen, among others.

That was until Frances Brown became the headline in November the following year. The *Daily Express* joined the *Mirror* in immediately pointing out her connection to the Ward trial. The *Express* front page was, 'Murdered: Ward case girl', and its story went further than the *Mirror*'s in asserting that detectives would be interviewing witnesses involved in the Ward case. Chief Superintendent John du Rose, who took over management of the Nude Murders investigation in

1965, would later confirm that all witnesses from the Ward case had been interviewed. This seems unusual because there appears no likely connection between the Ward and Nude Murders cases. If true, it suggests the police were desperate to uncover a solid suspect somewhere and somehow.

A year after the Ward case the media focus had shifted to the prostitute killings in west London and the fear that was gripping women who worked the streets. Vickie Barrett, who had known Frances Brown well, summed up the mood. She was quoted by journalist Brian McConnell, 'I last saw Margaret [Frances's alias] in the Rio Cafe, Paddington, a week before she disappeared. She and I shared rooms once.

'She was a jolly girl but she could sink into morose moods. You know we both gave evidence at the Stephen Ward trial. I can't help feeling the murderer is a man who knows all about us working girls in Notting Hill and picks his next victim carefully. Next time it could be me. It's all too Jack the Ripperish for me.'

Chapter 8

New Clues

The last time Frances was seen alive, the night of Friday, 23 October 1964, she was soliciting with another friend, 'Blonde' Beryl Mahood (an alias of a woman called Kim Taylor). They had gone out drinking earlier, with Frances wearing new clothes from C&A and other shops on Oxford Street that she had bought the day before, including a green two-piece suit with dark fur collar, blue and white check petticoat and black suede shoes. She also had blue gloves.

They had been on a long drinking session at the Warwick Castle pub on Portobello Road during the afternoon and evening. At closing time Frances and Beryl left and met two men who were in separate cars waiting at traffic lights by the junction of Portobello Road and Westbourne Park Road. The first man waved and directed them to go round the corner. The drivers overtook them and parked in a mews, Hayden's Place. They got out and were clearly interested in business. Brown suggested they go in one car to a quiet spot near Chiswick Green. The smaller man persuaded them to split up.

He was about 5 feet 8 inches tall, aged 30–35, with dark brown hair and a full face. He wore a white shirt and a tan suede jacket with sheepskin or lambswool collar. This man, according to what Beryl later told the police, did most of the talking. His mate was 5 feet 10 inches, of medium build, similar age, with thinning light brown hair, a round face, full lips and prominent ears. He had a London accent and was well spoken, while his friend was said to have a 'rougher' way of speaking.

The shorter first man talked Frances into his car, a darkish grey Ford Zephyr or Zodiac. Beryl got into the other car. The details she recalled about it were that it was newish, light grey, with a bench front seat and gear lever in the steering column.

The two cars went in a convoy, but when they reached Shepherd's Bush Green, they became separated. Beryl said her punter looked round for the other car and just said something like, 'It doesn't matter,' and he would meet his mate later 'at the flat'. They had sex in the car, probably in the car park on Young Street, just over Kensington High Street from where Frances's body would be found. Beryl's punter dropped her outside the Jazz Club on Westbourne Park Road. This is where she had an arrangement to catch up with Frances. But Frances was not in the club. No one had seen her. Later, at the club, Beryl saw Frances's partner, Paul Quinn, and he asked where Frances was. Beryl explained that they were split up…

It would be a week later, at 2pm on Saturday, 31 October, that Quinn would go to Hammersmith police station with his baby son in his arms and explain that Frances had not been home since Thursday, 22 October. The police sergeant Elizabeth Neale dealt with him and would say later, 'Mr Quinn appeared completely at ease and did not express any concern regarding the well-being or whereabouts of Brown. His only concern appeared to be for the child.' However, he denied he was the baby's father and said he was not worried about the mother because she often went missing for days at a time. He was referred to the child welfare department on Holland Park Avenue and said the mother was lazy and did not want the boy. The child went to a foster mother in Bushey. Quinn moved out of Southerton Road on 9 November, having given away Frances's clothes and the boy's cot and pushchair. In later life Quinn would bitterly regret becoming separated from his son at this time. Author Neil Milkins says in his book *Who Was Jack the Stripper?* that Quinn made several failed attempts after 1966 to regain custody of the boy, who was brought up by foster parents and then went to a children's home.

On Friday, 27 November, Quinn was in a pub in Maidstone, where he had been working on a building site, when someone said another prostitute had been found dead in London. The landlord showed him the front page of the *Daily Express* with a big photo of Frances on it, taken at the time of the Ward trial. Quinn was shocked, said he had lived with that woman and got out his own photo of Frances, before heading back to London to speak to the police.

That same day, the 27th, Beryl Mahood gave Detective Superintendent Bill Marchant's team, which was based at Kensington police station, her recollection of the night of 23 October. She described the two men who picked them up near the Warwick Castle, and an identikit picture was given to the media on 2 December. This was more than a month since Frances was last seen, and she and Beryl had been drinking heavily at the pub that day, so Beryl's recall of the details may have been cloudy. Nevertheless, this still looked like a big breakthrough for the detectives.

They thought there was a possibility the two motorists might have been attending that year's Earl's Court Motor

Show earlier that day. An appeal went out on Shaw Taylor's *Police 5* programme on ITV, a forerunner of *Crimewatch*. Local and national newspapers along with the BBC also carried details. The *Daily Mirror* plastered its front page on 3 December with the identikits, quoting Det Supt Marchant, 'It is vital that we find these two men.'

The appeals prompted a mass of information from the public, all of which was checked. After the Frances Brown investigation was then switched to Shepherd's Bush police station, where the previous cases were also based, detectives put out another appeal for the man who drove off with Frances to come forward. 'We believe he has information that is vital to our inquiries into the Nude Murders. The police are willing to meet this man anywhere, at any time, even through a third person. His identity will not be disclosed.'

This suggested that detectives did not necessarily suspect the short man in the tan jacket of being the killer. But he could clearly reveal where he had parted with Frances, which may also have been where she encountered her killer. Like many men who use prostitutes, he most likely did not want this to become public knowledge. Not that the police were taking any chances. Detectives hung around Portobello Road and the local pubs looking out for the two motorists.

In addition, plainclothes female officers were on the streets of west London talking to sex workers to glean as much detail as they could about Frances.

On 24 February 1965, the inquest at Hammersmith Coroners' Court heard from Dr Donald Teare that the cause of Frances Brown's death was again asphyxiation as a result of pressure on the neck. Verdict: murder by person or persons unknown.

Soon after, on the 27th, the identikit was reissued. Detectives also enlisted the assistance of Beryl Mahood again. She had been in custody in Accrington, Lancashire, on a charge of larceny. That would eventually be dismissed and at police expense she was brought to London on 4 March. She took the officers to Bayswater, Shepherd's Bush and Notting Hill and convinced prostitutes there to talk to them. They learned more about Frances's clients and the sexual practices they required, but despite all this work, the two motorists could still not be identified.

The press had ramped up its coverage. The *Sunday Mirror* on 29 November had a new angle – they had found the hairdresser's shop on Portobello Road where the paper claimed all the victims used to go. The man who did their hair was 35-year-old Derek Walter, who said, 'Whenever they had the money to spare for a hair-do they came to me. They changed the colour of their hair as frequently as they changed their names.

'I shall always remember the remarks that passed between them after the first girl vanished.

'They tried to laugh it off, and thought it would never happen to them. But I could see that underneath they were scared that they might be the next.

'Every time another body was found they talked of nothing else in the salon.'

The following day sister paper the *Daily Mirror* had a story with pictures of Paul Quinn on the rain-soaked streets of Shepherd's Bush. This stated that he had launched his own effort to find out what happened to his partner Frances. 'Paul Quinn, 28, put on his new blue suit yesterday and went hunting for clues to the killer of the girl he once lived with…

'Quinn – born in Dublin, Eire, and known to friends as "Pepe" – toured pubs and clubs, talking to prostitutes who had known Margaret McGowan [Frances Brown].'

He was quoted at length in the newspaper and his words give an insight into their relationship. 'Frances used to laugh about the other murders. She used to tell me nobody would ever kill her.

'She was small – but strong. She knew how to look after herself. She'd been around.

'I met her in 1962. I knew she was a good hustler. She would go out in to work in rain, snow – anything. All the money she earned she spent on our flat.

'Frances began staying away for two or three days at a time. I had to look after the baby.'

What he did not mention here was that she may have been keeping out of his way because he had been violent to her on occasion.

'The last time I saw Frances,' he said, 'was on October 22. I'd bought her a new costume and she was in high spirits.

'She went out and never came back.'

That weekend, the *News of the World* had had a different angle. 'Police build picture of kinky killer'. This suggested detectives were moving away from theories about pimps, gangsters or sugar daddies being the killer, and were instead coming up with what modern investigators would call a profile of a random murderer with no ties to his victims.

'Already he has murdered five girls [Elizabeth Figg and Gwynneth Rees were not included],' the report stated. 'Now police have pieced together enough data to suggest that the killer is middle-aged and hunts for victims between 5 foot and 5 foot 3 inches. He prefers the type of prostitute who is prepared to perform unspeakable perversions.' It was the *News of the World*'s style to use phrases such as 'unspeakable perversions' and 'kinky killer' without explanation, preferring to let its readers' imaginations run riot. The paper also said the

stalking murderer made frequent night trips cruising around
Queensway and Notting Hill in what it claimed, for some
unknown reason, was a car with a small, oil-stained boot and
numerous rust marks.

An interesting point the paper raised was that the murder
teams under Detective Chief Superintendent Jack Mannings
and Detective Superintendent William Marchant were
reviewing 3,400 statements taken since Hannah Tailford was
found on 2 February. This was in case they had already interviewed the killer without having spotted him.

It seemed that every corner of Fleet Street was able to come
up with a new theory about the killer. One of the more peculiar ones was in the *Daily Mail* on 30 November. This suggested the murderer might be a retired or struck-off solicitor.
'Scotland Yard detectives, seeking a man who preys on prostitutes, have a strangely written document, given to a West
London prostitute by one of her outwardly respectable once-
a-week clients. The prostitute has told police that this customer stopped his regular visits at the time 30-year-old
Hannah Tailford, found nude in the Thames last February,
was murdered.' The typewritten document listed the client's
sexual requirements; it was studied by detectives under Chief
Superintendent Mannings. The man, who was married but
picked up the 'frightened street girl' in Bayswater, was said to
have a grudge against prostitutes. Leaving aside the 'strangely
written document' for a moment, the *Mail*'s report was flimsy,
and soon forgotten.

The next month the *Evening Standard* gave the story a per-
plexing twist when it tracked down Beryl Mahood. Its report
on 1 December revealed that she had given detectives 'one of
their best leads so far', namely descriptions of the two motorists and the fact that Frances was driven away in a grey

Zephyr. Mahood was scared the mystery men would try to kill her, even telling the *Standard* that the previous night two men in a van had tried to run her down near the basement flat where she lived. Whatever the truth and relevance of her account to the paper, it is clear that the killings were sending a chill of dread through the prostitutes of Bayswater and Shepherd's Bush.

Then on 13 December the *News of the World* followed this up with another reported attack on Beryl. This time she said she had been attacked as she left a 'West London jazz club, used as a rendezvous for the car girls'. She was quoted as saying, 'The man kicked me and told me to mind my own business and keep my trap shut. I don't think he's the murderer, but with the hunt going on everybody is on edge.'

The story floated another police theory: that Frances Brown, Irene Lockwood and Hannah Tailford were part of a 'perverted network'. It did not specify what this was but claimed the victims all knew Julie Mollie, a woman who had died of a drugs overdose in Taplow, Buckinghamshire, but was 'well known among London's perverted party set'.

Because these three victims all frequented the Jazz Club on Westbourne Park Road, the *News of the World* added that the police were looking into the theory that the killer found his victims there and then followed them in his car.

The same paper had already reported earlier that month in a front-page splash, 'Net tightens on Nude Killer'. This carried the news that the police were using female officers as decoys pretending to be streetwalkers. They were watched by male colleagues also in disguise and had been ordered not to get into any punter's car but to record the driver's details. In one hour, the report stated, the incognito officers had netted 250 men trying to pick up prostitutes. 'And this was only one small area of Notting Hill,' it said.

The ongoing investigations into the murders of Gwynneth Rees, Hannah Tailford, Irene Lockwood, Helen Barthelemy, Mary Fleming and now Frances Brown finally seemed to have some tangible leads.

The most recent three victims were clearly linked by the dust and paint particles on their naked bodies. Once the huge effort being put into finding the origin of these particles was accomplished, and therefore the place where the killer had kept the bodies, surely then detectives would be very close to exposing the man responsible.

They now also had the descriptions of the two men who had driven off with Beryl Mahood and the latest victim, Frances Brown. Even if these men were not the killers, individually or as a team, then the man in the tan jacket might have invaluable information about Frances's movements later that night – or may even have seen who her next client was.

However, despite these promising developments, there were still many dead ends. All the manpower that was going into talking to prostitutes, clients and motorists in the Bayswater to Shepherd's Bush area, checking the car details and analysing dust particles had still not led to a breakthrough with a suspect at the end of it.

The appeal for information about the two motorists prompted hundreds of calls and letters from the public. These took time to clear, though many could be quickly dismissed. A male correspondent pointed his finger at a man he heard in a cubicle in the Gents at Paddington Station mumbling about prostitutes, though he didn't see the stranger's face, while another alerted the police to the possibility that one of the motorists was none other than Captain Yevgeny Ivanov, the spy from the Profumo affair...

Other hunches led nowhere. No pawn shop, jeweller's or second-hand shop in west London was found to have received any of Frances Brown's belongings, or a small gold ring that boyfriend Paul Quinn had loaned her before she went out with Beryl Mahood. The police even had the belongings of prisoners who had been taken into custody since 23 October checked in case something of Frances's was in their possession. Again, no luck.

Nor, despite the huge media coverage, did they ever find out who the two motorists who picked up Frances and Beryl Mahood were. No one could, or would, identify them, and they never walked into a police station to give their version of what happened on Frances's last night.

Even in depositing her body, luck had been with the killer. He had only covered Frances with a dustbin lid and some debris, and could not have hoped that she would lay undiscovered for nearly five weeks in a busy car park.

The police were certainly throwing considerable manpower and resources at the investigation – and the operation would grow further in 1965 with the discovery of the next body.

Shepherd's Bush police station, London's most modern in 1964, was the focus for inquiries into the murders stretching back to Gwynneth Rees, while the station at Kensington, the closest to where Frances Brown was found, became the base for the latest inquiry. Detective Superintendent Bill Marchant added the Brown case to his investigation into the death of Mary Fleming.

The size of the Nude Murders investigation was presenting problems. The hunt for the Yorkshire Ripper in the late 1970s would similarly be hampered by information overload in an era before the computerisation of data. This was still a time of index cards and filing cabinets. It was a very hands-on process.

During the 1960s, a detective superintendent would direct inquiries on most homicide cases. They would have a detective inspector as their deputy, while the murder office would usually be managed by one officer, a detective sergeant. All incoming data would be written on an A5-size message pad, which had boxes for details such as name of person calling, content of message, action taken and result. From these the sergeant would make up card indexes detailing names, addresses, car details, phone numbers and other facts relevant to that particular inquiry. The sergeant would then also make an Action Index to show inquiries made and the results.

Witnesses, fingerprints and forensic evidence were the foundations on which cases were built in this era before CCTV and DNA. But while every investigation had a card-index system in metal drawers, the actions were logged in different ways depending on the habits of the sergeant managing the office. For example, one sergeant might write actions up in an A4-sized book. This could create problems if investigations into separate murders showed a pattern and needed to be merged.

A detective superintendent and his deputy – usually a detective inspector – would generally not write anything down. They would keep details of a murder investigation in their head. This would have been a tight group, with the office manager (sergeant) and maybe one other detective sergeant as part of the inner circle. One former detective superintendent, who joined the Met in 1969, Chris Burke, told me, 'Other members of the enquiry were "mushrooms", kept in the dark and only told what the detective superintendent or inspector wanted them to know. They were terrified some of it would leak out to the press.'

Chief Superintendent John du Rose would eventually be brought in to coordinate the multiple investigations. Officers of this rank were a select bunch in the 1960s, and there were only a few of them in Scotland Yard. Some old detectives of Chris Burke's generation remembered this period fondly. He said, 'It was only in the 70s that the world went mad and made too many senior ranks of commanders and deputy assistant commissioners, who were, in the main, a pain in the arse. Normally, they were highly educated without any experience and a complete lack of common sense. However, the bosses of the 60s were mostly very experienced people who had spent lots of years in various ranks and positions in the Met before climbing the ladder. They were often bullies and feared by most, if not all. They could destroy a man's career in blink of an eye. Most were excellent detectives but would be heavy drinkers and "married to the job". If you didn't do your job to their satisfaction, the axe would fall.'

While the senior men could be working seven days a week, 14 hours a day, a heavy load was also taken on by those further down the hierarchy. Whether it was spending 12-hour shifts in a freezing van on a winter's night logging car number plates or doing a mountain of administrative work, a huge number of man hours were going into the hunt for west London's kerb-crawling killer.

This is perfectly illustrated in the efforts to trace the grey Hillman Husky spotted in Brentford and Chiswick. Today the Driver and Vehicle Licensing Agency (DVLA) holds computer records of all licensed vehicles. Ironically, the licensing system was only centralised in Swansea in 1965, just after these killings. At the time of the Nude Murders it was local councils that kept details of vehicle registrations. This was in the form of cards kept in order not of vehicle make or model but in sequence of consecutive registration numbers – and for the Hillman Husky, the police had no number. While today the police can easily conduct searches for vehicles by make, model, colour and so on, in the 1960s someone had to go to the London and Middlesex County Councils and go through every single card for every single car, van, lorry, motorcycle and coach registered. At Middlesex County Council there were 600,000 records kept, with another 1 million at the London County Council.

Here, once again, the police were out of luck. Both council authorities were engaged in a huge boundary revision scheme for the creation of the Greater London Council and could not spare any staff for the huge search the police required. So, the investigation had to devote its own officers to do the search. For this mammoth job, six female officers were detailed. This team was eventually increased to 11.

Amid all the tips and leads coming in, there was one piece of information told to the police that could easily be dismissed as just another bit of dross in a case full of dud information and unreliable players.

Or it might just be something more – a true encounter with the elusive killer. And if genuine, it would give a compelling insight into the killer's methods and how he may have won the confidence of his victims.

This account came from one of Frances Brown's friends, Vera Lynch. She recounted to detectives that Frances told her in October shortly before she disappeared that she had met a man on the street who had badly unnerved her the previous night.

He was driving a small van. He stopped and she got in. He

asked how much she charged and before she said anything he produced a black card with 'Metropolitan Police' on it in gold letters. The man said he was a CID officer. Frances countered that he could not arrest her on his own, to which he said he had a colleague nearby and would have no problem taking her in. This was a reference to the need for corroboration from two officers when arresting or giving warning to a prostitute.

The stranger then told Frances she had a 'laughing face' and mentioned the mad man preying on prostitutes. Frances asked how the victims were killed. The man outlined the method: the killer 'pulled the coat down over the shoulders, locking the arms and screwed whatever they were wearing underneath around their neck and strangled them'.

Frances got a chill from this man, opened the door and left the van. Before she got away, he gave her a pound, though there had been no sex.

Unfortunately, Frances gave Vera no description of this 'CID' man, or relayed what the make of the van was. But she did say he had a lot of junk in the back. And that the van was grey.

Was this just some creep who enjoyed freaking out women? That's possible. Or was he really an officer? The police at that time were indeed issued with small black folded cards with Metropolitan Police in gold lettering on them. He was driving a van the same colour as that seen in Chiswick and Brentford when two earlier victims were offloaded. And, most intriguingly, he seemed to have a very good idea how the actual killings were carried out.

If – and it is a big if – Frances did encounter the real killer in the same month that she disappeared, it would suggest that the man who had been so careful not to leave any clues behind may have got acquainted with his victims in some way before picking them up and killing them. Or perhaps he spotted them, followed them and picked them up away from the well-known kerb-crawling areas. That could explain why none of the victims was ever seen getting into a car on streets that were popular for soliciting, such as Queensway or Bayswater.

If he did stalk Frances before picking her up a few days later, perhaps she would have trusted him enough to do business with him, also knowing he was generous with his pounds. Who would be safer to go with than a police officer?

Vera Lynch's account did not create much interest during the ongoing police investigation. Lacking in vital details, it was obviously dismissed. But it raises tantalising possibilities, not least of which was that the Nude Killer may have been a police officer. Was this why he had so expertly evaded detection despite having left up to seven victims around west London?

Chapter 9

Noises in the Dark – Bridie O'Hara

As 1964 came to an end, sobering headlines roused readers from the heavy coverage being devoted to the Beatles or the love life of Peter Sellers. For the first time the number of serious crimes reported had topped the one million mark. There were fears that an increasingly consumerist, affluent Britain was becoming 'soft-living', more dishonest and violent.

The *News of the World* cited the Nude Murders as part of a murder wave that Scotland Yard seemed incapable of controlling. On 23 October 1964, just prior to Frances Brown's body being discovered in a car park, the paper catalogued a series of investigations into killings that had not been closed. 'As the unsolved lists grow, London alone has set the Yard a series of murder posers.

'Perhaps the biggest embarrassment for the Yard are the unsolved street-girl murders. The identity of the sex maniac who tours the vice areas of Bayswater and Notting Hill looking for slightly built prostitutes is still not known. This perverted murderer who may have killed four or five times has presented Scotland Yard with its most baffling problem since Jack the Ripper.'

The article speculated that the Yard's reputation as the world's finest police force was under threat. Challenges facing it included the loss of top detectives to retirement or promotion to desk jobs, overwork – 'often putting in 60 to 100 hours' work a week' – leading detectives having to investigate complaints against fellow police officers, and a complacent public failing to come forward with information.

While the *Daily Mirror* devoted a whole edition to 1964, 'The year that changed our lives' – skirts got shorter, boys' hair grew longer – the paper also had a different angle on the upswing in violence. 'London gun fury – Yard chiefs meet'. This was the front-page splash on Wednesday, 30 December 1964. Following a teenage thief firing a revolver at two police officers in Dalston, senior officers were meeting to discuss what action to take following this fifth shooting in north London in 11 days.

Yet another concern was the lure of vice for teenagers. Britain's new paper, *The Sun*, which had replaced the failing *Daily Herald* in September 1964, ran a front-page lead on Operation Innocents in November. This was a Scotland Yard plan to round up youngsters hanging around Soho's 'dimly lit coffee bars and basement jazz clubs' and call their parents to collect them. In view of the high volume of street prostitution in west London, police fears were perhaps understandable. A senior officer explained, 'Criminals, prostitutes and drug pedlars visit some of the places to which these youngsters are attracted... Young girls could fall under the influence of unscrupulous people who live by vice.'

The country was evolving in brash new ways. Labour's narrow defeat of the ruling Conservatives in October 1964 was partly a shrugging-off of the stuffy old, scandal-hit establishment. The capital was also famously swinging, with west

London certainly feeling the rumblings from the cultural shift. The Who's Pete Townshend, Roger Daltrey and John Entwistle were gaining a following with their early gigs in Acton and at the Goldhawk Social Club in Shepherd's Bush, while the Beatles were performing to screaming audiences at the Hammersmith Odeon during the Christmas fortnight of 1964.

BBC Television Centre opened just down the road from Shepherd's Bush on Wood Lane in 1960. A whole range of landmark series were launched in 1963–64, including *Doctor Who* and *Match of the Day*, while the hugely popular *Steptoe and Son* was not only set in Shepherd's Bush, it was filmed just round the corner at BBC Lime Grove Studios.

It is disconcerting now to recall that on the streets around these same venues and studios, the Nude Killer was cruising for 'slightly built' victims. Hannah Tailford's discovery on 2 February 1964 had been initially treated as a suspicious death. This had developed into a murder probe that ran until the end of April. By the time of the third killing in 1964, that of Helen Barthelemy, found on 24 April, it was clear that a pattern of murder was developing. This featured the targeting of petite women working with kerb-crawling sex customers, the victims being asphyxiated and left naked in public places. The Barthelemy inquiry, headed by Detective Superintendent Maurice Osborn, was also collating the facts from the cases of Tailford and Irene Lockwood, who had been found on 8 April.

News of the two most recent victims, Mary Fleming and Frances Brown, had ramped up the media scrutiny now focused on the murder squad. As pressure mounted on the police, it would seem the newspaper speculation about Scotland Yard's difficulties may not have been entirely incorrect. The investigation, although huge, was still short of the number of officers needed to conduct such a far-reaching and difficult murder hunt.

However, with the discovery of the next victim, on 16 February 1965, the investigation was set to suck in resources on an unprecedented scale.

Bridget 'Bridie' O'Hara was last seen by Shepherd's Bush Green on the night of Monday, 11 January 1965.

Earlier that night she shared a casserole with her husband, Michael O'Hara, a labourer working on a building site at Heathrow Airport. Theirs had been a chaotic life of drunken brawling and separations. At this time, Bridie, who was a prostitute, and Michael, with 11 past convictions himself for crimes including burglary, larceny and assault, were trying to reconcile and establish some kind of normal married life for themselves.

They had been together since 1955, marrying on 17 September 1962. By January 1965 they were living in a squalid top-floor flat at 41 Agate Road, Hammersmith, which had shared washing and kitchen areas for its tenants.

The couple only had 11 shillings between them on this January night. Bridie said she was going out to borrow some money from her friend, Jean Lovelock, who lived nearby in Shepherd's Bush. She was rather dolled up for such an errand, wearing a grey herringbone coat, black fringed scarf, light brown cardigan over a red and black speckled blouse, black skirt and matching calf-length boots.

In the event, Bridie did not go to Jean's, or she would have found that her friend was out. She turned up instead at the Shepherd's Bush Hotel, a grand old boozer on the corner of the green and Goldhawk Road. It was a music venue and a band was playing that night.

Once again, detectives would end up having a hard time sifting the witnesses' fog of booze and blurred vision when trying to reconstruct who did what with whom that night. Whenever the police tried to interview her husband, Michael, later on, he was nearly always drunk.

What is undisputed is that Bridie was seen at the Shepherd's Bush Hotel by Irish brothers Joseph and Edward Kelly, around 10.20pm. Joseph was a spray painter and Edward worked as a window cleaner.

Edward saw her drinking with a man called – confusingly – William John Kelly (no relation) – who was known as Jock. Later Bridie, drinking probably her favourite vodka and orange, and Jock were at the same table as Joseph. Edward was at another table (he and Joseph had had an argument), but later on Bridie went over to his table. Edward asked who her boyfriend was – meaning Jock, and she said Jock was just a friend. She rejoined Joseph and Jock. At 11.05pm, Edward left the pub.

Joseph Kelly, who had been hoping to have sex with Bridie and was waiting outside for her as the pub was closing, said he saw Bridie leave with Jock.

The police traced Jock and he made three statements. Much of what he said tallied with the Joseph's statement. But Jock disagreed that he had left the pub with Bridie. At closing time he went to the Gents and then stepped outside to see Bridie with a fourth man, who was aged around 40. Bridie and the man were standing by the telephone kiosks on Shepherd's Bush Green. Jock said that he had seen this man on another occasion the previous year. His description of Bridie's companion that night was 5 feet 6 inches, stocky build, full face, brown hair. He was wearing a trilby and three-quarter-length suede jacket with fleece collar. Bridie and the man crossed the road from the Green, passed Jock and set off down Goldhawk Road. Jock said he had heard that this man tried to strangle a woman in Acton or Chiswick during a row.

He also later told the police about the occasion on which he had first seen the stranger was at the Shepherd's Bush Hotel in Christmas week 1964. The man had been with Bridie, who had been there with a woman called Flo and two Welshmen, possibly brothers. Flo turned out to be Flora Forbes, a 31-year-old barmaid. Her description of the man with Bridie was similar to Jock's.

Mrs Forbes told officers that she and Bridie had danced with the Welshmen and the stranger at Coco's Club on the Green. However – and this must have annoyed detectives – despite being with these men till 2am, she did not know their names.

Fast forward a couple of weeks to 11 January, and Bridie was last seen by Jock Kelly strolling off into the night arm-in-arm with the trilby-hatted mystery man.

He recalled, 'When I saw her with this man she looked very happy...' As Bridie and the stranger walked down Goldhawk Road, Jock went into the Wimpy Bar for a coffee. 'I did not see Bridie again.' Interestingly, the three men who gave statements all said they only realised Bridie was a prostitute when they read it in the newspapers.

A description of the trilby-hatted man would later be given to the press and a search made, but neither he nor the two Welshmen were ever traced.

Was trilby man a punter she knew? It was a question the police were never able to answer.

Thelma Schwartz, aged 32, was hurrying to her cleaning job

at 5.45am on 12 February 1965. She worked at Zonal Film Facilities on Acton's Heron Trading Estate, and she was half-an-hour late.

Her route took her over a bridge to the busy but soulless industrial estate, where many factories and warehouses were based. The quiet two-lane bridge passed an open stretch of the Central Line Tube connecting West Acton and North Acton stations. The bridge carried Westfields Road into Alliance Road, which cut through the industrial estate and joined the A40 Western Avenue. The estate was not fenced off and was publicly accessible. The side of the railway bridge opposite the Heron Trading Estate was largely residential, including North Acton Playing Fields. At that time of the morning the area would have been peaceful.

Which is why, as Thelma crossed the bridge to the industrial estate, she was able to hear a noise coming from sheds backing onto the railway embankment, 30–40 yards away. She said later, 'It was too noisy for birds and I realised it was someone rustling leaves or some other dead vegetation.'

Being winter, it was also dark. Over the bridge and into the estate on Alliance Road, the rustling and movement, which was very loud at this early hour, continued. Thelma, wearing rubber-soled shoes, turned right onto a walkway between an engineering works and Union Cold Storage.

The noise stopped.

Had the leaf-rustler suddenly become aware of Thelma's approach? Feeling afraid, she started to run, not even glancing over her shoulder, and continued for 400 yards to the Zonal factory. She did not mention her fright to anyone at work that morning. 'I was behind with my work and the supervisor doesn't allow talking.'

Her experience would become of great interest to detectives when, three months later, she finally came forward.

Odd-job man Leonard Ernest Beauchamp, 26, worked at the Surgical Equipment Suppliers on the Heron Trading Estate. Four days after Thelma's scare, on Tuesday, 16 February 1965, Leonard needed to get some liquid soap for an empty dispenser in the Gents. He went to a shed at the side of his firm's building, alongside the railway embankment.

He habitually checked down the side of the sheds because people used those areas as a dump and sometimes he found useful cast-off property there. On this day he caught sight of something covered in bracken and grass in the narrow cut of undergrowth between the building and the fence abutting the embankment.

'I first noticed a pair of feet and I could see them up to the ankles,' he said. 'My first reaction was that I was looking at a dummy.'

Then he saw that the toenails were painted. Half-jokingly, Leonard told the storeman, Maurice Chester, that he'd found a woman's body at the back of the stores. It was difficult convincing anyone of this but it went up the hierarchy to production manager Gerald Marshall, who said it looked like wax, but told everyone not to touch anything. Acton police were called.

Bridget 'Bridie' Moore was born in Dublin on 2 March 1937, the sixth of 12 children. Dad Matthew was a plasterer, married to Mary. Bridie left school at 14 and for four years worked as a hospital cleaner and in factory jobs.

By 1954 she was living in Acton with an older sister. Her dad and brother William were also in London working. William heard from Margaret McEvoy, the woman she was living with in Gloucester Terrace, Paddington, that Bridie was staying out all hours – a pattern seen frequently with these victims as teenagers. Father and brother could not persuade her to return to Dublin. She ended up living with labourer Michael O'Hara in Shepherd's Bush.

In 1958 William made a distressing discovery. When he and another brother saw Bridie drunk in Shepherd's Bush and about to be arrested, they attempted to assist her, but instead were arrested themselves. In court, William heard that Bridie already had convictions for prostitution. He said, 'That was the first time I knew she was a prostitute.'

She received 11 convictions for soliciting, the first when she was 19. It was the familiar areas of west London that she worked – Bayswater, Notting Hill, Holland Park and Shepherd's Bush. Kerb-crawlers were her main clients, though she did meet men in pubs and cafes, charging them £2 or £3. A senior detective was not sympathetic to her, reflecting the views of the times. 'She was an unsavoury individual, who would prostitute herself in the lowest order, as did the other murder victims. From time to time she left her husband to cohabit with other men, having little regard for the type of person she lived with.'

Despite her chaotic lifestyle, she and Michael did get married and wanted to have children. She miscarried at home in 1962 and later went for a fertility test at Hammersmith Hospital in 1964, which was positive. However, a few days after the test in February she was in the hospital's casualty department, saying her husband had assaulted her. A pub booze-up on New Year's Eve ended in a row, broken plates and a smashed window back at their flat in Agate Road. The place was a shambles of broken glass, crockery, spilt milk and chips on the floor.

A couple of days later Bridie was with her friend Jean Lovelock, who said they had bumped into Michael on Goldhawk Road; he had had a few drinks. He was apologetic and later in tears, begging Bridie to go back to him.

The last time Jean Lovelock saw Bridie was on Friday, 8 January 1965, when, after another pub session with Mick, they all ended up back at her flat in Brook Green. Again, the good spirits eventually faded and Bridie and Michael had yet another fight.

It was on Monday, 11 January, that Michael, jobless for some weeks, finally started his job on a Heathrow building site. It was a last evening for the couple that had a semblance of normality. After eating Bridie's casserole, they watched the television. Then Bridie went out.

In the coming days Michael would check with Jean Lovelock and ask around after his absent wife. Finally, on 3 February he reported her missing at Hammersmith police station. She was not treated as a missing person but only entered in the Occurrence Book as a prostitute who had walked out on her husband. The feeling was that prostitutes in this type of district often left their partners to cohabit with other men, only to return later.

No one knew that the man who actually had Bridie was the Nude Murderer.

At 1pm on 16 February pathologist Dr David Bowen arrived at Surgical Equipment Supplies on Westfields Road. Detective Superintendent Bill Baldock, head of CID for this patch, T Division, was in charge and showed him to the gap between the storeroom and a chain-link fence.

The body was covered in bracken and grass, pulled from the ground to hide it. On her left forearm he saw a tattoo –

'Mick', her husband's name.

Dr Bowen conducted the post-mortem at 4pm. The naked body was that of a young woman, 5 feet 1 inch tall, weighing around 9 stone. Her dental plate could not be found, and she was missing quite a few teeth. On the upper jaw she had two back molars and the stump of an incisor, while the lower had nine front teeth and a solitary back molar. Pressure marks indicated the deceased had lain in her bra, stockings and suspenders after death.

On the left side of her neck the pathologist found two small abrasions. In her stomach were fragments of meat and vegetable, consistent with the casserole meal she shared with Michael. There were no sexual injuries, but there was a suggestion that she was suffering from venereal disease.

Estimating the time of death was difficult. Body markings suggested that the woman had been dressed/partially dressed when she died. She also appeared to have been left in a facedown position for a period. Then the killer seemed to have removed the clothes and put the deceased on her back.

The body was well preserved with no injuries. The skin on her back was soggy, which seemed to have been caused by lying on the ground. However, detectives believed she could only have been by the storehouse for a short time, perhaps up to a week. Dr Bowen decided the woman had been dead for around four weeks, possibly stored in a cold or even refrigerated area for two or three weeks.

Like the previous victims, Bridie had not been subjected to sexual or gratuitous violence and seemed to have died without struggling too much. The paint and dust particles were again present on the skin and matched those on Barthelemy, Fleming and Brown. Dr Bowen decided the cause of death was asphyxiation due to pressure on the face and neck.

A formidable cavalry of police were in attendance for this latest find, including officers from the Met's scientific laboratory, the fingerprint department and the photographic branch. The press were also on the scene quickly. The *Acton Gazette*'s reporter, Brian Collett, recalls, 'We had a call to the office. The deputy editor said get up to North Acton, there's a body on the embankment of the Tube abutting the trading estate. We shot up there. When we got there, coppers were milling all over the place. I looked across to where the body had been, and there was an old detective sergeant called McCann, who I knew very well. He waved and he opened his overcoat wide, to indicate she had been stripped, and then put his hands round his throat. They said it was another one of those stripped-and-strangled jobs.' This was confirmed at a press conference at Brentford police station later that day. 'The police said we've really got a nasty killer on our hands,' Collett said.

Forensic specimens found at the scene were taken away and the police called on residents of Highfield Road, a row of properties on the opposite side of the train line whose gardens overlooked the deposition site. The houses were 275 feet away across the line and the rear gardens. The chances of anyone there having seen something suspicious in the dark from that distance was highly unlikely. Nobody had.

However, the deceased's identity was confirmed quickly. Her fingerprints were checked, and Michael O'Hara and her brother William Moore identified Bridie, aged 28, on the evening of the day she was found. The deposition site was three miles by road from where she was last seen in Shepherd's Bush.

Meanwhile, Detective Chief Superintendent John du Rose was being recalled from his holiday bungalow in St Mary's Bay, Kent.

He would later recall Bridie's 52-year-old mother, Mrs
Mary Moore, travelling from Dublin. He said that on visiting
her flat in Agate Road, Mrs Moore broke down, asking, 'How
could this have happened to her?' Brian Collett, recalls, 'One
of our reporters went down to the dingy old room she rented
in Shepherd's Bush, I think it was. As he arrived her family
also arrived, and they were all wailing and sobbing. A poor
Irish family, who may not have known she was on the game.'
Du Rose agreed that Bridie's mother seemed to have no ink-
ling of her daughter's life in London. His recollection was of
Mrs Moore saying Bridie was 'the most beautiful of all my
family and a really kind, good girl'.

Chapter 10

Four - Day Johnny Takes Charge

The Nude Murders – a title that had attached itself to the crimes by February 1965 – became a huge story following the discovery of Bridie O'Hara's body. Where earlier in 1964 the press coverage had been more measured, largely covering the investigation when there was a development announced by police, now the reporting intensified.

'Big hunt for killer of Nude No 6' was the *Daily Mirror*'s immediate front-page lead on Wednesday, 17 February. It stated that every detective who worked on the earlier connected cases had been summoned to Brentford police station. Commander Ernest Millen was in charge of the latest hunt. The paper reported, 'His detectives were told to go back over the ground they had covered when they checked on the first five victims – all prostitutes in the Bayswater and Notting Hill districts – and their associates.

'That meant an all-night check on clubs, small hotels and boarding houses in those areas.'

The Sun's headline was 'Race to trap the strangler'. It also reported that Scotland Yard was drafting in its top investigators. 'Three superintendents of Scotland Yard's murder squad, who have studied the files on the previous killings, were assigned to the new all-out hunt.' These were Commander Millen, Chief Superintendent Jack Mannings and Detective Superintendent Bill Baldock.

The paper added that detectives were visiting prostitutes to seek their help, but also warned that 'any of them might be the next victim unless the maniac is caught'.

The coverage became more overheated. On the next day *The Sun* reported that the investigation's new top man, Chief Superintendent John du Rose, now had a description of the 'London strangler' and a partial registration for the killer's vehicle. The story claimed this information had come from a friend of Bridie O'Hara's, who had seen her get into the murderer's car on 11 January. 'That was the last time Mrs O'Hara was seen alive.' They got the date right, at least.

Reports followed that 150 cars sold in the previous 12 months were being traced and checked for links to the crimes, and that plainclothes female officers were patrolling west London to keep an eye on the prostitutes.

On Friday, 19 February, the *Mirror* reported that 'CID Boss Seeks Final Clue'. This report suggested John du Rose was expecting 'the final link in the puzzle to fall into place in the next 24 hours'. Either a detective briefing the press was getting over-excited or the reporters were making it up. It was true that du Rose and four senior detectives had been searching a house in west London for four hours and took away a bundle of women's clothing. 'Detectives were convinced that the killer – a pervert – is building up a "Black Museum" of his victims' clothes and jewellery, somewhere in the murder area.'

On the following Monday, 22 February, the *Mirror* had another story about du Rose and his team of scientists and detectives searching a property, this time in Hammersmith

Grove. Again the vice-ring theory was suggested. 'Police believe it has been used from time to time by a West London ring of married men and vice girls.'

The Sun elaborated on this angle. 'Detectives yesterday visited a number of addresses and questioned men who have attended sex orgies in West London during the last year.

'Police believe that although one man may be the actual killer, other members of the sex ring know his identity.'

Television was following du Rose and his squad as well, and the case was being covered by newspapers around the world. The pressure on Scotland Yard during what everyone agreed was its biggest ever manhunt was unforgiving. Surely, John du Rose, the detective known as Four-Day Johnny for the speed with which he closed cases, would be the man to nail this one.

In October 1931, as a 20-year-old novice copper, John du Rose had an early face-to-face encounter with death. At Horseferry Road mortuary he found himself staring at the strangled corpse of a prostitute on a porcelain slab. Decades later he still recalled her name – Nora Upchurch. 'I was smelling death for the first time, and I mean smelling, because the odour remained with me for days. I was mesmerised by the staring, glassy eyes which seemed to be imploring someone to answer why her young life had been cut short.'

He trained as a constable with C Division, which included the West End, and got an early insight into the world of vice there. Later in his 1971 autobiography *Murder Was My Business* he recalled, 'Life was never dull in the West End and there was always "business" for the policeman – arguments, fights, domestic disputes, endless questions, accidents, and always the prostitutes, busy all day and usually until four or five o'clock in the morning.'

Early on as a detective du Rose showed the quality that would be one of his trademarks – persistence. Looking into a case of car batteries stolen from a yard, he saw a stain in the road outside where battery acid had dripped. He followed the drops for 100 yards until they faded away, but then got on his hands and knees, picking out droplets, repeating this search for more than two miles. Eventually, he found the thieves' hideout. 'It was hard on the knees, but all the stolen batteries were recovered.'

Thirty-four years after that day in the mortuary, du Rose was a chief superintendent and one of the Big Five at the Yard – head of C1 Department responsible for overseeing murder inquiries. And he was again faced with such a challenge from prostitutes who had had the life squeezed from them. In between, du Rose climbed the ranks quickly as he helped to clear up some notorious cases.

As a detective sergeant he interviewed the Acid Bath Murderer, John George Haigh, becoming suspicious of the man's nervousness at a time when Haigh was just a witness. He reported his feeling to his superintendent that Haigh had probably murdered the elderly Olive Durand-Deacon – and would be proved correct. Haigh was executed in 1949 for the murder of Mrs Durand-Deacon and five other victims.

During the Yard's campaign against the Messina vice ring that thrived before and after the Second World War, du Rose was one of the officers who arrested Carmelo Messina in Kensington in 1958. In both of these cases du Rose had not been a leading figure, but his reputation was burnished by association with these successes.

He was called in to take over when the investigating officer on the Pillbox Murder Case fell ill. In 1960 Andrew Bonnick,

A woman arrested for soliciting in Soho, 1956, gives a photographer a piece of her mind. The sex trade was visible on streets from the West End to Shepherd's Bush, but by the early 1960s men were increasingly cruising for 'business' in their cars

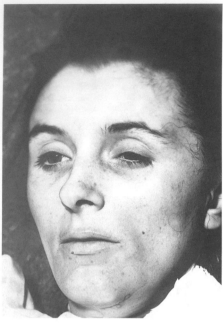

VICTIM Elizabeth Figg, found 17 June 1959 at Dukes Meadows

VICTIM Gwynneth Rees, found 8 November 1963 at Barnes rubbish dump

VICTIM Helen Barthelemy, found 24 April 1964 off Swyncombe Avenue, Brentford

VICTIM Mary Fleming, found 14 July 1964 on Berrymede Road, Chiswick

VICTIM Hannah Tailford, found 2 February 1964 on Thames foreshore, Hammersmith

VICTIM Irene Lockwood, found 8 April 1964 on Thames foreshore, Chiswick

VICTIM Frances Brown, found 25 November 1964 just off Kensington High Street

VICTIM Bridget 'Bridie' O'Hara, found 16 February 1965 on the Heron Trading Estate, Acton

ABOVE Bridget 'Bridie' Moore on her wedding day to Michael O'Hara in September 1962
RIGHT AND BELOW Paul Quinn, 28, boyfriend of murder victim Frances Brown, speaks to a prostitute in Shepherd's Bush in an effort to find out what happened to her

ABOVE CID chiefs leading the investigation: Detective Chief Superintendent John du Rose, Detective Inspector Ken Oxford and Detective Superintendent Bill Baldock at Shepherd's Bush police station

BELOW Det Supt Bill Baldock (second left) directs a team of CID officers at Shepherd's Bush police station in February 1965, the height of the Nude Murders Investigation

The final murder, 16 February 1965: a policeman looks over the spot on the Heron Trading Estate by the railway embankment, where Bridie O'Hara's body had been discovered by Leonard Beauchamp, 26 (below)

TOP George Heard, 34, had a shock when at 4.45am on 14 July 1964 he looked out of his window on Berrymede Road. What he thought was a shop mannequin on the drive opposite turned out to be the body of Mary Fleming ABOVE Later that day, while police stand guard, children play in the street

LEFT Police officers remove the body of Irene Lockwood on 8 April 1964. She had been found on the Thames foreshore near Corney Reach steps, Chiswick. BELOW Uniformed officers guard the path at Dukes Meadows, near where Elizabeth Figg was discovered in 1959

ABOVE A screen shields the spot where Helen Barthelemy lies, in an alley off Swyncombe Avenue, Brentford, while detectives inspect the crime scene

BELOW The car park on Hornton Street, Kensington, where Frances Brown was found under a bin lid on 25 November 1964

Detective Superintendent Maurice Osborn does not look happy to be greeted by photographers at Brentford police station as the investigation into Helen Barthelemy's murder begins on 24 April 1964

How the Daily Mirror covered the hunt for the Nude Killer

Daily Mirror   Saturday, April 25, 1964   No. 18,769   3d.

Nude Number 4 found strangled in an alley—riddle of night visitor

GIANT HUNT FOR MANIAC SEX KILLER

By TOM TULLETT, NORMAN LUCAS and BARRY STANLEY

A VAST hunt started last night for a sex-crazed killer, who is believed to have claimed four girl victims in six months.

The nude body of Victim No. 4—former striptease girl Helen Barthelemy, 20—was found yesterday in a lover's walk at Brentford. She had been strangled.

Brentford Yard detectives were told that her stripping and supper with a mystery visitor at her flat in Talbot-road, Willesden, late on Monday night.

She was never seen again by her neighbours in the rambling terrace house...

Helen Barthelemy ... strangled.

Murder by the river

Dumped

Victims

Continued on Back Page

Daily Mirror   Friday, February 19, 1965   No. 19,034   4d.

CID boss

NUDE KILLER HUNT—YARD MEN SEARCH A HOUSE

By TOM TULLETT and ALAN GORDON

SCOTLAND YARD'S top murder detective was searching last night for London's phantom sex killer will soon be hunted down.

Detective Chief Superintendent John du Rose—who broke his holiday to lead the hunt—expects the final link in the puzzle to fall into place in the next 24 hours.

The lead came shortly after 4.15 p.m. yesterday at Shepherd's Bush police station. Headquarters of the search for the man who is believed to have killed six...

2   DAILY MIRROR, Wednesday, February 5, 1964

...VER NUDE: MAN ...ELPS YARD

...d was helping police with ...quiries into ...d nude ...rly today.

...—a billiards ...er who knew ...oman well— ...o Lavender ...ce station.

Wandsworth, late last night.

Later he was taken to Heddon-on-the-Wall, Northumberland.

Last night detectives were searching for her daughter, a three-year-old named Linda. The dead woman also has an 18-month-old son.

The detectives know that the little girl has been looked after by friends.

Appeal

And they believe that if they find Linda, it may help them to trace her mother's killer.

Last night Scotland Yard issued a picture (right) of the dead woman...

about five years ago from Hammersmith.

The dead woman, whose naked body was found in the Thames at the weekend, was named yesterday as good-time girl Hannah Tailford, 31.

She came to London

Hannah Tailford ... she used several names

Museum

Rings

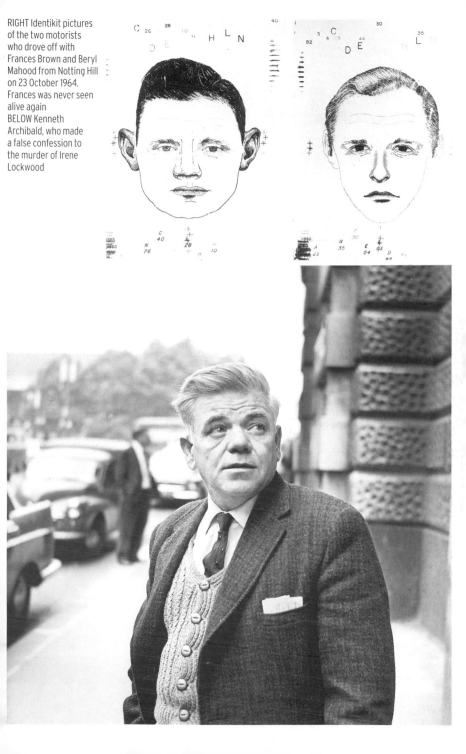

RIGHT Identikit pictures of the two motorists who drove off with Frances Brown and Beryl Mahood from Notting Hill on 23 October 1964. Frances was never seen alive again

BELOW Kenneth Archibald, who made a false confession to the murder of Irene Lockwood

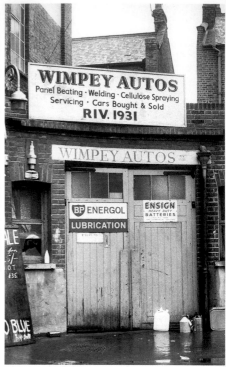

ABOVE Looking for clues at a property on Hammersmith Grove. BELOW Detectives leave the same basement property with boxes of evidence. RIGHT The Hammersmith garage that was investigated by police in 1965

TOP Detective Chief Superintendent John du Rose stands on the Thames foreshore at Hammersmith, near where Hannah Tailford was found. ABOVE Du Rose points to where Bridie O'Hara was discovered on the Heron Trading Estate. LEFT Du Rose and Detective Inspector Ken Oxford (wearing hat) at the Hammersmith Grove search in February 1965

BELOW AND LEFT John du Rose taking it easy in retirement after a police career that lasted almost 39 years. Retirement was not uneventful – his 1971 autobiography stirred up controversy over the Nude Murders

Leading geographic-profiling expert Kim Rossmo's analysis reveals two areas of West London that were likely to have been where the Nude Killer was based (see map overleaf). The peaks of his three-dimensional illustration show the highest probability of being where the murderer lived or worked. This is a tool used by modern-day investigators

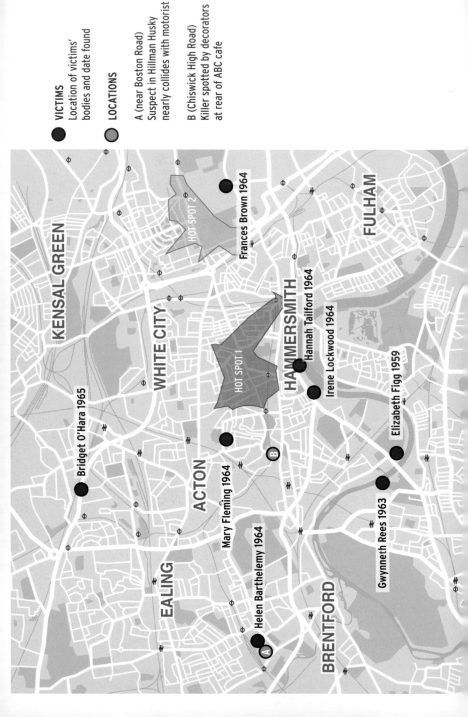

VICTIMS
Location of victims' bodies and date found

LOCATIONS

A (near Boston Road)
Suspect in Hillman Husky
nearly collides with motorist

B (Chiswick High Road)
Killer spotted by decorators
at rear of ABC cafe

KENSAL GREEN

WHITE CITY

FULHAM

HAMMERSMITH

ACTON

EALING

BRENTFORD

HOT SPOT 2

HOT SPOT 1

Bridget O'Hara 1965

Frances Brown 1964

Hannah Tailford 1964

Irene Lockwood 1964

Elizabeth Figg 1959

Mary Fleming 1964

Gwynneth Rees 1963

Helen Barthelemy 1964

14, was killed in a beach pillbox at the seaside village of Gileston, near Barry, Glamorganshire, in what appeared to be a sexual assault gone wrong. Malcolm Keith Williams, 20, went to jail for life for the crime.

Du Rose also cracked two double-murder cases, sending Ronald Herbert Benson to Broadmoor in 1959 for killing elderly spinsters Elizabeth Caroline Ivatt and Phyllis May Squire and helping to ensure that Henryk Niemasz was hanged for killing his lover Alice Bateman and the man she lived with, Hubert Buxton, in 1961.

He would later be involved in the operations against the Richardsons' fraud and torture gang, and the Kray twins.

His appointment to the Nude Murders case on the day Bridie O'Hara's body was found, 16 February 1965, was hailed by newspapers from the *London Evening News* to the *Los Angeles Times*. The *Daily Mirror* called him 'Scotland Yard's Top Murder Detective', while the *Chicago Tribune* went overboard in describing him as a detective 'who has never failed to solve a murder case'.

Behind the headlines, what kind of man was 54-year-old du Rose? He certainly worked incredibly hard and made many personal sacrifices for the sake of his career. His investigative skills on homicide cases were clearly formidable, almost certainly superior to Bill Baldock's, the superintendent whom he replaced as top man on the Nude Murders, though Baldock carried on as du Rose's right-hand man. Du Rose was aware that his men called him 'big bad John', and he could be dour, whereas the urbane Baldock, 48, was an admired leader, but friendly and well liked, too. He was not delighted to have to move aside for Four-Day Johnny.

What seems clear today, however, is that du Rose and his colleagues, with all their experience, had never encountered a case like the Nude Murders. His previous successes involved culprits who had some relationship with their victims or became visible to investigators in some way. This killer was different. He had no ties with his victims and was frustratingly efficient at leaving only microscopic clues behind.

Shepherd's Bush police station became the nerve centre of the operation. An incident room was set up and John du Rose trawled through all the statements and exhibits connected to the murdered prostitutes. Detective Inspector Ken Oxford was his assistant, while Bill Baldock's right-hand man was Detective Inspector Edward Crabb.

The media ran stories about du Rose and his squad when there were no stories about the actual investigation to print. The *Daily Mail* staged a corny photo feature of the chief superintendent addressing a semi-circle of detectives – including 'Woman Sergeant P Perkins' – all with pens poised over their notebooks. 'The briefing was held after scientists had found a clue which indicated the killer had slipped up when he murdered Bridie O'Hara,' it stated hopefully.

ITN ran a report about du Rose's 'specially picked squad… grappling with one of the most sordid, brutal and baffling crimes of all time'. Du Rose and Baldock were filmed leaving Shepherd's Bush police station and getting into a police car, part of a 14-hour day on a seven-day week. The station was shown at night, upstairs offices aglow, before detailing the women officers gathering prostitute statements and night patrols monitoring the sex trade on the streets.

On Tuesday, 23 February, the *Mail* asked, 'Has It Occurred to You How Little Wives See of These Men in the Nude Killer Squad?' This recounted how du Rose had returned from Kent to take over the Nude Murders investigation, worked for

52 hours straight before finally returning to his Morden home for four hours' sleep.

'After 32 years his wife accepts the long hours he works,' the story said. 'He even had to go to court on his wedding day.' At present, he was riding around London's back streets where women officers were posing as prostitutes so that he could personally meet and quiz the genuine streetwalkers about the victims and their punters. The punishing hours were common to most officers on the case, from junior to senior ranks.

Behind the scenes, the most promising early lead after du Rose's arrival was focused on a garage in Hammersmith. The original tip about a possible suspect came from a prostitute on 9 December 1964, during the investigation into Frances Brown's killing.

The woman had been approached by a man who called himself 'Cyril' at a coffee stall in Shepherd's Bush. This man told her he had a couple of pals who liked young girls and were looking for business. They were joined by the two men. The woman thought these two looked like the pair in the recently circulated identikit pictures, who were wanted for questioning after driving off with Frances Brown and Beryl Mahood on Frances's last night.

These men took her to the Hammersmith garage. Masturbation was the service provided. Afterwards, the woman left, going straight to the police. The men were soon identified and it was found that one of them owned the garage, one was a mechanic and the other occasionally assisted there.

Suspicion fell on this garage, Wimpey Autos in Barb Mews, because of dust samples taken from the premises. The pattern of coal dust and paint particles on Bridie O'Hara matched those on the previous three bodies – 10 x 50 microns in size (1 micron = 1/25,000th inch); the paint was globular (from a spray rather than brush); with red globules predominating and turquoise, brown and cream also found; all seemed to be cellulose (non-flammable polymer).

Chief scientific officer Thomas Jones revealed to the investigation on 18 February that, although his analysis was not complete, the sample taken earlier from the Hammersmith garage was similar to that on the bodies. None of the hundreds of previous samples painstakingly gathered from many other premises was so close a match.

Suddenly, the Hammersmith garage seemed a promising prospect. It was thoroughly examined by the forensics team, the three men made lengthy statements and their homes were searched, though nothing incriminating was found. The garage owner, William Chissell, was detained overnight. It was his garage, after all, and he was sole key holder. When he was about to be released, a Luger pistol and ammunition were found in his garage's roof area. He said he knew nothing of them but was charged with receiving and not having a firearms certificate. Both charges were eventually dismissed in court and he was awarded 20 guineas from public funds.

Detectives also became interested in a pal of the garage owner's, a car dealer called Anthony Holland, who often visited Wimpey Autos. An informant had revealed that this man often used the services of prostitutes. The police searched his Hammersmith flat and his garage in Hanwell. But where was he? The *Sunday Mirror*'s front-page lead was 'Yard seeks man's help' and Bill Baldock was quoted as saying they wanted to speak to this car dealer in connection with the Nude Murders.

Could it be that Four-Day Johnny's arrival had coincided with an immediate breakthrough?

Detectives also remained suspicious of the mechanic at

Wimpey Autos, Cecil Spurgeon. He drank in the pubs around Shepherd's Bush, admitted knowing Bridie's husband, Mick O'Hara, as well as occasionally having a 'bunk-up' with prostitutes in the back streets. He also resembled the stocky man in the identikit. If this mechanic, or any suspect, could be linked to Bridie O'Hara's killing, they could surely be connected to all the other deaths. In an identity parade on 21 February, however, William 'Jock' Kelly – who had been in the Shepherd's Bush Hotel on Bridie's last night – did not pick the mechanic out.

Meanwhile, Holland's solicitor got in touch with the police on his behalf. He was quizzed at Shepherd's Bush by John du Rose, with Bill Baldock present. This man said he had had a car sprayed at Wimpey Autos around two years previously, had never seen prostitutes there, had not been to the Shepherd's Bush Hotel for years, and did not know Bridie O'Hara or any other prostitutes.

All four men – Chissell, Spurgeon, the man who assisted there, James McCarthy, and Holland – were finally eliminated from the inquiry (Holland had been in Brixton prison awaiting trial for burglary between June and August 1964, when Mary Fleming was murdered, before eventually being set free).

In addition, Bridie's husband, Mick, despite his known violence towards her, was also ruled out, along with her companions at the Shepherd's Bush Hotel that last night – Edward Kelly, Joseph Kelly and William 'Jock' Kelly, who had all been investigated and questioned at length (the latter did not even own a car). According to the police, Bridie often boasted to people she knew about one or two sugar daddies, as she called her generous clients. One of these, a 53-year-old man, was successfully located, but again was discounted by the police. Detectives concluded that she had been boasting when referring to men like him as sugar daddies.

It was becoming clear that there would be no sudden breakthrough for du Rose and the murder squad.

Instead, teams of officers called at pubs in Shepherd's Bush looking for the man who was seen walking down Goldhawk Road with the victim on 11 January. The *Daily Mail* was assuring readers on Monday, 22 February, that a breakthrough was coming. 'An important development is expected in the next few days in the investigation of the six deaths. Criminal scientists working round the clock at Scotland Yard may produce evidence linking clues discovered by detectives.'

It was beginning to sound a little desperate, but as the *Mail* had also warned, du Rose had 'landed the toughest job of his 32-year career'.

Chapter 11

The Biggest Manhunt In Britain

What the public and media were never made aware of in the coming months was that the investigation was under strain. The inability of the murder squad to locate one truly compelling suspect meant that they were having to undertake a huge number of searches and chase a scattergun pattern of leads and tips simply on spec. Chief Superintendent John du Rose soon found himself commanding a huge force, but the Nude Killer always seemed to be ahead of his pursuers.

On Friday, 26 February 1965, a housewife resembling Bridie O'Hara was dressed identically to the victim on her last night and posed in a press and TV photocall. But the appeal failed to spark recollections of any sightings of Bridie.

A few weeks later, on 17 March, Sir Ranulph Bacon, Scotland Yard's assistant commissioner, went on television to appeal to the public for information. 'Amongst those watching this programme, there may be one of you at least who knows or strongly suspects the person responsible. If so, I am speaking directly and personally to you. It may be because of your affection for this person or because of a misconceived loyalty that you hesitate, but the means of bringing to notice the identity of the person lies within your power. I expect you must be a very worried person. Should you fail to carry out this moral and public duty there could rest on your conscience the possible death of yet another young woman. I appeal to you to come forward and I can assure the utmost confidence and discretion to anything disclosed.'

Bacon's appeal attracted huge coverage, even internationally, but no one emerged who could name the man behind the crimes.

'I wanted the whole of West London to be flooded with policemen – and it was,' John du Rose said in later years.

He had a 200-strong CID murder force under his command, with around another 100 men and women of the uniformed branch. He also asked the commissioner, Sir John Waldron, for additional backup by requesting the newly formed Special Patrol Group (SPG) of 300 officers to be added to his contingent. He got them. This was a formidable force.

Detective Superintendent Bill Baldock later revealed that part of the strategy was to have police on the ground in readiness for the killer. There was clearly some frustration that so far this man had struck six times in 12 months even while the police presence had increased with the growing investigation. Baldock's approach was that now 'no stone was left unturned'.

While the investigation had unavoidably been pulled into futile searches for sugar daddies, vice rings and orgy participants, police thinking had crystallised on the most likely type of suspect. This was a man cruising the Notting Hill/ Shepherd's Bush/Bayswater area picking up streetwalkers. He had asphyxiated and stripped them, before keeping them in a place where they came into contact with a particular mix of paint and dust particles.

While finding his storage spot was one vital part of the police strategy, the other was identifying his vehicle. The killer was looking for his victims in a vehicle – possibly a van or Hillman Husky-type vehicle with closed sides like that spotted in Brentford and Chiswick – picked up his victims and deposited his victims with it. Identifying this vehicle would surely expose the guilty man.

Night observations around west London were established. There was logic in this, but trying to monitor and note the movements of every vehicle, investigating suspicious incidents and journeys against registration details, was daunting. However, it was hoped that in the event of any further killings the perpetrator's licence registration would have been recorded. Observation points were set up around a 24-square-mile area.

The early murders of Hannah Tailford and Irene Lockwood, prompted the River Police being called on to watch the river from Hammersmith Bridge to Chiswick Bridge, particularly around Dukes Meadows, and this continued.

Before all du Rose's requests for officers could be met, the 'pathetically few men' available, in Baldock's words, were sent out on night observations from 19 February 1965, just three days after Bridie O'Hara was found. Baldock was referring to the lack of officers in relation to the scale of the observation task they had set themselves across a huge swathe of London, but this did ease a bit as more men and women were drafted in. Because most of these watchers were on foot, a few days later authority was given for 28 officers to use their private cars to carry out patrols. Some officers would soon be clocking up to 100 miles a night covering roads from Dukes

Meadows to Kensington, monitoring all kinds of shady spots where prostitutes took their punters.

On 9 March the night squad got an additional six CID officers, 58 aids to CID (aids were essentially detectives on a trial period), four female plainclothes officers and eight uniformed officers in plainclothes. The squad came under a detective inspector. In addition, dog handlers were detailed to work alongside the SPG.

A typical night-observation detail was at Ealing Common, where an officer sat with a civilian driver in a baker's van. During a 12-hour shift on freezing nights, wrapped in blankets, the detective constable would stare through slits in the van's sides watching the local prostitutes as they waited for customers to come by in their vehicles. These women cooperated with the officer, clocking on and off with him in the van, and if a new woman turned up, he would take down her details on a form. He would also log the cars cruising for business. To kill the boredom, they would listen to Kenny Everett on Radio Caroline.

Roger Crowhurst, a temporary detective constable, was on duty here. 'There was a steel seat which spun round, a bit like an office seat with a cushion on it. The other seat was a biscuit tin with a cushion on it. We had to pee in another biscuit tin – and shit as well.'

Meanwhile, at murder HQ, Shepherd's Bush police station, there was a wall map covered in red and blue flags. The blue markers denoted cars seen entering the murder area twice, while the red ones were for vehicles seen in the area three times. The red-flagged drivers were visited by detectives and discreetly asked about their journeys.

Notting Hill, Bayswater, Kensington and Shepherd's Bush were all under surveillance. Car parks, cul-de-sacs, lovers' lanes, railway arches, parks, all were watched.

Officers were also stationed in old-style 'TARDIS' police boxes, at key points such as on the approach to Chertsey Bridge, monitoring passing vehicles. After midnight was the period officers were recording, with cars seen on main roads and side streets all going on the forms. Particular attention was paid to vehicles that could convey a body, with one occupant driving.

Du Rose tried to maintain morale among officers on these tedious shifts by briefing them about how the many forms they filed were being followed up with checks and interviews. Many veteran detectives recalled the investigations into Acid Bath Murderer John George Haigh and Rillington Place killer John Reginald Halliday Christie, but the scale of this current operation dwarfed those. Du Rose was determined to provide the manpower the investigation now demanded.

Young officers reporting for duty were stunned by the number of officers on the inquiry as it expanded in late February and March. Most also discovered an upside to the long shifts. One officer, David Cant, recalled, 'I worked briefly as a DC on the case towards the end. At that time CID officers were paid £17 or £18 per month detective duty allowance plus a plainclothes allowance of a couple of pounds. Now this was averaged out over the whole of the Met, and it never varied, so no matter how much overtime you did, that's all you got. And then John du Rose declared this to be a "special occasion" and everything suddenly changed. You were working 14, 15,16 hours a day and you could earn a fortune, or what seemed like a fortune then.' In exchange for having their social lives curtailed for six months, some officers were clearing enough money to buy a new garage, a new Morris 1100 or even put down a deposit on a house.

In his memoirs recounting 19 years on the Met, David I Woodland captured the dark humour around at this time. 'Some wag on the murder squad reckoned [the killer] had to be one of the team who, after each murder was wound down and the "special occasion" status removed, went out to do another to benefit from all the overtime we were clocking up.' Gallows humour also got to the street women. In the Warwick Castle on Portobello Road, they put money on the bar and ran a sweepstake on which of them would be the next victim.

Officers were also instructed to spend time in pubs, cafes and clubs from Soho to Shepherd's Bush. Here the job was to mingle with prostitutes and punters.

One aspect of this intelligence-gathering that attracted headlines around the world was the use of decoy female officers. A dozen women volunteered for this tricky duty, and their experience ranged from eye-opening to downright dangerous.

Four women dressed as prostitutes worked in pairs each night in the usual kerb-crawling areas of Queensway, Westbourne Grove, Pembridge Road, Kensington Church Street and Shepherd's Bush Green. Accompanying each pair at a discreet distance was a male officer. By simply standing in the street – not actively soliciting business – they drew a queue of cars and could chat to the drivers and note number plates, driver descriptions and any other details useful to the inquiry. On some nights a continuous line of cars ran the length of the street waiting to speak to these decoys.

Some women had tape recorders with mics concealed in their clothing, but often notes were scribbled on scraps of paper within the woman's coat. Du Rose said of the women volunteers, 'Until then few of them had realised what odd demands men could make upon women. One "client" wanted to watch a woman as she took a bath and was willing to pay a fiver for the privilege. Another was anxious to undress while a nude woman in high-heeled shoes paraded before him. Flagellation, beating the girl or being beaten by her, was another mode of sexual excitement frequently asked for and there were others interested in witnessing love-making between two women.'

To deceive the punters that the decoys were genuine, a male colleague would occasionally pull up in a car and drive the WPC away for a while before bringing her back. Her female companion, who remained on the street, would still be closely watched by yet another officer.

The real street prostitutes saw the decoys as allies and helped by sharing information about their punters. The police gained a lot of intelligence about the kerb-crawling trade – 'travelling brothels' as the prowling cars were called by some – and senior officers were stunned by the high volume of men looking for sex, often the same drivers out night after night cruising all the areas in which the decoys were operating.

The female officers were under strict orders not to enter any punter's car, and the male officer's job was to jump in if a client turned nasty. David I Woodland recalled his time as backup to a prostitute decoy. 'One man tried to bodily drag my protégé, WPC Purvis, into his car, a large pink Vauxhall Cresta. It had mock leopard skin seat covers and pink plastic flowers on the rear window shelf, all done in the best possible taste.

'The consequences didn't bear thinking about and I bounded across the road and dragged her clear.' The driver got out of the car and came at Woodland, but the police officer punched him in the stomach, leaving him sprawling in the road. 'We both realised what a close shave she'd had.'

All car details were placed on index cards the following morning. Drivers who approached prostitutes or were seen regularly in these areas were then interviewed and dust samples taken from their vehicles. These punters were often professional types – doctors, clergymen, lawyers, company bosses.

David Woodland gives an insight into the delicacy of turning up at a man's house to quiz him without causing embarrassment in front of his family. He recalls one obnoxious chap who tried the patience of under-pressure detectives by snapping, 'If you have anything to say to me you can do it in front of my wife, we have no secrets.'

To which the officer replied, 'In that case, sir, perhaps we could begin by asking why a man answering your description and driving your car accosted a prostitute in Queensway last Saturday night and tried to forcibly drag her into your car?'

The police index of vehicles in connection with the Nude Murders eventually ballooned to 300,000 entries, while 1,700 drivers were interviewed and had dust taken from their cars.

The 'special decoy patrol' ran from 22 March to 18 June, while night observations continued until 3 July. In addition to gathering valuable data about the sex trade, 59 arrests were made for attendant crimes such as robbery, larceny and possessing offensive weapons. But again, the killer was nowhere to be seen. Had du Rose's plan to flood west London with officers left the fugitive no dark corners to work in?

Another squad of six CID officers, eight aids to CID and three uniformed officers was formed on 8 March 1965 to search for the spot where the most recent four bodies had been stored.

The mix of dust and paint particles found on these victims was the team's starting point. If they could locate the place where that rare particle mix originated, then they would have hit the jackpot. It would surely be a short step to sift through men connected with the storage site and find the Nude Killer.

However, this was a daunting task. First of all, the area they had to cover included the boroughs of Kensington, Paddington, Hammersmith, Fulham, Ealing and Hounslow. Every street had to be visited and dust/debris samples taken from garages, rooms, sheds, empty shops – anywhere a body might have been hidden or spray-painting done. Evidence gathered was then forwarded for laboratory tests.

This was a herculean job. In all, 648 streets were visited and something like 120,000 people seen; the perseverance required to go back time and again to locate key-holders and get access to premises must have been immense.

And yet again a breakthrough was elusive. None of the lab results tested positive on the dust samples.

Bill Baldock was certainly aware that the trawl for the storage site should have covered the same 24-square miles as the night observations because it was probably within this zone that the killer lived or worked and would likely have kept his victims. However, the large number of officers that du Rose and Baldock's investigation had called on had created a manpower drain on other Met divisions, so this part of the operation was halted unfinished on 28 August. Only half the targeted area had been checked.

A 'Husky squad' was set up to trace the grey van seen in suspicious circumstances in Brentford and Chiswick back in April and July 1964.

These were the occasions when Helen Barthelemy and

Mary Fleming were dumped. A grey Husky-type vehicle almost collided with another driver at the junction of Swyncombe Avenue and Boston Manor Road. On the second occasion decorators frightened off a man driving a similar vehicle who was behaving oddly in the early hours at the back of Chiswick High Road.

In neither incident did the witnesses get the registration number of the small van or estate, resembling a Hillman Husky, Hillman Estate or Commer Cob. There was a team of 11 women officers ploughing through 600,000 vehicle files at Middlesex County Council and a million more files at County Hall (London County Council). To make the job even more brain draining, the files were sequenced by registration number rather than make or model. To find Hillman Huskys meant going through every single record.

The first task was to sift Husky and Cob vehicles from these records into lists. These lists showing owner names and addresses were taken to Shepherd's Bush police station, where it was necessary to check that owners had not moved away. Finally, action lists could be prepared and owners visited and interviewed, with dust samples taken on sticky tape from their vehicles.

On 28 April a quartet of Flying Squad officers was added to the Husky squad to ease the load a little. In all, 783 Hillman Husky cars were examined and the drivers interviewed. As data came in from the night patrols, the Husky officers also checked these owners and vehicles, regardless of colour or make.

On 6 May 1965 the positive development that detectives had been desperate for finally came.

While the paint and dust particles found on Barthelemy,

Fleming, Brown and O'Hara were very similar, other debris from the surrounding crime scenes on the bodies were all completely different. However, in Bridie O'Hara's case, the paint and dust on her body matched that from the local area in which she had been found. Could she – and therefore the other victims – have been stored on the Heron Trading Estate?

Analysis of foliage in the vicinity where Bridie O'Hara had been found led to further tests by the forensic laboratory on samples from the Heron Trading Estate. These were taken from the railway embankments, factories and roads. There were 35 factories on the estate, and samples were taken from them, with the sequence of particle tests pinpointing one vacant premises, Napiers Aero Engines Ltd, as the site where their bodies had been kept.

The disused building had been in full operation before closure in August 1963. Between then and May 1964 all the machinery was cleared out, leaving the place empty. There was no security on the premises, and anyone could get into it – it was even used as a shortcut to a cafe on Westfields Road by factory workers on the estate. At night, courting couples spent time there.

It was concluded that the precise spot where the bodies had been stored was probably an outbuilding housing transformers. This was entered through a large double-door in the factory, secured by sliding bolts. To keep the place cool there were large wire-mesh openings, 6 feet by 3 feet. Even in summer the building was decidedly cool, and dust from the area could easily blow in there. It was 150 yards from where Bridie O'Hara's body was found.

It seemed clear that at least the most recent four victims had been stored on the estate (because the first two victims in

1964, Tailford and Lockwood, were pulled from the Thames, they were not tested for dust/paint particles). They had been hidden for periods from one day to four weeks, with Bridie stored for the longest time. Her body had not been frozen or left in the open for that period, so the cool transformer shed during a chilly winter (average 4.6° Celsius) fitted this scenario.

The good news for investigators was that this must be place the killer used to store his victims. The bad news was that it was empty and abandoned. Another hard slog began.

On 6 May 1965 it was decided that CID would interview all employees and visitors to the Heron Trading Estate. Fifteen officers were devoted to this, their first hurdle being to consult management and unions to get their cooperation in making employees available during working hours.

The operation was huge. There were 6,154 people working on site, with another 1,060 former staff to trace. Nevertheless, interviews were conducted with all of these people. Anyone with a criminal record was closely scrutinised, women employees were asked about any dodgy men they may have encountered, and vehicles and visitors to the estate were also checked. There was found to be very little traffic at night, another helpful feature of the estate for the killer. Night staff and security men were also spoken to.

A lot of attention was paid to a BBC building that housed outside broadcast gear, which was on Kendal Avenue. The site was unoccupied from 1961 until May 1964, during which time it was being refitted, but it overlooked the spot where Bridie was dumped. Three porters working there reported seeing women's clothing in a bin on the BBC site, one of them sure they were there on 11 February, five days before the body was found. Cotton dresses, petticoats, a bra, knickers and cardigan were among the items. Bin men were interviewed and the dump at Gerrards Cross was sifted, but the clothes could not be found.

Officers called at shops, pubs and cafes in the locality, but again no useful information was forthcoming.

The whole effort was complicated by the fact that during the period of the murders several factory buildings had been demolished and the paint/dust samples came from several premises, which required a lot of cross-checking, and that the estate was wide open to every Tom, Dick and Harry passing by.

So, having put so much effort into finding the hiding place for the bodies on the assumption that it could connect the killer to the crimes, Scotland Yard found another line of inquiry turning metaphorically to dust.

The killer had been ahead of the police once again. He either had no connection with the Heron Trading Estate or managed to cover it up completely.

Which also begged one further question. He had so far deposited his victims on the bank or in the Thames and in residential areas. So why this time had he left Bridie right outside his secret storage place? He was virtually pointing detectives there and saying, 'Look, fellers, this is where I've been keeping them.'

Unless he knew Bridie O'Hara would be his final murder, his sign-off? Or could he not risk driving around west London with another body in his grey van?

'I don't read detective novels, you know,' John du Rose told the *Daily Express*. 'I haven't seen a play for years and I don't think I've read a piece of fiction for 25 years. But I do know that real-life detection is far more exciting than any fiction could be.'

Was he really finding the Nude Murders investigation exciting? He gave this interview on 3 May 1965, when he was nearly three months into the case. No one was using the Four-Day Johnny tag these days, and his murder squad kept finding themselves in a maze of leads that led nowhere.

The *Express* article was another one describing du Rose's heavy working day. It recounted how, rising at 7am at his south London home, he would grab his note pad from the bedside – there in case he needed to jot something down in the middle of the night – and then head for Shepherd's Bush police station. This was his 12th week on the case, but he still could not believe they would fail. He was quoted as saying, 'Make no mistake about this case. When I see the man we're looking for I shall know him without any doubt whatsoever. And there will be absolutely no problem about proving his guilt... It's a question of going over the ground again and again and checking and re-checking. There are hundreds of police involved in this inquiry... more than ever before.

'We'll get him. Oh yes. We'll get him. You can be sure of that.'

During these weeks, on top of the night observations, the WPC decoys, the Husky squad, the house-to-house checks and the Heron Trading Estate inquiries, du Rose and Bill Baldock had overseen further searches for a truly incriminating lead.

Officers were checking mental hospitals, every prostitute who complained of being attacked by clients, telephone and letter tip-offs. They sifted their Stop Books, which had details of anyone confronted by the police on the street in suspicious circumstances. There were 73 of these books from B, D, F, T and X divisions. Every instance of suspicious activity at times relevant to the murders meant the suspects were questioned again and their stories checked.

Because all the victims had had venereal diseases or were suffering from one, an idea was explored that they may all have had contact with the same man. Checks were made at Holloway Prison and special clinics in west London, but no man with connections to all the women could be found.

Press conferences were held twice daily at Shepherd's Bush police station. This could result in new alerts – perhaps a woman not seen in her usual haunts for a while had become the latest victim of the Nude Killer. For example, the police issued an identikit for 25-year-old Susan Smith, alias Goldie, who had not been seen for ten days. 'Nude murders alarm: girl missing' was the *News of the World*'s headline on 21 March. Susan was close to the profile of victims, being 5 feet 4 inches and missing her top front teeth. However, after the press and TV coverage she was found to be safe.

From 15 March tracing missing prostitutes became another duty for female CID officers in case they had become victims, which the police wanted to be aware of as quickly as possible.

In total, the whereabouts of 29 women reported missing by other prostitutes or pimps were traced, and all found alive.

During the first half of 1965, under du Rose's lead, a virtual police army pored over every tip and lead to find the man behind the campaign of death on London's streets. At this time the media supported the investigation with a lot of column inches and airtime, and Scotland Yard received hardly any criticism.

Would public pressure on John du Rose's team to catch the Nude Killer have been more intense if the victims had been housewives or nurses? That seems likely. In April 1979, when Peter Sutcliffe, the Yorkshire Ripper, departed from his apparent pattern of murdering prostitutes and bludgeoned to death 19-year-old building society clerk Josephine Whitaker in Halifax, there was a huge response from the public with more than 1,000 phone calls from people with information to share. One female detective even said, 'Before that I just thought, well, he seems to be hanging around prostitutes, I'm OK, but after that one, I thought no one was safe.'

Another telling moment from the Yorkshire Ripper inquiry occurred after the murder of Wilma McCann in 1975. The head of Leeds CID, Dennis Hoban, wanted to appeal to the public for information about the victim's final movements. However, as author Michael Bilton reveals in his book on the case, *Wicked Beyond Belief*, Hoban felt that Wilma McCann being a 'good-time girl' would be a 'major complication'. Bilton writes, 'Labelling a victim a prostitute in this situation was unhelpful. Experience showed the public were somehow not surprised at what happened to call girls.' So, on this occasion the Leeds police directed attention to the victim's children, hoping to appeal to the public's sympathy. This was the level of disconnection between the general public and street prostitutes in the 1960s and 1970s.

During the Nude Murders case the press largely portrayed prostitutes as being outside of decent society. Newspapers enjoyed giving their readers a glimpse of the prostitutes' red-light world in features such as the *Daily Mail*'s 'Behind the Nude Murders... a highly organised underground in vice'. This suggested the Street Offences Act 1959 may have cut the number of prostitutes arrested for soliciting but the trade had not gone away. It had morphed into organised Soho vice rings run by pimps, with sex workers soliciting in cafes and clubs or operating as call-girls. None of the Nude Killer's victims worked in this way but the story was still an excuse to look at a shady world where Soho prostitutes advertised their services by sitting in lighted windows, with maids in attendance.

It is a sad fact that there was little, if any, compassion expressed for the dead women amid all the media prurience. The mood of the time was a general unspoken disapproval of a lifestyle that had led to their murder. Brian Collett covered the killings for the *Acton Gazette* and he recalled, 'I used to do the police calls and they said very little about the Nude Killings. Shepherd's Bush nick was the centre for three really big inquiries – the Nude Murders, the Braybrook Street police killings [also known as the Shepherd's Bush murders, concerning the three officers shot to death in 1966] and the escape from Wormwood Scrubs of George Blake.

'I don't honestly think there was as much drama with it [the Nude Murders] as you might expect. There was more with the police killings.'

The murdered women all had basic educations, poor or stormy lives as young people and had ended up in a degrading struggle to earn money on the streets – a fate that made them the perfect target group for a serial killer. The stigma that came with prostitution was much greater 50 years ago. That their deaths should be so publicly unlamented made the crimes much more tragic.

However, it was not just the UK media that showed a lack of feeling for the victims. The foreign press went completely over the top. The *Los Angeles Times* was not alone in writing about London's '10,000 soiled Cinderellas', as it called the capital's street women. On 14 May it said, 'The police investigation has given the public a rare glimpse of the murky depths under the tourists' London of jolly beefeaters, prancing horse guards and Olde English tea shoppes.'

Which was a good distraction for reporters and readers just then. Behind closed doors at Shepherd's Bush police station, du Rose and Baldock were circling several major suspects for the Nude Murders. However, each man would end up pointing the finger at completely different potential culprits, starting a controversy that would last to this day.

PART 2

THE GALLERY

Chapter 12

What Kind Of Monster...?

Detective Superintendent Bill Baldock would eventually write the final 1965 report summarising the entire investigation for the Scotland Yard hierarchy. By the time it was submitted in September, he had built up a picture of the kind of man he thought they were hunting.

The newspapers had called the culprit a 'maniac sex killer', 'twisted', 'sex-crazed', 'perverted'. Baldock's outline was more mundane – and realistic. He thought the killer was outwardly respectable, a professional or businessman. He could be married, obviously drove a vehicle, was calm under pressure and calculating. He was cunning enough to get rid of his victims' belongings, thereby hiding evidence, though this would have been a challenge for him because undressing corpses was a difficult task. The killer had an excellent knowledge of west London, including out-of-the-way spots such as Dukes Meadows and the Heron Trading Estate.

Baldock suspected that he did not operate at weekends, with the victims last being seen on weekdays (Tailford, on a Friday night/Saturday morning; Lockwood, Tuesday night; Barthelemy, Monday night; Fleming, Friday night/Saturday morning; Brown, Friday night; O'Hara, Monday night).

The superintendent and his colleagues did not view the killer as having a 'vendetta' against prostitutes, which seems to have meant an excessively violent grudge against them, but he was obviously targeting them. This was no doubt either down to their accessibility or his internal obsessions, or a bit of both. The attacks were callous and lethal, but not excessively violent.

The actual method of murder led to a lot of speculation. Baldock also considered that the killer could have embarked on his murder campaign by accident, that having inadvertently smothered his first victim he developed a taste for it.

One view of the senior investigators was that the neck marks and patterns suggested the women had been asphyxiated by having their clothes pulled tightly round their necks. A hand may have been placed over their face, and perhaps their neck. As was noted several times in the post-mortems, finger marks suggested the victims had tried to release the lethal pressure.

But some time was also spent looking at whether the victims had been smothered while fellating the killer. Dr David Bowen, who examined Bridie O'Hara, agreed that asphyxiation during oral masturbation, while the victim was leaning over the man in a car, might be a possibility. Slight facial bruising on the victims might have been caused by their being pressed into the killer's lap. Bowen had never come across such a mode of murder but had examined bodies with some similar signs to those in O'Hara's death. He was thinking of mentally impaired patients who attempted to cram an object such as an apple down their gullet, resulting in immediate asphyxiation. With the mouth and jaw fully occupied by the object, coupled with the victims' all missing several teeth, defensively biting down on the object might have been prevented.

Baldock seemed to favour this 'death-by-blowjob' theory. Despite being experienced in providing oral sex to punters and having what the detective called 'animal' cunning and wariness of men, the victims had still died without being able to put up much of a struggle. So, the theory was that the women were possibly ambushed and overpowered during oral sex. Today, the idea seems highly speculative and far-fetched, but it was a serious line of thought back then. Du Rose apparently concurred with Baldock on this 'death-by-blowjob' scenario, signing the report in which Baldock outlined the idea. In addition, in his 1971 memoirs du Rose wrote that the killer 'certainly wasn't satisfied with normal inter-course' and indulged in 'his particular perversion', becoming frenzied at the moment of orgasm – no doubt these were euphemisms for oral sex.

One incorrect conclusion was that the killer would strike again soon. In fact, the Nude Murders ceased with the discovery of Bridie O'Hara in February 1965. Why?

Before looking at the men who came under serious suspicion, it is worth reviewing why detectives thought one man was responsible.

There were clear links in the pattern of the crimes. The murder squad eventually excluded Gwynneth Rees – found in a decomposed state on the Mortlake rubbish site in 1963 – from the victim list because there was a strong possibility she either died at the hands of an abortionist or one of her very many violent acquaintances. In addition, the cause of her death had been difficult to ascertain and it was not clear that she been murdered. They did, however, think Elizabeth Figg, discovered at Dukes Meadows in the summer of 1959, could be included as potentially the first victim.

That made seven – Elizabeth Figg, Hannah Tailford, Irene Lockwood, Helen Barthelemy, Mary Fleming, Frances Brown and Bridie O'Hara. Figg will be reviewed separately, but common features linking the final six were:

Height: All were quite small. They appear to have been carefully selected regarding height, all being between 5 feet and 5 feet 2 inches.

Cause of death: The first two bodies found in 1964, Tailford and Lockwood, were thought to have drowned, based on river water found mixed with air in their lungs. But in light of the remaining victims all having been asphyxiated, investigators later considered that Tailford and Lockwood may have been killed in the same way. They had similar bruising on their faces and marks on their necks as the four later victims. Detectives wondered if the movement of the swirling Thames could have caused Tailford and Lockwood's diaphragms to have drawn in river water, making it appear they had drowned. In addition, Tailford's body had marks from her underwear that were visible from the blanching of her skin after death, which was inconsistent with drowning (such a lividity pattern, caused by blood settling in dependent, lower portions of the body, is usually absent in water deaths because of buoyancy). All the victims had these marks, though it was unclear whether Lockwood also had them because few pictures were taken of her body.

Naked: Of the six linked murders from 1964–65, only in the case of Tailford was any clothing recovered, namely the stockings she still had on when found, the pants thrust in her mouth, and her coat, discovered in a boat's propeller. With the subsequent victims, the killer succeeded in eradicating all trace of their clothes, jewellery, dentures and bags. Elizabeth Figg in 1959 was wearing a cotton dress and undershirt, but it is not clear that she was the first in the series – John du Rose certainly discounted her. If she was, it was possibly a bungled or accidental killing committed by the perpetrator, which could explain why he failed to take all of her clothing.

Prostitutes: The women were categorised as 'low-class street prostitutes' by the police. Very few did not perform oral masturbation, which was in great demand, according to senior detectives. They worked the streets in the Notting Hill/Shepherd's Bush area, often after midnight. They were picked up by kerb-crawlers, though none was apparently seen getting into a car with the killer. All came from outside of London, from other parts of the UK and Eire.

Four bodies stored: Because the paint/dust particles found on the final four bodies matched those at the Napiers site on the Heron Trading Estate, the police were convinced they had been hidden there for periods of one day to four weeks, with Bridie O'Hara kept for the longest time. If he picked up his victims in his vehicle and killed them in it, then storing the bodies would obviously give him the chance to remove all of their belongings and dispose of them when he felt ready and it was safe. The first two victims in 1964, Tailford and Lockwood, were pulled from the Thames and were not tested for dust/paint particles. Tailford was last seen at home on 24 January 1964 and was found on 2 February – but her movements in between were hard to pin down, though one witness said he saw her on 1 February. Lockwood was definitely seen the day before her discovery, so both may not have been stored.

Teeth: All the victims had lost teeth. In addition to their missing clothes and belongings, no dentures were ever recovered at the crime scenes. Baldock speculated that the killer may have preferred women with missing teeth and that this could 'be connected with sexual satisfaction', and that if he took their dentures it was probably 'an attempt to destroy identification'.

Alcohol: The victims were heavy drinkers, often seen in local pubs until closing time.

Clients: Mostly kerb-crawlers, often professional or business-men. Police put a lot of emphasis on the high social status of these car-driving punters. But was this accurate? Witnesses sometimes cited kerb-crawlers as being servicemen, cabbies or tradesmen. Ernest Forrest, for one, who drove and was with Elizabeth Figg on her last night, was a decorator.

Venereal disease: All had suffered from venereal diseases, though this was ruled out as a revenge motivation for the killer.

Sexual violence: None of the victims showed signs of this, with the only abrasions appearing above the neck and on the face. Three victims did, however, show signs of having been punched – Tailford (jaw bruises), Barthelemy (swelling on nose and cheekbone), Fleming (large bruise on chest).

Disposal: Here the killer changed his method as he continued his grim campaign. Tailford and Lockwood were thrown in the River Thames. Two panicked disposals followed. Barthelemy was left in the alley off Swyncombe Avenue just two weeks after Lockwood, the shortest period between killings, and the fleeing killer seems to have nearly collided with another motorist. Fleming was left in residential Ber-rymede Road after the killer was apparently spotted behind the ABC restaurant by decorators. After these near misses he was inactive for about 15 weeks. With his next victim, Brown, he was careful to cover her up in the Kensington car park. Twelve weeks later O'Hara was killed, stored for four weeks before being partially covered and found after four days.

So, these were the similarities in the cases of the victims found from February 1964. But on closer scrutiny, the police felt the case of Elizabeth Figg, found five years before, had common features.

She was discovered under a tree in Dukes Meadows overlooking the Thames, 500 yards upstream from where Lockwood was found and 800 yards from the Chiswick Church Street slipway where it was thought Tailford and Lockwood were put in the water.

Figg, 21, an unconvicted prostitute, was still clothed in her dress and underskirt, but her underclothes, shoes and handbag were not located. She was found to have been manually strangled. Injuries included abrasions apparently caused by fingernails on the front of her throat, a similarity with the later cases, and a small injury on the anus (probably caused by a fingernail), which was not.

Her death was therefore similar to the later victims. She had been a prostitute for only a short time and solicited men in vehicles around the Harringay and Holland Park Avenue areas. She was discovered in a similar part of the Thames as the next two victims. One difference was that she was a little taller than later victims – 5 feet 5½ inches. There was little doubt she had been driven to Dukes Meadows and either killed on site and abandoned or murdered elsewhere and left there shortly afterwards. Another difference was that there was no sign that she, unlike at least five of the other victims, had been stripped after death.

How to explain the five-year gap in killings if Figg was victim number one? Perhaps a sojourn abroad, imprisonment, living in another part of the UK. Or maybe the man had initially been frightened by his lethal act.

Nevertheless, while media coverage rarely included Figg among the victims, as the investigation progressed during 1965 the murder squad did consider her a possible additional victim.

The media and public never heard about the men the murder squad were quizzing and checking as suspects. These included anyone who knew or was close to the victims, as well as various criminals and assorted oddballs who had any suspicious aspect to them. But by filtering the various dead ends, the squad would eventually come to strongly focus on a couple of suspects.

Going right back to the beginning, on 11 June 1959, Ernest Patrick Forrest, 34, a builder from Stoke Newington, was with Elizabeth Figg on her last night. They had sex in his car and he dropped her on Holland Park Avenue at 1.10am. He said they arranged to meet back there at 3.30am, but she never appeared. As the last person to see her alive he was thoroughly checked by detectives. Nothing was found to connect him with Figg's killing or the subsequent murders.

In relation to the later crimes, Essex police alerted the murder squad to a 45-year-old man from Fulham who had been convicted of murdering a prostitute in 1952. Having been found insane and sent to Broadmoor, he was released on licence in 1961 and returned to London. He was questioned and his vehicle examined but there were no links to the murders.

A 52-year-old newsagent from Brighton drew police attention during the Husky inquiries. He liked to dress in women's clothing, but when checked none of these items was found to belong to the victims.

Kenneth Archibald's fake confession over Irene Lockwood in 1964 was not the only one that detectives had to deal with. In June 1965 a man charged with robbery was in jail in Bradford and told his solicitor that he had murdered a woman called Bridie. He claimed he met her in Shepherd's Bush on 10 February. After a row with her, he said he killed and dumped her in a mews off Bayswater Road. The car he claimed to have hired and picked her up in could not be traced and no dead prostitute could be found. More wasted police time.

Other wild goose chases included investigating a retired 55-year-old electrical engineer from Tunbridge Wells. A prostitute reported him because he had a taste for being whipped while the proceedings were recorded on a tape recorder. No connection with the murders could be found.

A company director from Kent came under suspicion after a report from another prostitute. She was picked up outside Ladbroke Grove Tube in a Vauxhall Victor and taken to the Civil Service Sports Ground near Dukes Meadows. The man wanted sex 'up the rear' but she refused and he then agreed to the 'right way'. However, during intercourse he put his hands round her throat and choked her. She started crying and he apparently said, 'You're too young, I can't do it to you.'

The prostitute jumped out of the car and got its number, but the man nearly ran her down. The police traced him. He turned out to be married with three children. He also denied being with the prostitute, saying he was instead at a Catholic church on this particular Sunday night in July. His wife and another man also gave him an alibi, saying he had been home. No evidence in his car or at his home or business could connect him with the crimes. In addition, the prostitute could not identify him at Shepherd's Bush police station. Despite police doubting his insistence that he was not the man seen driving through Kensington in the early hours on a subsequent occasion – as reported by WPC decoys – his alibi, failures to identify him and further doubts about the trustworthiness of the prostitute finally ruled him out.

A 42-year-old mortuary assistant looked like another potential suspect. He was reported by a prostitute who lived on Hornton Street in Kensington, right by where Frances Brown was found in the car park. He paid the prostitute £15 and £25 on two occasions to get partially undressed and watch him masturbate. It was his work in a mortuary (at this stage the police were wondering where the victims had been stored) that really alerted detectives to his potential as a suspect. But again, they could not link him to the murders, though he was charged with stealing hospital equipment and articles from bodies at the mortuary.

More alarming was a report that came in about a 42-year-old stoker who lived in East Acton. A workmate told the police that he hired prostitutes and bragged of his exploits with them. One of these women was located and she told officers that in February 1965 she was taken to the boiler house of a west London hospital. She had intercourse with this man for £2, but then he refused to let her go for a time, though she did eventually get away. He owned a Bedford Utilibrake van and had worked on the Heron Trading Estate, both for Napier's and another company. Despite these promising links and the fact that detectives found him to be a peculiar character, they could not associate him with the murders.

A 36-year-old engineer from Kingston, Surrey, was looked into after he was accused of attempted rape in Epsom in April 1965. He had threatened a woman in his Commer van with a knife and his wife confirmed his violence towards her, but his van did not turn up in the murder squad index of vehicles and no evidence could be found against him.

Interpol was asked for assistance with another inquiry. Suspicions developed about a Belgian man who had been a strong suspect in the murder of Ann Noblett, 17, who was found in a wood at Whitwell, Hertfordshire, in January 1958. This case became known as the 'Deep Freeze' murder and its association with refrigeration interested the murder squad. They had wondered if Bridie O'Hara had been kept in a fridge. Both O'Hara and Noblett appeared to have been kept somewhere cool before being deposited. The Belgian was a refrigerator engineer at the time of the Noblett killing and, though heavily suspected, was released for lack of evidence. He returned to Belgium (he had dual nationality). It was found he had committed fraud concerning a refrigeration business he ran in the UK, and it was thought he may have slipped back into Britain via Holland. His movements over the previous two years were pieced together with Interpol's help. His picture was circulated around the Heron Trading Estate, but no evidence against him in the Nude Murders was unearthed.

Another strange character came up during the probe into activities on the Heron Trading Estate. A 63-year-old engineer at Ultra Electronics had been suspected by Hertfordshire police in 1961 of sending a homemade bomb to a company director at another firm where he used to work. The bomb exploded in the recipient's face. Though he seemed to recover, the man committed suicide a month later. The suspect was seen by detectives hunting the Nude Killer dumping cartons of burnt material and soil in the bins at Ultra Electronics. Samples of this stuff were taken and checked, and the man was followed. Nothing incriminating was found. When questioned, the man said he was dumping bonfire debris. Under questioning his behaviour was weird, at times he was unable to speak. Despite his troubling behaviour, no incriminating evidence against him was uncovered and this inquiry eventually ground to a halt.

A macabre twist here is that Ultra Electronics had once also employed John Christie, the Rillington Place killer who was active in the 1940s and 1950s. He even met one of his victims there, Muriel Eady.

A 45-year-old Harley Street dentist who was also a justice of the peace was questioned. His Ford Zodiac was seen several times cruising around Notting Hill and Holland Park Avenue between 2 March and 29 April 1965. He told detectives the Zodiac was his father's and that his own motor was a Rolls-Royce. This was also seen doing the rounds in the areas under surveillance. Was he trying to pick up prostitutes? No, he said. But he had approached decoy WPCs, and the detectives pointed out he was driving round in circles. It turned out the dentist also owned a couple of boats, including a 90-foot sea-going vessel. Could he have dumped Tailford and Lockwood from one of his boats? Once more, a promising theory fizzled out. The boats were berthed at Sunbury and there was no record of his having taken them through the locks during the times Tailford and Lockwood were found. Samples of dust taken from his cars and boats all proved negative.

One man who was connected to the Heron Trading Estate would become hugely significant in the Nude Murders case.

He was 46-year-old Mungo Ireland, who lived on Tildesley Road, Putney, with his wife, Elizabeth. He worked as a patrol man on the estate for Night Security from 6–24 October 1964.

He was a heavy drinker and his home life was fraught with problems. Mungo Ireland committed suicide on 3 March 1965. His suicide note read:

I can't stick it any longer. It may be my fault but not all of it. I'm sorry Harry [the name of Ireland's brother] is a burden to you. Give my love to the kid,

Farewell, Jock.

PS To save you and the Police looking for me I'll be in the garage.

It is a sad sign-off from a man clearly at a low ebb. He was due to appear at Acton Magistrates' Court on the morning of his death to answer a summons for failing to stop his car when required to do so. Instead, after watching the TV the night before his court date, he got into his car and drove to his garage in Solna Avenue, a few streets away. Elizabeth was alarmed to find his note in the morning and asked their 22-year-old daughter to check on him. What a shock for the young woman. Ireland had left the engine of his Ford Consul running and died of asphyxiation.

Could he have been the man who eluded the massive manhunt for so long?

As with many of the other suspects, Ireland had tantalising circumstantial links to the case. During just under three weeks as a security man on the Heron Trading Estate he was on site during the nights. He left Night Security on 13 November 1964 and joined the New Century Cleaning Company in Harlesden, before moving on again on 28 November to be foreman cleaner on contract at Jute Industries in Dundee.

That job ended and he returned to London on the day before it was thought that Bridie O'Hara's body was deposited on the Heron Trading Estate, which was 12 February 1965. He committed suicide during the high point of media publicity caused by the latest discovery of a body.

The police also discovered that a member of Ireland's family worked as a 'maid' to West End prostitutes, a job that usually entailed cleaning, running errands and greeting customers. So, it was clear that Ireland had several connections with the trading estate and with prostitutes (he usually collected this family member from their job). One other detail was that detectives had no idea of his movements on 23 October 1964, when Frances Brown was killed.

However, it is clear that despite these circumstantial links, Bill Baldock did not consider Ireland that strong a suspect. Ireland's car, number plate YUL 333, did not crop up in the police index of cruising motorists. Dundee police also confirmed that Ireland was working as a foreman cleaner in their city on 11 January 1965 – the date Bridie O'Hara was last seen.

One other trait of the man might also have counted against his potential to be the killer. On the night of 17 October 1964 he had been found near Renaults Limited on the Heron Estate with minor head injuries. He was taken to Central Middlesex Hospital, saying he had been attacked by two men. But it was clear he had been drinking and had probably fallen down. He went back to work but was absent on 23 October, when Frances Brown died. Nevertheless, there must have been a nagging doubt that someone who got falling-down drunk could also be the cool, calculating killer out-thinking the biggest police manhunt in Britain.

It appears that the investigation did not delve into Ireland's job history before his short time working on the trading estate. So what he was up to before Frances Brown and Bridie

O'Hara's deaths was not known. This further suggests rather strongly that he was not highly rated as a suspect.

What is more, the murder squad were not aware of him until two months after his death. It was then, in May 1965, that the importance of the Heron Trading Estate was realised. It was also at around that time that a check on the suicides index brought Ireland's name up. This is an important point because later on it would be suggested that the Nude Murders investigation, in a game of cat and mouse, pressured him to commit suicide. Whereas in fact his house, garage, car or his wife's car, were never inspected. He was never interviewed.

So, it is not a surprise that no one from the murder squad attended Ireland's inquest. Coroner Dr Gavin Thurston said it was significant that Ireland's death had taken place on the morning he was due to answer a court summons. He also referred to the man's recent 'change in habits' and heavy drinking. At this point the assumption was clearly that Ireland appeared disillusioned with his life rather than racked with a murderer's guilty conscience. The verdict was suicide, caused by asphyxiation from inhaling car-exhaust fumes.

When Bill Baldock summarised the investigation in a report for his Scotland Yard bosses in September 1965, he outlined the suspicions about Ireland and the points that appeared to exonerate him, but laid no great emphasis on his being the guilty man. Indeed, Baldock devoted as much or more space to several other suspects.

A significant point here is that Baldock's boss, Detective Chief Superintendent John du Rose, signed off Baldock's report, because later on du Rose would contradict that report. He would go on to claim that he had known all along who the killer was – Mungo Ireland.

However, when the investigation was at its height of activity, du Rose and Baldock were united in strongly suspecting another man. Had their suspicion been made public, it would have sent shockwaves through the media and public, because the man they were pursuing was a former detective.

Chapter 13
The Ex-Cop – Killing for Revenge?

The man who Detective Superintendent Bill Baldock viewed as a 'strong suspect' was still alive as this book was being researched. For that reason he will not be named, but the investigation of him back in 1965 was one of the most extraordinary episodes during the Nude Murders case.

This man came to notice a couple of weeks after Bridie's O'Hara murder. At that time the man was a car salesman in west London, but prior to that he had been a detective constable whose career ended in disgrace.

The suspect joined the Met in 1956 and moved to CID in 1961. He served in Fulham and then as an 'aid' or probationer in Notting Hill. He became a CID officer at Kensington police station, then Hammersmith and in June 1962 he transferred to T division, working at Acton and Brentford stations. Interestingly, during this time he lived in police married quarters in Eastfield Court, East Acton Lane – half a mile from the Heron Trading Estate where victims had been stored and Bridie O'Hara found.

At best the man could be described during his police career as a misfit, at worst a spiteful loner. In 1961 and 1962 there were complaints and suspicions about him. In one incident at Kensington station, a detective sergeant returned from an evening drink to find his court papers burning in a toilet bowl. Someone had taken them out of his tray. Later, the office's crime book went missing. It was found in the street by a passer-by and handed in. The feeling was that the office loner was behind it. His former sergeant was quoted by author David Seabrook in *Jack of Jumps*. 'Well dressed, always spotless... He had no pals that I remember. Normally in the CID you'd pal up with somebody, but nobody seemed to be his pal.

'He was a creepy type of bloke. He always seemed to be hanging around... bloody listening to other people's conversations.'

The man failed his detective sergeant's exam in January 1962. It was during the next month that he was sent to Hammersmith for supervision. There, a WPC's handbag was stolen. The thief was spotted running down a corridor and she and several others chased him towards Shepherd's Bush Green, but he got away. Again, word was that the thief was recognised as being the loner.

Then on 17 September 1962 his police career crashed permanently. He was suspended from duty and charged with office-breaking. A psychiatrist's report concluded the man knew right from wrong, and the break-ins were a display of vindictiveness towards his former colleagues. He was sentenced to 12 months' imprisonment and dismissed from the Met.

He was found guilty at the Old Bailey of breaking into properties around Brentford and Isleworth and stealing a bizarre array of goods. From Sycamore Ltd, Commerce Road, Brentford, he took nine paintbrushes and 12 files; from Permutit on the same road, a spanner and £11; from Coley Thermometers, London Road, Isleworth, tobacco. He also attempted to break into Admiralty Oil's laboratory on the Great West Road, Brentford. He pleaded guilty to these charges, but not guilty to breaking and entering the Julius Sax factory on Commerce Road. This latter plea was accepted in court.

A security man at the Admiralty laboratory, Arthur Cox, testified that he had seen a man on the roof on 16 September. The intruder had a chisel. He then clambered down a drain-pipe and got away on a moped. Cox noted its registration number, and it was found to belong to this detective.

It appeared that the guilty man had attempted to cover his crime earlier. He had been the only CID officer on duty when the Admiralty break-in was reported to Brentford police. A uniformed officer took down the moped's number, and this note was later found ripped to pieces in a bin.

Having denied his involvement, the detective was told he would face an identity parade with the security man attending. The detective under suspicion then told his superintendent, Maurice Osborn, who would later be heavily involved in the Nude Murders case, 'There is no need for that as I was at the [Admiralty] laboratory. I have not been feeling too good lately and have been doing queer things.' He confessed and explained his actions by saying he had received a bump on his head during CID training when a loose sash window slammed on him. He claimed to have been plagued by head-aches since then.

He also said that when he joined Kensington CID he felt other officers were watching him. He became unhappy. 'I found I was doing stupid things and then developing a tech-nique whereby I convinced myself I had not done these things,' he told the police. At Hammersmith he said he was happy for a time, but his stint there was 'marred by an incident' for which he was blamed. At Brentford he was accused of theft and felt persecuted. He said, 'My feeling, wrong as it was, was that if they thought so strongly that I was a black sheep, I will show them and be a black sheep.'

A recollection told more recently in Dick Kirby's *Laid Bare* by an aid to CID who worked with the disgraced officer in Brentford during this time reveals his rule-breaking tendency. While on night duty the disgraced officer asked the aid if he had ever seen mass killer John Christie's house in Notting Hill. He then committed a disciplinary offence by driving miles from their night-duty patch to view the exterior of the Rillington Place house of horrors.

Testifying in court later, Detective Superintendent Osborn explained why he wanted to transfer the difficult officer from Kensington to Hammersmith. 'I felt he was not mixing with his colleagues as he ought to do and in his work he was inclined to be rather careless.' The man had also been dealt with for gross negligence, prompting the move to Brentford.

In a short police career of almost six years, the man had made a lot of enemies with his irresponsible, impulsive, deceitful and criminal behaviour. This is how he explained his crimes. 'I would like to point out again that when I broke into the premises I have mentioned I did not set out to steal but rather have the satisfaction of doing something which I knew my colleagues would have to work on but get nowhere.'

Were the Nude Murders a similar poke in the eye for former police colleagues? An escalation of crimes intended to drag detectives into a time-consuming and ultimately fruitless investigation?

The ex-cop became the most compelling suspect for Bill Baldock. Not only had he lived half a mile from the Heron

Trading Estate and had a self-confessed grudge against a police service that rejected and exposed him as a crook, he also worked throughout the whole area where the murders were committed. This stretched from the pick-up streets of Notting Hill out to the Heron Trading Estate, as well as the car park off Kensington High Street where Frances Brown was left.

Baldock said the ex-cop started to figure in the investigation two weeks after Bride O'Hara's murder. What brought him to the superintendent's attention is not clear. A tip-off? Someone such as Baldock's colleague Maurice Osborn mentioning the disgraced detective following his involvement in the ex-cop's career and court case? Or had Baldock simply recalled the man himself for his reprehensible behaviour and odd hostility to former workmates. He had been at Kensington police station at the same time as the ex-cop was stirring up a bad atmosphere.

Once the suspicions against the man who I will call the Disgraced Cop surfaced, another disturbing fact became apparent. Each victim had been discarded in a different police subdivision: Hannah Tailford in the FD subdivision (Hammersmith); Helen Barthelemy in TB (Brentford); Mary Fleming and Bridget O'Hara in TA (Acton) and Frances Brown in FK (Kensington). Irene Lockwood broke the pattern, having been discovered on the Thames foreshore in FC subdivision, which was Chiswick. But even here, there was the chance that she was put in the river upstream and floated to that spot. The point for the investigators was, who else but a cop – or ex-cop – would know these police sub-divisions? Or was the body distribution just a coincidence?

Baldock needed hard evidence and an extensive investigation into the Disgraced Cop got moving.

He came out of Ford prison in June 1963 after serving seven months of his sentence for breaking into the business premises. This, of course, was almost eight months before the first of the six confirmed victims, Hannah Tailford, was found in February 1964.

He went to live in Essex with his wife and family, and found a job as a travelling salesman until February 1964. Making discreet inquiries so as not to alert the Disgraced Cop, detectives then discovered that he moved on to become a car salesman for a firm based on the Old Brompton Road in west London. The firm's managing director told officers the Disgraced Cop had been employed at their depot in Hadleigh, Essex, and was eventually dismissed for being inefficient.

Essex police were asked to keep a watch on the suspect, to record which vehicles he drove and search any premises he might use to store the victims' clothes or their bodies.

It was discovered that the Disgraced Cop had been sick for two days in July 1964, an important month as this was when Mary Fleming was murdered and found in Berrymede Road, Chiswick. The ex-cop's wife called in and said her husband could not come to work because he had a problem with his nerves. Frustratingly, the car firm could find no record of the specific days during which the suspect had been absent. It then turned out that the branch manager who had told officers of these sick days was a bit of a drinker and could not be trusted.

Meanwhile, the doctor that the ex-cop saw during his mental health troubles in 1963, who was based on Goldhawk Road, Shepherd's Bush, told the police that the man had not been back for further treatment.

It did not take long for the Disgraced Cop to realise that the murder squad was talking to people about him. By late February 1965, after Bridie O'Hara was found, he had been asking several associates if the police had contacted them. Even this seemed to make the police suspicious, because once he was aware the investigation was interested in him, he made no attempt to come forward and assist.

Stories had gone round, which are still remembered by retired officers today, that the suspect had been spotted up a tree spying on a woman in her bedroom, and that he visited strip clubs. But when pubs, clubs and west London's streets were canvassed – with locals being shown enlarged photos of the Disgraced Cop – no one could place him. In addition, none of the many cars he used as a salesman turned up in the police index of cruising motorists.

It was time to interview him. The Disgraced Cop had moved house as stealthily as possible, presumably to make it difficult to trace him, but his new address was eventually found. He told officers he knew they were investigating him and was not surprised they had called on him. He also denied any knowledge of the Nude Murders. In a statement he said he had only been to London during the evening three times. These were two occasions when he attended the Motor Show at Earl's Court (23 and 30 October 1964), while the other was for a Volvo sales course at the Washington Hotel, Curzon Street (25 January 1965). He had used public transport and taxi, always returning home no later than 11pm. He said he avoided London because of his past troubles, no doubt a reference to his humiliating police career. He confirmed he was now working for another second-hand car dealership in Hadleigh, Essex.

His wife added that he did not go out late at night since he had been home from prison. She said she 'would not stand for it' and would leave him if that happened, clearly fearful after her husband's disastrous spate of burglaries. She also said she could not remember his being sick in July 1964.

The wife did recall the trips to the Motor Show and sales course. Also remembered was another time he was out late, but not in London. This had been when he went to a party given by someone in the car trade, and he arrived home at 2.30am. The man throwing the party, which had been in Hadleigh, confirmed the ex-cop's attendance.

Baldock wondered if the Disgraced Cop's wife was covering for him as an alibi. He felt she had almost been expecting the detectives' visit. When they arrived the Disgraced Cop told her, 'They have come about what I mentioned the other month.' When she referred to another matter, the ex-cop said, 'Not that, the other business we joked about.' His wife laughed at that. 'Oh, not the Nude Murders.'

Before working for the car dealer in Hadleigh, the Disgraced Cop had been employed by another motor business in Leigh-on-Sea. The managing director of this outfit told the police that the suspect had been a good salesman and confirmed his trips to the Motor Show and sales course. He said the Disgraced Cop had manned the Volvo and Saab stands at Earl's Court on 23 and 30 October 1964, which was confirmed by another witness. The Disgraced Cop finished work on both nights at 9pm. He was given a white Saab saloon to use with a five-gallon petrol allowance – which he exceeded and had to be warned about. However, his expenses for attending the show seemed to further confirm that he was there.

Another tantalising possibility arose when it was learned that the Disgraced Cop had recommended to his superiors a firm where repairs and spray jobs were done cheaply. Would this tie in with the dust/paint particles found on the victims? The premises, in Canvey, had samples taken, together with many others in the area, but the results were negative.

Detectives were also particularly interested in the first date at the Motor Show – 23 October. This was the night Frances Brown went missing after being separated from her friend when they were driven from Portobello Road by two motorists. Suspicions at the time were that the two men who had picked up the women, and had never been traced, were themselves attendees at the Motor Show. So, Beryl Mahood, the prostitute who had been with Frances Brown, was shown a photo of the Disgraced Cop. She did not pick him out as being one of the two mystery motorists. This was frustrating because the police felt that the Disgraced Cop resembled the identikit picture Mahood provided of the man who drove with her on Frances's last night. Clearly, it was the other man, the one who drove Frances, who was the killer, but a positive ID from Mahood might have implicated the Disgraced Cop as being an accomplice. However, this turned out to be another dead end.

The question remained – what had the Disgraced Cop done after finishing at the Motor Show? Did he really go home by public transport? The investigation could find no way to disprove this. The directors of the Saab and Volvo stands were spoken to in an effort to piece together what the suspect's movements and activities had been, but eventually this line of inquiry had to be dropped. Detectives did not have the time to track down and interview the 130-odd representatives who had been present on each of the Motor Show stands.

By September 1965 when Bill Baldock wrote his report on the case, seven months had elapsed since the discovery of Bridie O'Hara on the Heron Trading Estate. No further victims had been found and the massive investigation team was being wound down. There was no media outcry that this was happening. It is perhaps a sign of the public's general lack of empathy with the victims that once the killings stopped, the crimes faded from the headlines and most people's memories.

The conviction among senior detectives was that the killer would strike again, but until he did the huge drain on Metropolitan Police resources could not be sustained. John du Rose and Bill Baldock were frustrated by this, but even before du Rose had been put in charge of the investigation it was already engaging a far larger number of men and women than was usual on a murder case. Du Rose had a 200-strong CID murder force under his command, which was then supplemented by about another 100 uniformed officers and 300 members of the Special Patrol Group. The day-to-day workload of the Metropolitan Police, particularly the CID, had been under pressure for months by this diversion of manpower and could not continue.

However, when the Nude Killer did re-emerge, as detectives assumed he would, the police would again pull out all the valuable data amassed on the cases and restart the manhunt. For Bill Baldock, the Disgraced Cop could not be eliminated from the inquiry and remained a strong possible suspect. But they had so far found no positive identification of him from witnesses such as Beryl Mahood, and had uncovered no evidence linking him to the victims or crime scenes. Not a shred. Baldock concluded, 'The circumstances surrounding his mental history, knowledge of the area and background are ideal in every respect for his being the murderer. If he is the man responsible he will certainly kill again in the absence of any precautions.'

How frustrating for Baldock, John du Rose and the murder squad to expect a horribly elusive villain to kill again while knowing their hunt for him was being wound down.

That there had been strains in the relationship between du Rose and Baldock was a well-kept secret of the investigation so far. Also hidden was the fact that there had been many logistical tensions in attempting to have officers check and process so much evidence and cover so much ground. For a time the appearance of unity among Scotland Yard's finest was maintained. But perhaps nothing breeds resentment like a major failure. Eventually, the friction between the two men leading the manhunt would break into the open.

What followed was an inappropriate spat in the press fed by police sources, with both sides proposing completely different men as the true Nude Killer.

Chapter 14

The Investigation Ends and the Controversy Begins

The inquest into Bridget O'Hara's death was finally concluded at Hammersmith Coroner's Court on Wednesday, 9 February 1966 – 13 months after she went missing. Dr Harold Broadbridge came out of retirement to oversee proceedings that he had adjourned 12 months previously. This was the fifth inquest into the murdered prostitutes that he had led.

Michael O'Hara recounted that he and Bridie had married in Dublin in 1962. He recalled that they had just reconciled after a separation and had shared a meal at their Agate Road flat in Hammersmith on the last evening he saw her alive. Further witnesses followed including a police officer who testified that Bridie was seen leaving the Shepherd's Bush Hotel and was last spotted near the Green with a man. The jury's unanimous verdict was that Bridie had been killed by 'person or persons unknown'.

Since the discovery of her body on the Heron Trading Estate, the investigation had reached a high pitch of remorseless activity, with hundreds of officers involved. By the autumn of 1965, however, the operation was winding down. Detective Chief Superintendent John du Rose had left Shepherd's Bush and returned to his duties at Scotland Yard in October. A team of seven officers continued on the case for a while, but this was ended on 15 January 1966, a year after Bridie O'Hara's disappearance.

The expectation had been that the Nude Killer would strike again. But by early 1966 he had been inactive for a whole year. Was he waiting for the massive police presence in west London to scale down before resurfacing? The answer, we now realise, was no. The killer was apparently not compelled to keep taking the lives of prostitutes, at least not in west London and not using the same methods. He remained totally unknown and hidden.

The huge operation to trap him had put a tangible strain on the Met. On 3 July 1965 the night observations were scrapped because of the shortage of staff on other divisions. Officers returned to their divisions immediately. If another murder occurred later that month, the police would not know which cars were cruising west London, but it was a chance they felt they had to take in the circumstances.

The following month, on 28 August, the Husky squad and the house-to-house checks were wrapped up too. With the house inquiries, only half the 24-square-mile area had been covered, with dust samples having been collected from around 500 premises and processed. Senior investigators had become convinced that the killer lived within this part of west London, from Paddington out to Hounslow, but again the drain on staff across police divisions meant that officers were sent straight back to their normal duties. Despite the painstaking search through vehicle registration records and 783 Hillman Husky cars having samples taken from them, this ambitious search had to be abandoned before completion as well. Moreover, an effort to make inquiries with the various armed services to pinpoint any personnel who could have been culpable for the killings was also dropped.

Detective Superintendent Bill Baldock would have liked to go over again a lot of the earlier work done in the individual cases, but this effort was also left incomplete. Perseverance was his mantra, as it was with his boss, John du Rose, and it is clear he found it frustrating that they were not able to follow through with these investigations. Even tracing the 130 representatives on each of the two stands at the Earl's Court Motor Show to find out more about the Disgraced Cop's movements could not be finished.

Despite the massive effort to catch this prolific killer having effectively petered out, Scotland Yard could still count on a positive press. During the 1960s there was a reluctance to criticise what was still lauded as the finest police force in the world. The Fleet Street newspapers of that decade were more respectful than their brashly partisan children are today. *The People* on 10 October 1965 sounded at first as though they were going to attack the investigation. 'Scotland Yard murder hunter Chief Det Supt John du Rose, the man who for months has led the vast search for the London "Nudes' Killer"', returns to his office desk tomorrow – his expensive bid to catch the murderer a failure.

'The hunt cost between £5,000 and £10,000 a week, month after month. Hundreds of detectives took part in it.'

But then the article swings behind the police. 'Its failure to trap the killer was no fault of du Rose and his men.

'It was due to one gruesome fact – the sex maniac who has killed at least six women has never struck again.'

The report's logic was that the Yard had such a huge team lying in wait following the last killing, monitoring every vehicle, that if the murderer had attempted another homicide he would certainly have been caught. It concluded that every penny had been well spent in halting the murder spree.

A few weeks later the *News of the World* ran a strange report that was again supportive of Scotland Yard, almost in awe of its near mythical powers of detection. Headlined 'Guilty secrets in a red diary', the 21 November piece regaled readers with the potency of John du Rose's desk diary. 'The book records the activities of outwardly respectable businessmen who move at night in the twilight of London's seamy vice areas at Notting Hill, Paddington and Bayswater.'

What is interesting about this article, which was probably written with the chief superintendent's cooperation, is that it suggests that among these names were some secret suspects. 'Most of the men listed in this diary are frightened that their guilty secret will be uncovered. But it is a groundless fear. Their secret is safe. Chief Supt du Rose, a man noted for his discretion, will only ever disclose one name in the diary – and only if it can be proved that the man is the Nude Killer.' Perhaps du Rose was stung by the word 'failure' that hung over the previous month's story in *The People*. Now the angle was that the detective was still on the case – despite having gone back to Scotland Yard – and ready to pounce.

'Every day a stream of information pours into his office, much of it from his undercover squad,' the story read. 'And every day he flicks through his murder diary searching for a link between the old information and the new.' One of his big clues, it was stated, was the two men who had driven off with Frances Brown and Beryl Mahood on the night Brown had gone missing. Both men still refused to contact the police and the article reprinted their identikit pictures, appealing again for information about them. The hunt was ongoing, not on the massive scale of before, but 'patiently and methodically'. The story concluded, 'Theories abound. One is that the killer is dead. It arises from the fact that two suspects committed suicide.'

This was likely to be a reference to the Heron Trading Estate night watchman Mungo Ireland and another man investigated by detectives. In a bizarre coincidence, both men killed themselves on the same day, 3 March 1965, the second with a drug overdose. He was an accountant from Wembley, who spent a lot of money on prostitutes and was briefly scrutinised, but, among other factors, he could not drive so was ruled out as being the killer.

The suggestion that the killer was a man who had committed suicide, however, was one du Rose would return to controversially within a few years.

With no further murders or lurid details to print, the press coverage quickly evaporated. And now that the murders appeared to have stopped, there was almost a collective sense of relief. The news agenda moved on. As did the police.

Bill Baldock moved from T Division to the Yard's C1 Department, the central CID office, 18 months later, before retiring in 1967.

John du Rose went on to feature in high-ranking supervisory roles in two of the 1960s most notorious cases – that of the torture/extortion gang of Charlie and Eddie Richardson, and the Kray twins' organised crime outfit. Both investigations were successful, with Charlie and Eddie imprisoned for 25 and 10 years respectively for robbery with violence, grievous bodily harm and demanding money with menaces. Ronnie and Reggie Kray received life sentences in 1969 for murder. Though not lead investigator on these triumphs, du Rose was a senior member of the operations. During these years he moved further up the hierarchy, becoming CID Deputy Commander in 1966, then Commander CID in 1968 and Deputy Assistant Commissioner the following year. He received an OBE in the 1969 New Year Honours list.

Despite the spectacular career, du Rose was rueful when he stepped down in 1970. He said in his autobiography, 'On looking back on my career I am convinced that I should have retired 15 years earlier than I did. With crime ever on the increase the strain became that much greater and I came to realise that men of senior rank should be rich in experience but young in years.'

He had certainly sacrificed plenty for his career, and not just his holidays, from which he was recalled several times, including for the Nude Murders inquiry. Precious time he might have enjoyed in retirement with his wife, Constance – having put in so many long days, seven days a week, getting in at 2am – was denied him when she died in 1968. Shortly before retiring he married again, this time to detective con- stable Merle Taylor, aged 35. She had been one of the first officers to volunteer for the decoy patrols. He became head of security for National Car Parks and eventually settled in Great Yarmouth with his new wife. He died aged 69 in 1980.

Of course he had not solved every case with which he had been involved. The Countess Lubienska homicide back in 1957 was an investigation he was part of that ended in failure, while the Nude Murders case was obviously a major disap- pointment. While there may have been no discredit in these setbacks, his apparent attempt to take credit for having known the identity of the Nude Killer all along was more dubious.

A first taste of what was ahead came in a big feature in *The People* on 2 November 1969, nearly five months before du Rose left the Yard. Headlined 'The day the murders stopped', this announced that 'Officially the file is still open but... Scotland Yard believes it knows the secret of the Nude Killer'.

It revealed that the 'eight unspeakably bestial killings will remain unsolved – for ever', but that the search for the killer was over. Reporter Michael Wells had something of a scoop here. 'Though they can never declare it officially some of Scotland Yard's top brass believe they know the identity of the sex maniac who, between 1959 and 1965 murdered at least eight London prostitutes. It seems that "Jack the Stripper" will never be brought to trial. He is dead. He committed suicide just a few hours before detectives, having finally secured the evidence they needed, were to swoop on his home to arrest him.'

So why had Scotland Yard allowed everyone to assume their hunt had failed? Why had they never taken credit for one of the 'most painstaking and inexorably efficient investigations in criminal history'? The answer, *The People* suggested, was, 'Because of a remarkable act of fairness and humanity that perhaps could only happen in this country.' The killer was dubbed 'John X', a man in his 40s living a quiet, apparently respectable life in a London suburb. It was to protect the wife and several children of this loving family man that Scotland Yard had not revealed his 'bestial' secret. Instead, the family were allowed to believe he had killed himself because of stress. The article, stretching over two pages, stated that the police preferred to appear to be failures rather than confront John X's family with the truth. 'In the fairness of British justice they can never accuse a man who cannot now defend himself.'

What evidence were the police said to have? John X's car registration was spotted in a kerb-crawling area where victims were picked up. His face fitted the description of a man seen at the times of the killings. John X was revealed to have been in London when all the murders were committed and was away from home on every occasion that a body was deposited. He also worked 'alone and undisturbed' at the factory where the bodies were kept. Finally, the report explained how the pressure built on the guilty man. 'John X must have known the net was closing when he learned that detectives had made a minute inspection of the garage where he kept his car. He did not wait for them to come for him. He killed himself. And the nude murders came to an end.' To clinch the case, after the man's suicide, detectives found dust particles in the back of his car that were identical to those found on the naked bodies.

An open-and-shut case! And the police were such paragons of discretion.

The truth was a different matter. Going on the obvious implication that John X was Mungo Ireland, only the point about his connection to the factory bears any relation to the facts. He did work for a few weeks in October 1964 on the Heron Trading Estate. But his car was never spotted by the night-observation teams, there was no man fitting his description seen at the time of the killings and he was not in town when all the murders occurred – he was working in Dundee when Bridie O'Hara vanished. Neither his garage nor his car was ever searched, either. Murder squad detectives were not even aware of Ireland's existence or that the trading estate was where the bodies had been kept until two months after his suicide – that is, not until May 1965. So there was no way they could have searched his garage and thereby inadvertently put pressure on him. As for protecting the feelings of the dead man's wife, of course the police could not do that when they were investigating a serious crime. Mungo Ireland's wife was eventually interviewed once he came under suspicion.

Moreover, nothing had been stopping du Rose from appearing at Bridie O'Hara's inquest in February 1966 to state officially that he had known who the killer was a year ago. Instead, it had been Bill Baldock who was present to tell the court that 120,000 people had been interviewed by the police and more than 4,000 statements taken. Hence the verdict of 'murder by person or persons unknown'.

Further indication that this new spin on the killer's identity was probably coming from John du Rose arrived in 1970, the year after *The People*'s bombshell. Deputy Assistant Commissioner du Rose, then aged 58, had just retired from the Met. He was interviewed by Tom Mangold on 2 April for the BBC programme *24 Hours*. Here du Rose took all the credit for cornering the guilty man. 'Now the man who stopped the inquiry is free to say what happened...' it was announced on air. Du Rose explained that stories had been fed to the media every day to pressure the killer and perhaps force him into making a blunder and exposing himself. He said, 'It didn't have the effect that we desired, but he obviously became so frightened he took his own life. And this was within a matter of weeks of this inquiry started by me in February 1965.' The fact that the murders had stopped confirmed that the killer had taken his own life before he could be caught, du Rose claimed. He stated that the suicide victim was a suspect already known to the police.

He also revealed how the killer had been cleverly boxed in. Du Rose's team had started with a shortlist of 20 suspects, which was gradually whittled down to three names. It was one of these last three that had killed himself. 'Now we couldn't talk to him,' du Rose said, 'he was dead... We could only make enquiries about him, check his employment, check his activities, his movements, where he associated and so on. And when you bear in mind that there were six takings of the women [between 1964-5], and six droppings of the body, we had 12 occasions on which to check an individual out. A wonderful set of circumstances, really, to pinpoint an individual.' The clear implication is that the dead man's movements confirmed that he was the killer. In fact, as we have seen, his car was never spotted by the night patrols, it seemed his whereabouts before October 1964 were not investigated, and in any case Dundee police said Mungo Ireland was working in their city on 11 January, the day Bridie O'Hara disappeared.

It is extraordinary that so little scrutiny was given to du Rose's assertions. Which stories placed in the media had tipped the Nude Killer over the edge? Would claims that the 'net was closing' really be enough to make him think he should kill himself? And, of course, this supposed strategy of the shrinking shortlist contradicted *The People*'s earlier suggestion that it was the police search of his garage that made the killer realise his time was up.

But no one was looking closely at these claims, and du Rose was careful to keep it vague. Events had unfolded 'within a matter of weeks'. If the actual date when Mungo Ireland came under scrutiny had been known publicly – which was two months after his suicide – then the holes in du Rose's account would have been glaring.

Crucially, Ireland had taken his life on 3 March 1965. In which case why had du Rose, who apparently knew the killer's identity, gone on to escalate the investigation so spectacularly by launching the mass road surveillance, house-to-house inquiries, WPC decoys, the forensic tests on the Heron Trading Estate and the taking of thousands and thousands of additional statements? All of these efforts began in the days and weeks after the suicide and continued until the summer. Why would Scotland Yard waste tens of thousands of pounds on all this if du Rose knew who the killer was?

Why would Assistant Commissioner Ranulph Bacon have made a TV appeal for information about the killer on 17 March 1965? And why, two months after the police had inadvertently driven the guilty man to suicide, would du Rose himself have been featured in newspaper reports such as the *Express* interview of 3 May 1965 saying, 'We'll get him. Oh yes. We'll get him. You can be sure of that'?

It seems there was then an attempt to water down earlier claims in *The People* that detectives had proof against the night watchman. A follow-up feature in *The Observer* magazine on 3 May 1970, which most likely again had du Rose as its source, indicated that the suspect was a 45-year-old night patrolman who visited factories and workplaces in west London, including the premises where the bodies came into contact with the paint/dust particles. However, this article stressed the circumstantial nature of the evidence, whereas *The People* article had pointed to the deceased's car being spotted cruising and having incriminating paint/dust elements in it. Perhaps du Rose felt the earlier version given to *The People* had gone over the top.

Why did du Rose claim to have secretly solved the case when this seems to contradict many of the facts? Professional pride may have played a part. He enjoyed a tremendous reputation as Four-Day Johnny – the *News of the World* called him 'brilliant' – he had risen high and been honoured. But he had not cracked the biggest case of his life. Did this rankle?

He also had an autobiography coming out. In *Murder Was My Business*, published in 1971, du Rose outlined his theory about the Nude Killer. 'It was assumed from the manner in which all these girls had died that their killer was a man of some strength and virility. He certainly wasn't satisfied with normal intercourse... In obtaining satisfaction he became utterly frenzied and at the moment of his orgasm, the girls died.' It seems as though du Rose or his ghostwriter over-egged the description here. The killings were not 'frenzied', there was no sexual violence and as du Rose says elsewhere in the book, the 'girls died extremely quickly'.

The retired detective repeated his claim that he and his team engaged in a war of nerves with the Nude Killer via radio, TV and the press. He begins the chapter on the case boldly. 'Justice caught up with the Boston Strangler. A hundred writers have, since 1888, speculated on the identity of Jack the Ripper who murdered seven prostitutes in three months in London's East End.

'I know the identity of Jack the Stripper – but he cheated me of an arrest by committing suicide.'

The police had 'leaked' stories to the media about how close they were to the killer. 'We could never forget the fact that no woman was safe until the killer was in our hands,' du Rose wrote, 'but it was not to be and within a month of the murder of Bridie O'Hara the man I wanted to arrest took his own life. Without a shadow of a doubt the weight of our investigation and the enquiries that we had made about him led to the killer committing suicide.' Here there are no mentions of the suspect's car being recorded in the kerb-crawling areas or any forensic evidence against him.

It may have previously appeared that the Nude Killer had outsmarted John du Rose and his team, but the detective had made a determined effort to set the record straight on his own terms. But, of course, Mungo Ireland was no longer around to defend himself or contest these claims.

If John du Rose was blowing his own trumpet with these claims, what did other members of his team on the Nude Murders investigation make of them?

Bill Baldock, du Rose's right-hand man at the time, wrote and signed the final report on the investigation. The press and public had no access to this confidential document. It made no mention of cat-and-mouse games that drove a prime suspect to suicide or any strong evidence implicating Mungo Ireland. It was also signed by du Rose, who only added an addendum that a few selected CID officers should be posted on special night duties in case of another murder. The disparity between Baldock's summary of the murder hunt, which du Rose endorsed, and du Rose's later revelations is jarring.

It became clear in later years that Baldock had not been a fan of his boss, that he may even have shared the view of writer Dick Kirby that du Rose was a 'bullshitter'. Author David Seabrook even spoke briefly to Baldock well into the former detective's 47-year retirement (he died aged 97). From his Finchley home a few years before his death a 'still angry' Baldock said, 'John du Rose should never have been called in. He hindered more than he helped. "Four-day Johnny!" And if he couldn't solve it in four days he wasn't interested.'

The year after du Rose's autobiography appeared, his version of events was rudely dismissed in a still more sensational story in *The Sun*, which by now was looking more like today's *Sun*, following its 1964 relaunch out of the ashes of the *Daily Herald*. This series of reports was written by Owen Summers, who had covered the Nude Murders for the *Daily Mail* some years before. His scoop was given to him by 'certain senior officers', now thought to be Bill Baldock. This special investigation, which ran over several days from 8 February 1972, was headlined 'Was the maniac killer a cop – and could he strike again?'

The story began with a reminder that six women (though the police thought it might have been seven, if Elizabeth Figg was included) had died at the hands of 'London's most vicious killer since Jack the Ripper'. The bid to catch the man was 'Britain's biggest-ever manhunt'.

However, while the 'brilliant' John du Rose claimed that the killer committed suicide, Owen Summers believed there was a lot more to it. 'It is my belief – after an investigation in which I have retraced the steps of the killer, and those of his hunters – that du Rose could be wrong.' The phantom killer could still be alive, and could even strike again.

The features were a shocking repudiation of du Rose's claim about the security man who committed suicide. 'The murderer, I am convinced, halted his killing spree only because he knew that a police net would surely have caught him if he had struck again,' Summers wrote. 'How? Because he may well have been a policeman, perhaps retired, who knew the area better than most men, and could have been in touch all along with the progress of the murder hunt.'

Summers reminded his readers that the Nude Murder case was not closed, despite the suggestion – which is still believed by some today – that the killer did away with himself. The series of articles, coming seven years after the final 1965 killing, were published at a time when the Nude Killings had faded completely from the headlines and the investigation seemed to have run its course long ago. It was probably the longest and most detailed newspaper examination the case had received during or since the investigation was at its height. In addition to recounting the crimes and some flowery speculation from a psychiatrist, there was a lot of detail about the thousands of statements taken and the flecks of paint and dust samples. It is clear the writer must have had good police contacts in compiling this series.

It concluded with Summers' chilling speculation that the killer was still around. First, he attempts to dismantle du Rose's claim that the guilty man was the security guard, Mungo Ireland. He pinpoints the moment that the police learned of Ireland's suicide. 'When three months had passed without another victim being discovered, du Rose ordered a check on all inquests around the time the body of victim No 6 Bridie O'Hara had been found,' Summers wrote. This turned up the security guard, who Summers does not name (Ireland's identity would not become known for many years). Even though Summers does not emphasise this time scale, it again strongly indicates that du Rose first learned about Mungo Ireland in May 1965, so he could not have suspected and put pressure on him in early March that year, when the night watchman committed suicide.

Summers then questioned du Rose's assertion, pointing out that Ireland's car was never spotted by 'the army of police who checked on scores of thousands of cars and vans'. No victim clothing or other items were found at his home and no conclusive scientific evidence exists linking Ireland to the paint/dust particles. The suicide note makes no mention of the killings, and his family had no reason to suspect he had a secret life. It does seem strange that a man committing suicide over a guilty conscience should make no mention of that in his final note. Summers also highlighted the fact that Ireland had been working in Scotland when Bridie O'Hara disappeared. He acknowledges that it was feasible for him to have got an overnight train to London, picked up a prostitute, murdered her, hidden the body, then caught a train straight back to Scotland, but he questions the likelihood of this. And that seems a fair question. If he was in his hometown of Dundee and felt the urge to kill, would he not do so there instead of making a frantic 724-mile round trip by train? His contract as foreman cleaner ended on 8 February anyway, so why hurtle down the length of the country and back when he would be returning to west London in a few weeks? In addition, Dundee police confirmed his attendance at work in January when Bridie O'Hara disappeared. Were they so slipshod they did not do this properly?

Finally, Summers outlined his guilty police officer theory, which was also a strongly favoured line of inquiry by the murder squad. Summers cited the killer's detailed knowledge of the alleyways and deserted places of west London. The killer had somehow gained the confidence of his victims, which during the climate of fear at that time would have been easier for an officer to do. He was also a 'resourceful man who acted quickly and cleverly under personal stress' to avoid detection; and the killer appeared to have been aware of the 'master plan' to check every vehicle in the killing area (he stopped killing just as the mass surveillance of vehicles began in spring 1965).

If Baldock, as seems likely, was attempting to put the record straight himself by talking to Summers, he was also careful not to pass on details of the ex-cop he really did investigate (see chapter 13). But the intention of the source seems clear: to be a forceful rebuke to John du Rose's claim to have known who the killer was within weeks of taking over the investigation.

The claims and counter-claims were a sad and rather undignified final word from the investigation's top men. They had the effect of sowing confusion and doubt about what had been a tremendously ambitious and dedicated campaign to catch the Nude Killer. It was also a disservice to the relatives and loved ones of the victims. In particular, du Rose's dubious assertions to have known who the murderer was showed a lack of respect to the families. They no doubt had hopes, and may still have today, that there might one day be justice for the women who lost their lives. Those hopes have been trampled in the uncertainty over whether the killer committed suicide or not.

If he did not, which seems a very strong possibility, then he got away with his secrets intact and could be walking the streets today.

Chapter 15

Afterwards – Books, Hitchcock and New Theories

In his 1972 exclusive, *The Sun* journalist Owen Summers stated his surprise that public awareness of the Nude Murders had faded so quickly. 'This orgy of killings, only seven years ago, and still open on Scotland Yard's files, has been virtually ignored.'

This falling away of interest was hardly expected around the time the murders were committed. John du Rose predicted that the Nude Murders were 'certain to have as prominent a place in the annals of crime as that of Jack the Ripper and the Boston Strangler'.

While that has not happened, and today the crimes and the victims are largely forgotten, a few authors – non-fiction and fiction – and even the police themselves have on occasion revisited the events of 1964–65.

Early on, there was novelist Arthur La Bern, whose crime tale *Goodbye Piccadilly, Farewell Leicester Square* was published in the immediate aftermath of the murders in 1966. La Bern drew on several notorious British murder cases for his crime story about a serial strangler and rapist, including Neville Heath, John Christie and the Nude Murders. Britain's master of suspense Alfred Hitchcock refashioned the novel for his 1972 movie *Frenzy*, whose opening directly referenced the Nude Murders with the discovery of a woman's body in the Thames.

More closely revisiting the Jack the Stripper events and setting was 2009's novel *Bad Penny Blues* by Cathi Unsworth. This noirish take on the period is more sympathetic to the victims than the media were at the time. It also mixes true events with fiction, along with one of the strangest theories about the identity of the killer. This pointed the finger at boxer Freddie Mills.

Mills was an English fighter who became world light-heavyweight champion in 1948. After retiring from the ring he emerged as a popular celebrity, appearing in films, presenting the BBC's music show *Six-Five Special* and running a nightclub.

How did he get shoehorned into the Nude Murders mystery? *The Observer* reported in 2001 that a book was being written that would name him as the killer. Since the 1970s rumours had got around that Mills was Jack the Stripper, sometimes even spread by police officers, which just goes to show that they are as prone to gossip as everyone else. Brian Collett, the reporter who covered the west London murders, was among those who heard a whisper from an officer. 'I was in hospital in Bristol and in the bed next to me was a youngish PC. He said, "You know who did those murders? Freddie Mills."' Collett relayed the gist of this conversation with the constable. 'Mills was known to be a bit sex-driven and it was said he had done the murders. The police turned up one night to arrest Mills [at the West End nightclub he owned] for the murders. He got out the back door, jumped in his car and blew his head off.'

The facts are more prosaic. Born in 1919 in Bournemouth, Mills learned his trade fighting in fairground booths, having his first professional bout aged 16. Fearless Freddie won British and Commonwealth and European light-heavyweight titles, and beat the American Gus Lesnevich at the second attempt to take the world title at White City in front of a 46,000 crowd. While he was a popular celebrity following his retirement in 1950, being featured on *This Is Your Life* in 1961, these years had their problems for Mills. During his career he had fought a lot of punishing bouts – 64 fights in three-and-a-half years in his early days – and he suffered from frequent headaches. In addition his nightclub business eventually got into trouble. On 24 July 1965, six months after the final Nude Murder, he was found shot to death in his car in a cul-de-sac behind his Charing Cross Road club. The inquest found he had shot himself in the right eye with a rifle. A number of malicious rumours started – that gangsters had actually killed him in a feud over his club, that despite being married he had been arrested in a public toilet for indecency, and that he was the Nude Killer.

The Observer story said that 'reformed south London gangster' Jimmy Tippett had interviewed three generations of criminals and boxers for a book he was writing and that he claimed to have uncovered the truth about Mills. Tippett was reported as saying 'he had been told' that the former champion feared the police were closing in on him for the Nude Murders and took his own life to avoid arrest. However, that book has never appeared.

Nevertheless, the rumour was pursued by other authors, notably David Seabrook in his book on the Nude Murders, *Jack of Jumps*. He devotes a long, turgid chapter to Mills, which is full of lurid speculation. Did Mills marry his wife, Chrissie, because he needed cover for his homosexuality? Was Mills murdered because he would not pay a protection gang? Were the Krays behind it? Did a bent officer cover it up?

As for evidence of involvement in the Nude Murders, even circumstantial, there is not a jot. The assertion is so devoid of facts, it cannot even qualify as a conspiracy theory.

A more intriguing theory involves a convicted killer called Harold Jones. As a conniving and brutal 15-year-old, Jones had murdered two girls in Abertillery, south Wales, in 1921. As he was too young to hang, Jones was jailed for 20 years, emerging from prison in 1941. It was the discovery of author Neil Milkins, outlined in his 2011 book *Who Was Jack the Stripper?* that Jones ended up living in west London in the 1960s. Milkins' research revealed that Jones' addresses showed he had lived near to Mungo Ireland and later to Bridie O'Hara and Frances Brown. Had the boy psychopath grown into an adult psychopath?

Forty-four years previously, the teenage Jones had served eight-year-old Freda Burnell in the seed store where he worked in the quiet town of Abertillery, Monmouthshire. It was the morning of 5 February 1921 and the girl was on an errand to buy a bag of poultry grit. She never returned home to Earl Street. Her father, Fred, searched for her and, unable to locate her, reported her missing to the police at lunchtime. It was a measure of Jones' sick callousness that he twice called on her family pretending to be concerned for Freda. He had in fact murdered her and attempted to rape her. After a search involving an army of miners and locals, Freda was eventually found the next morning in a lane just 100 yards from her home. Her hands and feet were bound. It was estimated that 100,000 spectators lined the streets for Freda's funeral on 10 February.

Two Scotland Yard aces, Detective Chief Superintendent Albert Helden and Detective Sergeant Alfred Soden, were dispatched. Freda's handkerchief was found on the floor of the warehouse belonging to Jones' employer, off Princess Street. This turned out to be the murder scene. Police became convinced she had been murdered there after leaving the seed store, around 375 yards away. They suspected Jones, but he was alibied by his employers, Herbert and Rhoda Mortimer, who said he could not have left the store, gone to murder Freda in the warehouse and come back without their noticing. Three of Jones' friends also said they had spent part of the remaining day and evening with him. After 12 days on the case without a breakthrough, the detective duo returned to Scotland Yard. The inquest recorded that Freda had been strangled and had injuries to her genitals.

Evidence given at the inquest, however, implicated Jones and he was detained at the police station. The detectives returned to Abertillery and arrested him on 7 March. The magistrates' court sent him for trial at Monmouth assizes, with Harold Jones shouting in court, 'I am not guilty.' His trial began on 20 June. The case against him, that he had directed Freda to the warehouse where he would give her the grit she requested and there killed her, was circumstantial. The prosecution suspected that the store-owning Mortimers could not believe in Jones's guilt and had thereby given him an alibi. Other witnesses either further backed up his alibi or gave him character references. The jury unanimously found him not guilty. He was cheered by crowds in the streets and welcomed back to Abertillery by a brass band.

How sadly ironic that an 11-year-old girl should be the one to point the finger at Jones. Florence Little, a school chum of

Freda's, said to him in front of friends, 'I know you killed Freda.'

Two weeks after Jones's acquittal, Florence Little disappeared. When word got round that Jones had been arrested again, the Abertillery crowd turned ugly. Popular suspicion was that the police were victimising the local lad to vent their frustration at failing to secure his conviction for killing Freda. The police station was besieged and officers threatened. So, imagine the shock when Superintendent Henry Lewis came out and addressed the crowd. 'I have found the body of the child in the attic of Harold Jones' house foully murdered...'

Florence lived at 4 Darran Road, a few doors from Jones' family at No 10. She vanished on the evening of 8 July 1921, the day before the angry scene at the police station. As another huge all-night search got under way, Jones joined in, going through the motions of being a concerned resident until 3.30am. When he left his house the following morning, the police searched it and in the rafters found the body of Florence. Her throat had been cut. Jones denied all knowledge.

He stood trial again at Monmouth assizes on 1 November. This time he pleaded guilty, not through remorse but because his lawyer warned that if he went for a not guilty plea and the case was in court beyond 11 January 1922, his 16th birthday, he would be eligible to hang if found guilty. He made a written confession to the murders of both Freda and Florence. This told how he had cut Florence's throat in the kitchen of his home, letting her bleed over the sink, before he shoved her into the garret and cleaned up. He had used his own sister, Flossie, to invite Florence in with the promise of a lemonade.

Jones ended up in Maidstone prison, where the senior medical officer and governor were impressed by his callousness and disregard for his victims. Milkins quotes the governor. 'Sad as it may seem I can see no hopeful prospect for

Jones in the future…' All the more astonishing then – and disheartening – that when Jones was sent to Camp Hill Prison on the Isle of Wight in 1940, the Commissioner of Prisons, Alexander Henry Paterson, thought Jones richly deserved a second chance by being enlisted in the Royal Engineers, noting, 'One day he should be the father of happy children.' Jones was released in December 1941. He stayed clear of the armed forces.

Milkins gives several reasons for suspecting that Harold Jones went on to become the Nude Killer (perhaps in allegiance with Mungo Ireland). He lived in west London, moving from Hestercombe Avenue, Fulham (1947–62), to Colinette Road, Putney (1962–65), and finally Aldensley Road in Hammersmith (until his death in 1971). These addresses gave Jones proximity to several figures in the Nude Murders case. Colinette Road is a short walk from where Mungo Ireland lived in Tildesley Road. Meanwhile, his last address of Aldensley Road is a couple of streets from the homes of Bridie O'Hara (Agate Road) and Frances Brown (Southerton Road). Milkins also says Jones told prison authorities he had no wish to be free of his inclination to murder. He was in the Hammersmith area using various names – Harry Stevens, Harry Jones – during the period of the Nude Murders. Milkins sees parallels between the taking of the prostitutes' false teeth and clothing with Jones having in his possession a collection of seven ladies' handkerchiefs. These, the prosecutor in the Florence Little case said, were probably a part of his 'perverted lust'. The prostitutes' diminutive stature could have made them childlike to Jones. Milkins also cites theories suggesting that Jones could be responsible for other atrocities before the Nude Murders, in particular the murder of 12-year-old Swansea girl Muriel Drinkwater in

1946. In a case that became known as the Little Red Riding Hood Murder, the schoolgirl was raped in Penllergaer Woods, near Swansea, and shot with a First World War-era Colt 45.

That Jones may have been the Nude Killer is certainly a thought-provoking possibility. Milkins' book is painstakingly researched and won the respect of leading British criminologist Professor David Wilson of Birmingham University, who said it shone new light on the Nude Murders. But while the Jones theory may do that, it does not solve the case. Jones had a revolting past as a vain and callous child killer, and he lived in west London during the prostitute-killing spree. But other people were also murdered in this neighbourhood during these years. Jones's proximity to all these crimes is not proof of his guilt.

However, what is clear is that it may have been a badly missed opportunity that Harold Jones did not come under closer police scrutiny in 1964–65. And here one chilling 'what if' rears its head. Jones moved to 51 Aldensley Road in Hammersmith in the autumn of 1965 or 1966, some months after the final Nude Killing and at a time when the house-to-house inquiries had already been terminated. However, as will be outlined, leading geographic profiler Kim Rossmo's analysis reveals two hot spot areas in west London where the killer may have lived, worked or with which he had some association. Aldensley Road is in the middle of one of these hotspots. It was here that Jones died in January 1971 from cancer. Did Jones, whose movements and identities were always sketchy, have a connection with the Aldensley Road/ Hammersmith area – a job, accommodation – before he moved there?

The nagging 'what if' is this: if in the mid-1960s detectives had been able to employ the tools of geographic profiling – a

method analysing the locations of connected crimes to determine a perpetrator's probable whereabouts – and focused on
this hot spot, would Harold Jones have come to their attention? And if he had, what might they have discovered about
his activities?

The Survivor is a 2001 memoir by former underworld figure
Jimmy Evans, which carried the provocative question on its
jacket 'Was Scotland Yard's top detective a serial killer?'

It's a lurid tale of violence and gang feuds in which Evans,
born in London in 1931, claims bent Scotland Yard detectives
falsely accused him of being Jack the Stripper. In turn Evans
accuses one of the most famous detectives of the time, Tommy
Butler, of being the killer.

The book claims to have 'shocking evidence' to back this
up. In reality it offers broad speculation. Detective Chief
Superintendent Tommy Butler was the head of the Flying
Squad and the man who played a big part in catching the
Great Train Robbers. But, according to Evans, he was also in
a prime position to know when the police surveillance was
getting close to catching the Nude Murderer. Butler was born
in Shepherd's Bush and knew west London well, living in
Hammersmith with his mother. Evans claims Butler, who
died in 1970, was a loner and secretive. But as he also says in
the book, 'Hold on, you may be thinking: this stuff is so circumstantial that it's just a wild theory tied in with a few coincidences, all put together by a villain bent on revenge. But the
coincidences keep piling up.'

Not enough to come close to being convincing.

It was the efforts of another writer, David Seabrook, that
prompted the police to revisit the case in 2006. While writing

Jack of Jumps he made contact with the police, and it eventually fell to Scotland Yard's Specialist Crime Review team to look over the case once more. I spoke to one of the veteran detectives on the review, former Detective Chief Superintendent Albert Patrick. He confirmed that it was after David Seabrook contacted the police that the review was launched. 'Somebody wrote to us, the guy who had a bee in his bonnet about it being an ex-copper. So that had to be looked at again.' Mr Patrick explained that Operation Yetna was also a factor, in which Scotland Yard was reviewing hundreds of unsolved cases, some from the 1960s.

The review was concluded nine months later. That was a decent amount of time in which to scrutinise the murder files, which will be kept away from public scrutiny for 84 years, until around 2050. This is because the murders are unsolved and the investigation could be reopened if there was new evidence, however unlikely that is now. About half-a-dozen files – on Hannah Tailford, Irene Lockwood, Helen Barthelemy, Frances Brown and on the work of the WPCs – are being kept secret for up to 100 years. What is so sensitive about these particular files is not stated at the National Archives in Kew, London.

For the 2006 review, a team of former detectives were tasked with re-examining the case and giving it a modern reassessment, but the outcome contained no surprises. It is hard not to feel the review may also have been a missed – and final – chance to find a new line of inquiry. The team apparently did not interview any of the suspects still living and it could not find any physical evidence from the original case, including slides with oral and vaginal swab samples taken from the victims. It concluded that the man who committed suicide, Mungo Ireland, was the most likely suspect.

Apart from the fact that this flatly contradicted the 1965 report by Detective Superintendent Bill Baldock, which strongly favoured the Disgraced Cop as chief suspect, the review appears a little half-hearted. Why were none of the suspects who were still alive in 2006–07 not spoken to? Maybe officers at the time did an excellent job in quizzing them, but surely if the case was being reviewed 40 years on there was scope for a fresh approach to interviewing them again?

As for all of the evidence being lost, with so many police buildings being sold off to the nearest property developers and evidence in storage being moved around as the decades passed, this may not be a huge mystery. Sadly, even though it may have been a very distant prospect, the loss of the physical evidence means there is no chance now of any DNA being available to verify or discount suspects, alive or exhumed. And if the evidence were found today, the possibility of presenting DNA in a murder trial that would not be challenged by defence lawyers as having been corrupted in the intervening years is just as improbable.

Albert Patrick told me, 'My conclusion was that they actually got the right guy, the guy who committed suicide… They had a massive team on it, people undercover, WPCs, the lot. It was a huge effort. Nowadays you'd never get 100 staff on a murder, it would be impossible. The guy who committed suicide, I was relatively happy it was him. Whoever did it is dead now anyway. I forget his name now.'

The night watchman, Mungo Ireland.

'That's him.'

So, what about the disgraced detective?

In fairness, Mr Patrick was trying hard to remember details of the case he had looked at 10 years before. 'For me, weird as he was, he didn't fit. Yeah, you've got to keep an open mind, but there was nothing [to make] him the perpetrator.'

What about evidence that Mungo Ireland was in Dundee when one victim vanished?

'You say that, yeah, it's interesting. But that wasn't concrete, he could still have had time to get back down to London. Look at [serial killer Robert] Black, he lived in Stoke Newington and he went all the way up to the borders of Scotland, catching little kids in his van. You're right, he [Ireland] was up in Scotland, but there was still an opportunity to be back in London.'

So, despite the fact that he found Bill Baldock's final report summarising the investigation to be 'brilliant', Mr Patrick did not go along with Baldock's proposal that the Disgraced Cop was the most likely suspect.

'Listen, for me it was a very thorough investigation, they just didn't have the luck. Bear in mind they didn't have DNA, they had fingerprints. But that type of venture is solved by clothing, fibres, eye witnesses.'

Certainly, if there was any luck going round, the Nude Killer had it all. But were there weaknesses in the Nude Murders investigation? By looking at the case through modern eyes it is possible to see how contemporary police practice has been built on past failures, and to get some idea of how the killer cheated the massive hunt to find him.

PART 3

THEN AND NOW

Chapter 16

'This Is a Weird Spot. It Reeks of Desperation'

Driving through west London with two retired detectives in May 2016, it was almost bewildering to see how the area still closely resembled the 1960s city terrorised by the Nude Killer, while at the same time having changed so dramatically.

We were visiting the body-deposition sites, as would be done in a cold-case review. This was at the suggestion of Brian Hook, who spent the majority of his police career serving on specialist investigation units and was a crime-scene examiner way before CSI became sexy. It was a sobering tour to get into the mindset of the murderer and consider the original investigation from a modern perspective. It was also a chance to consider why the huge investigation had ultimately failed.

Brian and his colleague Andy Rose, a former Met detective inspector, both now lecture in forensics, investigative skills and criminology at the University of West London. Andy has 30 years' experience and is a former senior investigating officer. Brian's career as a detective included time with the Anti-Terrorist Branch and as a crime scene manager and investigator. In addition to his academic work, these days he also advises television production companies on how to make their police dramas more authentic. Away from their new jobs, Brian likes to go hunting and Andy is a keen pilot. They share an ironic sense of humour that police officers seem to specialise in and between them have a wealth of experience in dealing with serious crimes.

'There's no doubt society had a different view in the sixties,' said Andy. 'From my experience of investigating sexual offences against prostitutes even into the 1980s it was seen as a case of, "Why would you [bother to] do that?" The women are putting themselves out there. Whereas obviously they are just as much victims as anyone else, probably suffering more than many.'

With Brian driving, we went through Chiswick to Dukes Meadows, where Elizabeth Figg was found under a willow tree in June 1959. This is one spot that has not changed much, a stretch of quiet, lush parkland overlooking the River Thames and Barnes Bridge. The tree is still there right outside Chiswick Boathouse. A wonderful spot to go for a jog, take the dog for a walk or leave a body at night. I asked Andy whether the killer might have had run-ins with the police prior to his killing career. He said, 'Often they [perpetrators] are abusive in their relationships. But that [being noticed by the authorities] comes down to whether the woman reports it. Certainly, 50 years ago the police response would have been poor.' Statistics for domestic violence against wives in the 1960s are thin because it was largely seen as a private matter. Even today, however, the charity Refuge says that only 35 per cent of domestic-violence incidents are reported to the police. So, if the Nude Killer was a violent or abusive husband, it was probably a trait he easily kept hidden.

Though Gwynneth Rees is generally excluded from the series of victims – the cause of her death had been difficult to determine – we looked at the Barnes Borough Household Refuse Disposal Plant on Townmead Road. What was once an open-air dump, where her decomposing corpse was uncovered by a digger, is now a modern recycling centre, though bizarrely a private housing estate has been built next to it. In 1963 this spot, near to North Sheen Cemetery, was very quiet and out of the way. 'You'd have had all the time in world here,' Brian said.

It is easy to understand why the Figg and Rees discoveries were sometimes linked to those of the next two in the sequence, Hannah Tailford and Irene Lockwood, because it is such a short drive along the river to where they were found. The Corinthians Sailing Club on Upper Mall, Hammersmith, where Hannah was found under the landing stage, is still there amid a terrace of old houses overlooking the river. The area further west where Irene was found on the foreshore by Corney Reach looks very different. The wharves, cranes, transport depot, engineering works and industrial premises have gone. By the 1990s they had been replaced by a dull, but no doubt expensive, private housing development.

Brian's first impression was of how close the crime scenes were. 'All the deposition sites are within two or three minutes' driving.'

'In the days with little traffic, fewer traffic lights,' Andy pointed out.

'It's quite a schlep from Holland Park, but it would have been a quick drive in the sixties.'

And a pretty stress-free one for the killer, who had few fears of being pulled over. The tour of the deposition sites brings one fact home with force – just how anonymous the killer was driving around west London with a corpse in his car back then. Not much traffic (1965's 12 million licensed vehicles compares to 2011's 34 million), few police patrol cars, and little incentive for the police to stop cars when they had no on-the-spot means of verifying vehicle ownership. 'You think about him marauding around and getting stopped by the police, but it was unlikely,' Brian said. 'There was no national computer to check for stolen vehicles, so why would a police officer begin stopping people? There were not many police cars. You would have one area car for the whole district. Today you would have area-response cars, but these were the days before Panda cars [introduced in the mid-60s, first in Lancashire]. Back then, people walked, simple as that.'

However, the dangerous moment for the killer was getting the body out of the vehicle, as the next two deposition sites made clear. The alley off residential Swyncombe Avenue was the first occasion on which the murderer almost gave himself away. It was around 6am when he reversed a short distance into the 200-yard track linking Swyncombe and The Ride on 24 April 1964. It would have been daylight as he lifted the naked body of Helen Barthelemy and dropped her by a fence. Then he tore off, swinging into Boston Manor Road without slowing and almost colliding with motorist Alfred Harrow, who had to brake violently to avoid a vehicle he described as a Hillman Husky or Hillman Estate.

'He took a huge risk here,' Brian said. Then he recalled the press photographs of detectives standing all over the crime scene. 'The forensic capabilities now are far, far more advanced. To have a body found in these circumstances and then three hours later to have a post-mortem, you're like, Oh, hang on.' By which he meant the forensic examination at the scene would have lasted many more hours. 'And the cop standing there on potential tyre tracks peering over the screen [that had been erected to protect the crime scene]. It's not a question of blame, it's just a lack of knowledge and training. So those actions would be different today.'

The killer described in the police report as 'cool and calculating' was certainly not so in July that year. The two detectives were, like their 1960s forebears, struck by how close the Berrymede Road disposal of Mary Fleming was to where the decorators spotted the van driver acting strangely behind the ABC restaurant on Chiswick High Road. 'This is a weird spot,' Brian said. 'It reeks of desperation.'

He speculated that perhaps the killer risked the daylight disposal because he feared the body would be found where he had been hiding it. "There could have been a catalyst for that – some activity up at the industrial estate [where the victims were being stored], which means it's got to go. He's got up there in the early hours of the morning. Where can I dump it? Or it may be that he's got spooked. It's suddenly got light, busy on the roads – Sod this, I can't drive round with this in the back of the car because I've got to go to work. It could be the simple thing of he's passed two police cars.'

Both former detectives concurred that the killer was very likely to have been a local person. The area where the prostitutes were picked up were the obvious kerb-crawling streets, such as Bayswater and Queensway. But the deposition sites – down by the river, an alley, the side of a storage shed – these reveal his local knowledge. Brian said, 'It's down to someone frequenting them to use for sex or he might have actually worked or lived there. Or it's a route he travels.'

The car park on Hornton Street in Kensington is gone, with a new Kensington and Chelsea Town Hall replacing it alongside the central library in 1976. While it is clear the killer switched tactics by hiding the body of Frances Brown under debris in the old dilapidated car park in November

1964, the area is certainly not without risk. It is close to the shopping thoroughfare of Kensington High Street and surrounded by grand residences. 'The amount of potential eyes here, compared to the remote spots chosen before, is astonishing,' was Brian's comment.

Twenty-first-century Notting Hill, an area of spectacular wealth just north of Kensington, is a stunning contrast to the boarded-up houses, piles of trash and peeling plaster work that was the norm in so many streets there half a century ago. Mary Fleming once slummed it in a multi-occupancy flat with several families sharing facilities on Lancaster Road – that same property costs around £3.5million today. The kerb-crawlers and street workers have largely vanished from Queensway and Bayswater, the trade having migrated to the internet.

The Heron Trading Estate, scene of the last deposition, has also changed considerably. It was constantly being redeveloped even back in the 1960s. The spot where Bridie O'Hara was left between the warehouse and the railway siding has gone, as new industrial units have replaced many former businesses.

This was the final Nude Killing. Because the murderer had effectively drawn attention to his body-storage site by leaving Bridie outside the building where he had been keeping his victims, it was tempting to view this as a sign-off by him. So was that a final flourish to taunt the police? I'm done and this is where I've been keeping them…

Brian did not think so. 'It's circumstances again. I don't think it was a decision consciously made not to do it anymore. There's been an event [that diminished his need to kill]. The body was in an area where nobody goes – behind the shed by the railway line, partly covered up. It could have been there for months and months if somebody hadn't made effectively a chance finding. Maybe he had decided to go and play again, so he needed the room in the storage space. Or maybe he becomes aware that there was going to be some activity around that premises, renovation, demolition. So, let's get rid of that body, I don't want it to be found.'

'People don't always make rational decisions,' Andy pointed out. 'You're giving credence to somebody who may not have had that process.'

'He may have thought,' Brian said, 'I've been driving around with a body in the car, I'm going to get caught. The less I do of that the better. So he thinks, I can just walk round the corner and dump it here. You think about what he's been going through, and the fright he had in Chiswick [spotted by the decorators] – "Jesus, I nearly got fucking discovered there."

'I think there was an escalation and a closing down, almost a self-imposed pressure. He's been fairly free and easy. Now there's been an avalanche of media, and he's driving around in it. Baddies have this paranoia that they're being watched. It does alter the way they behave and react. I've had people say to me, "I knew you were behind me," and I'll say we weren't. They say, "You're only saying that." No, trust me, we weren't. This person was living with that. The killing is one, two per cent of their life; the other 98 per cent they're sitting there thinking about it. They're waiting for the knock on the door. Driving around with a body in the back of your car – that ain't good.'

So, why did he stop?

Andy outlined some possibilities, including that not all murderers are compelled to kill all the time. 'He might have been arrested, might have died. Everyone's an individual.' He cites the example of Ipswich serial killer Steve Wright, who had been violent to one wife and had a string of female partners, all the while showing an obsession with using prostitutes, but who only turned to killing them at the age of 48.

'He hadn't killed anyone but had demonstrated all the traits up to that point,' Andy said. 'If someone is driven to do this because something is missing in their lives and they find what's missing, then they don't need to do it until that thing gets missed again, and maybe it never will. Some people will kill because they enjoy a certain thing and they can't get it anywhere else, some don't need it on the first occasion and then they find they get quite a thrill out of it. Some people enjoy killing but they wouldn't do it to someone they were close to, so they take someone they have a dismissive view of or someone they see as not even in society.'

Andy concluded. 'If you're dealing with someone who is in or around the criminal arena, he might get arrested, might get kidnapped, they die. Or does it stop in London because he moved away? He could have been charged with a murder that no one linked to these murders...'

It is ironic that the University of West London, where Brian Hook and Andy Rose have just launched degree-to-PhD level courses for police officers, is a few streets from one of the deposition sites, Swyncombe Avenue. It was at the university that they outlined how a modern murder investigation would be structured, using Swyncombe Avenue as a hypothetical example. Comparing then and now, they were able to highlight potential flaws in the original inquiry.

Leaving aside technological advances that were simply not available to John du Rose's murder squad – DNA, modern forensics, CCTV, tracking of mobile phones and the like – there were problems with the way the 1960s team was set up in the face of what was a particularly complex and data-heavy investigation. Looking at how today's murder inquiries work – which have been built on and corrected past investigative failures – it becomes clear where du Rose's squad got bogged down. Two major inefficiencies become obvious. First, the Nude Killer investigation was too unfocused, and, second, the squad's dictatorial hierarchy – standard for the time – could not cope with the huge amount of statements and data generated by six major murder probes during 1964–65.

Crime fiction fans will have heard about the importance of taking control of an investigation in that first 'golden hour', when clues and memories are freshest. In the 1960s a lot of early decisions were taken by constables who were first on the spot and awaiting the arrival of their inspector. 'In those days there wasn't a permanent murder team,' Brian said. 'That was the thing. Whoever got called down to the crime scene was whoever was on duty. Never mind if the on-call detective inspector was good at murder investigations or not.'

Andy adds, 'A murder would happen and two or three detectives would just get taken out of the office – right, you're on this murder now. The likelihood was you chose people who didn't have a lot on. You were reliant on them being paired up with somebody who knew what they were doing.'

Today's priority is to get a specialist expert team there as fast as possible. A car carrying the Homicide Assessment Team would aim to be at the crime scene within 10 to 30 minutes. Their job is not to go onto the scene but, if required, to call in a specialist homicide unit, alert a senior investigating officer and get efforts such as house-to-house inquiries under way.

Forensics are obviously more advanced today. The scene assessment of the body in situ would probably last for many hours more than it did in the mid-sixties, more samples – soil, vegetation, tyre tracks – would be taken, and the victim may even be examined on the spot, with temperatures taken for potential time of death.

The point is to gather as much information in the golden hour or first few hours. The second phase of the investigation is to gather the team together. 'You've got your SIO [senior investigating officer] and you're going to have your office meeting,' Andy said. 'These are very open and while they are led and directed, everyone's view is listened to equally. It's not hierarchical.' This open approach was not the norm in the 1960s. It recalls the comment of former detective superintendent Chris Burke: 'Other members of the enquiry were "mushrooms", kept in the dark and only told what the detective superintendent or inspector wanted them to know.'

Brian expands on this. 'There was nepotism. You had a system of bag carriers. You would have a detective superintendent and a detective sergeant, and the sergeant would be the superintendent's bag carrier, basically a PA. It was very much a closed team at the top.'

It is a point that had been made to me by several former detectives. The attitude was that the top detective was the clever, experienced one. This may have worked on smaller, less complicated investigations, but when faced with the tidal wave of tips, statements, car sightings, house-to-house inquiries, dust samples and the rest, there is no knowing what connections or possibilities were missed.

Consider the 'immensity of the operation', as Bill Baldock referred to it, of interviewing more than 7,000 current and past employees on the Heron Trading Estate, where the bodies were stored. As Brian explained, 'The SIO has to read every single statement that is relevant. Now, even if 10 per cent of those 7,000 statements are relevant, that's 700 statements. There is no way John du Rose could ever have read those and assimilated where they fit in at all.' And there were tens of thousands of further statements on top of that for du Rose, Baldock and the 'closed team' under them, including inspectors Ken Oxford and Ted Crabb, to get through.

Andy pointed out, 'When you look back, historically you've got named detectives: Jack Slipper, who was known as Slipper of the Yard, and Nipper Read. You couldn't do that today. Unless you are working in this environment [a modern murder squad], you wouldn't even be able to name all the senior investigators on one murder team. The picture that was painted then was that they were the brilliant detectives, and of course they believed their own publicity.'

Brian adds, 'TV programmes still go back to that – Oh, it's this person that solves it. That's because what happens now in reality wouldn't make good TV.'

'Doesn't make good TV,' Andy added, 'because you'd have to have too big a cast.'

'If you read between the lines about the SIO in this case [John du Rose],' Brian said, 'that was very much what was happening there, this kind of self-belief.'

'I think that is the biggest difference,' Andy said. 'Nowadays, you can't have a dictatorial SIO. The system doesn't allow it, the review processes don't allow it. Within 21 days of a crime, somebody's already started to review those first 21 days – what have you done, how did you do that?'

The culture now is of having outside detectives quickly moving in to review the decision-making on an investigation. Senior investigators are scrutinised more closely and have to fill out decision logs detailing what they did and did not do, why and at what times.

'Which would never have happened in the 1960s,' Andy said with a laugh. 'They wouldn't have countenanced anybody else coming in to somebody at that [du Rose's] level and saying, "I want to have a look at the way you're running this investigation…" Initiative was not encouraged. A senior officer's justification used to be we're doing it this way because I say so. That was rarely questioned. That's not the case anymore.'

However skilled were John du Rose and his inner sanctum, it is clear they were swamped by the investigation. Du Rose knew the investigation was a drain on the whole of the Met, while Bill Baldock lamented that so many lines of inquiry had to be prematurely cut short in 1965 – the night-time vehicle observations, the Husky squad, the house-to-house inquiries, the search through the records of armed services personnel and more.

Was the killer's identity lurking in one of those unfinished searches?

Baldock voiced his frustrations in 1965. He mentioned how 'thinly' spread were his teams across 24-square miles of west London and in particular that they had simply not had the time to trace everyone they wanted to interview about the Disgraced Cop at the Earl's Court Motor Show.

'You can see what they were doing but it was so unproductive,' Brian said. 'Trying to find out the registered keepers of all those cars – all that actually did was take a huge amount of time and resources. It was so unproductive, it wasn't focused. It was a case of, "Let's cast the net out and see what we drag in", which is just nonsensical and counterproductive.'

The huge efforts that went into investigating the four men associated with the Hammersmith garage and the frustrating campaign of having three squads of officers sweeping west London to find the premises where the paint/dust particles originated both came to nothing. Brian had these in mind when he said, 'Some huge tangents were gone down, and you can actually see the inquiry going off track. They've got their theories and hypotheses and they're following them slavishly.'

We also know about the daunting hours and overtime that went into these efforts. But again, often all that was achieved by the long hours put in by senior and junior officers was to generate a mass of useless information. Think of the effort devoted to the night observation of vehicles, for example, sitting in vans for 12 hours at a time, peeing into a bottle, taking down numbers. 'Hard to maintain focus and motivation,' Brian said. 'But it was all they had. It was such a long shot. The problem they had was that it creates such a huge amount of work.

'You had fixed observation points all round Kensington, Chiswick and Shepherd's Bush. If they're told they are looking for a Humber van, they would take the number of every single Humber van. What that means is that in the morning, when they give their lists in, they had to cross-check the lists for vans that appear more than once, and then phone up the councils or take the lists to the councils, who had to physically search for them. Out of, say, 50, 10 won't be registered to anyone now... And that's every single night.

'What you're doing is creating a huge wall of administrative shite, basically. All in the hope that when you knock on their door, someone's going to say, "Oh, you're too good for me, copper, you've caught me."'

The two former investigators were in no doubt that this kind of hugely labour-intensive, potentially dead-end investigation could have been scaled down and managed far more effectively today. Investigation is all about elimination, and they point out that a modern inquiry would be able to eliminate far more vehicles and suspects to allow the murder team to focus on fewer targets.

Even without all of the 21st-century technology, however, Brian and Andy are adamant that today's more collaborative approach to investigation, with its decision-logging and constant assessment, would have greatly enhanced the investigation back then.

'You had officers from different divisions who may not have worked together, with different levels of knowledge and experience,' Brian said. 'And because there was no Murder Investigation Manual [a thick book outlining procedures and methods], there was no structure to it. Now there are far more studies into how murders are solved and what helps to solve them. The SIOs who solve the most crimes are the innovative ones, who'll say, "This has never been done before but I'll try this."'

'It was very blinkered and prescriptive,' Andy added.

The corollary is clear: such open-mindedness was far less common in the 1960s.

Perhaps the greatest failure of the old autocratic management style came in the area of information sharing. The drivers of 1,700 vehicles were questioned and dust samples taken, 783 Hillman Husky owners traced, 120,000 residents and business owners seen during the house-to-house operation, and thousands of statements taken. All of these separate bits of information were gathered by individual officers. It would have been impossible for John du Rose and his select senior group to collate and make sense of all that.

Today murder teams have two advantages. One is

technological. There are suites of inputters who feed HOLMES 2, the database used by the police since 1994, with statements, forensics, descriptions of witnesses, vehicles, phone numbers, addresses, even details of tattoos. The miracle of the system is that the police can use it to cross-reference data to reveal unsuspected connections – who has phoned whom, witnesses who frequent the same pub – all of which can expose suspicious discrepancies in witness statements. The other advantage is in the more open organisation of modern investigations, as cited above, with team meetings to share information where suggestions would be listened to and initiatives encouraged. Had that been standard practice in 1965, who knows what unforeseen evidential links might have turned up? What vital connections were staring them in the face but never made?

With the data the police today have access to, it is also possible to sift car owners by make, year, colour, locality of vehicle – an undreamed-of advantage in Bill Baldock's day.

Modern investigative processes are there because of mistakes of the past. The Nude Murder team threw everything they had at finding the killer; they were not the first or last to have difficulties in understanding and trapping a serial killer. Mistakes had been made in the much quoted case of John Christie. The Rillington Place monster killed his first victim, Ruth Fuerst, in 1943, but was not exposed, tried and executed until 1953. In the meantime he murdered his wife Ethel, and at least four others. He also testified against his neighbour, Timothy Evans, helping to secure Evans's conviction for the murder of his own wife and daughter, Beryl and Geraldine, when it was very likely Christie who had killed them, too. When searching Christie's garden for the bodies of Beryl and Geraldine, the police failed to notice the femur of another of his victims propping up a trellis. Had they done so, Christie would surely have been exposed as a mass killer sooner.

In the 1970s, the police would struggle to stop Peter Sutcliffe, the Yorkshire Ripper, during an investigation that was badly bungled. Detectives here ran into similar problems to those that Scotland Yard had in 1964–65 – a stifling command structure and serious information overload that swamped the police and obscured possible leads. Even today, with all the latest technology and knowhow, things still go wrong in serial killer cases. In 2014–15, the investigation of the so-called Grindr Killer, Stephen Port, in east London, made serious oversights. These included the failure to initially realise the deaths of his four victims, all dumped within a few hundred yards of each other, were linked and not accidental.

When I asked Andy and Brian who they thought had committed the Nudes Murder, the police's trademark bleak sense of humour emerged. 'It was either a friend, a relative or someone they didn't know,' Andy said.

That is the challenge in catching serial killers, a term not even coined when the Nude Killer was operating. Where perhaps 80 per cent of murders are committed by someone who knows or is related to their victim – wives, husbands, lovers, friends – serial killers are that minority who most often target strangers.

A look at contemporary methods of profiling reveals how a better understanding of the Nude Killer's mind and habits could have made a vital contribution to the original investigation.

Chapter 17

Hunting the Hunters

The Nude Murders were a shocking and callous severing of innocent lives. The killer was viewed as depraved, a pervert or sex-crazed beast. Today it is more common to talk about such a murderer as a psychopath, a term that is scarce in news and police reports of the 1960s. In the vast majority of murder cases the perpetrator's motive is clear – lust, a grudge, jealousy, betrayal. Such crimes often happen in the heat of the moment. But serial killing is different, being perhaps the rarest form of homicide. Serial killers are calculating; they target strangers, which makes it harder to track them down. They hunt their fellow humans as part of some grotesque inner obsession. If the Nude Killer's rationale could have been better understood at the time, it might have given detectives a clue about what kind of man he was and where to look for him.

To gain such insights has been the quest of criminologists and psychologists in increasing numbers since the 1970s and 1980s, a time when serial killers became more prevalent. There have always been individuals who murdered strangers, but several features of modern society have created an environment of anonymity in which serial killers have increased opportunities to prey on strangers. Mass urbanisation is one historical upheaval that contributed to this. Where a medieval village dweller would rarely meet people they did not know well, today we can encounter hundreds of strangers on the way to work. Dense modern cities are ideal for those routine impersonal encounters that are a trademark of serial killing.

In this context it is hard not to think of a victim such as Hannah Tailford, in the middle of a twilight network of strangers with phoney names, tearful, wandering round Victoria, getting by on the generosity of Arnold Downton and his wife, Elizabeth, people she barely knew. She and the other victims were members of a marginalised group, prostitutes, who along with the elderly, homosexuals, young adults and the homeless are among those frequently targeted by serial killers. British criminologist Professor David Wilson has written of four phases of serial murder in the UK: 1888–1914, 1915–45, 1946–78 and 1979–present. He notes there were three serial killers and 11 victims in the first period, while the last produced 16 serial killers and 269 victims. He also makes the point that less caring, less equal societies – as arguably Britain has become since 1979 – mean that marginalised groups will be more vulnerable to serial killers. This is the background to what became a collective mission of scientists and investigative professionals to understand these killers and aid the police in catching them. In comparison, 1960s detectives had far less knowledge of the motivations and behaviours of offenders who set out to repeatedly murder strangers.

It is hard to imagine today, when fictional serial killers such as Hannibal Lecter and Dexter Morgan are part of popular culture, that back in the 1960s the term 'serial killer' did not exist. Infamous killers such as Scotland's Peter Manuel and John Christie were simply viewed as monsters and little understood. They tended to be caught because of their mistakes: Manuel spent traceable banknotes he had stolen from victims, while Christie left his victims barely concealed in Rillington Place for new tenants to find.

Like many serial murderers, the Nude Killer presented a huge challenge to the police. He was not disorganised and did not kill in a jealous rage or fit of anger, recklessly leaving behind evidence and a motive. He planned his crimes, no doubt stalked his victims, waiting for the type he preferred – petite, vulnerable women selling sex. He did everything he could to stay ahead of the police. He was never seen kerb-crawling and he apparently took all his victims' belongings, even their dental plates, thereby leaving as few traces of himself behind as possible.

As we have seen, Scotland Yard did not know where to look, so they looked everywhere. Theories included a sugar daddy, a vice ring, a pimp, gangsters, a pervert with a grudge against prostitutes, a 'monster like Christie', a man linked with a group of prostitutes who killed them when they were no more use to him, members of a ring of orgy enthusiasts. Under suspicion were punters from the car mechanic to heavy drinkers at the Shepherd's Bush Hotel, figures involved in the Stephen Ward case, the Disgraced Cop, a dental surgeon, security man, accountant, architectural assistant, decorator, spouses, an engineer, stoker, ex-cons, a mortuary assistant, company director, bar porter, labourer, pipe fitter and on and on.

Professor David Canter, the UK's leading criminal psychological profiler, has written that British police learned a lot from the blunders and bad decisions made during the Yorkshire Ripper investigation of the mid-to-late 1970s. 'The confusions and inefficiencies in that investigation cast a long shadow over the work of the police even today. No longer do you hear the police talking of the completely ineffective strategy of "leaving no stone unturned". Instead, they now have highly trained and sophisticated teams that work steadily through the appropriate options. These actions will be guided by behavioural and other scientists...'

In reference to the west London night observations, 'no stone unturned' was precisely the phrase used by Detective Superintendent Bill Baldock. The Nude Murders investigation was a textbook example of this now-redundant approach. It is also clear that the dictatorial management structure of the squad was not fit for purpose in efficiently managing such an immense multi-inquiry. Since the sixties, academic study of serial murder has expanded exponentially and new disciplines developed to assist law enforcement. A look at contemporary profiling techniques further reveals how the search for the Nude Killer could have been narrowed down, improving the chances of exposing him.

Serial killers have been around a lot longer than their label. Britain had two particularly notorious multiple murderers in the 19th century. Mary Ann Cotton may have poisoned as many as 21 people, including several husbands and 11 of her 13 children. Fifteen years after she was hanged aged 40 at Durham Gaol in 1873. Whitechapel in London became the scene of five grisly prostitute murders attributed to Jack the Ripper. News of these ghastly crimes was relayed around the world and the case is still the subject of books and speculation today. The Whitechapel case bore similarities to the Nude Killings and comparisons were constantly made between the investigations in the media during the 1960s. The victims in both cases were impoverished prostitutes and the murderer was never identified.

Dr Thomas Neill Cream, George Chapman and George Joseph Smith were three killers who all preyed on women in the two decades after Jack the Ripper. Cream, the Lambeth Poisoner, was executed for the murder of four prostitutes in 1892, while Chapman and Smith were hanged in 1903 and 1915 respectively. Chapman had poisoned three women while Smith embezzled and murdered three women in what became known as the 'Brides in the Bath' case. There were no serial killer cases between that of George Smith in 1915 and 1943, when John Christie committed his first murder. Prior to the Nude Murders, the police managed to end the killing careers of Acid Bath Murderer John George Haigh (hanged 1949) and spree killer Peter Manuel (1958).

The Nude Killings came at a point in the post-war era when serial murder became more common. The Moors Murderers Myra Hindley and Ian Brady shocked Britain by torturing and killing five children and young people the year after the Nude Killings ceased, while during the 1970s serial murder cases would hit the headlines with the trials of Patrick Mackay, Donald Neilson, Trevor Hardy and the duo of Archibald Hall and Michael Kitto. The most traumatic manhunt would be for Peter Sutcliffe, which lasted five long years from 1975 to early 1981 and saw police repeatedly miss opportunities to arrest him while the death toll rose to 13 women and seven attempted murders (some argue it was more). The 1981 Byford Report on the investigation highlighted the failures of West Yorkshire officers, including that they allowed themselves to be misled by a hoaxer, their paper-based incident room was deluged with information they could not assimilate, and that despite Sutcliffe being repeatedly interviewed, the right connections were never made to indicate he was the prime suspect. The prospect of inefficient management during the Nude Murders hunt cited in the previous chapter still seems to have been around a decade later during the Ripper investigation. Here the Byford report noted, 'The senior detectives were not well equipped in management terms to control an inquiry of the size and scale which the Ripper inquiry proved to be.'

Meanwhile, the USA experienced a similar eruption of serial killer cases. The quintessential horror figure from this era was undoubtedly Ted Bundy, rapist, burglar, kidnapper, necrophile and serial killer of numerous women. The FBI reported that motiveless crimes – the category that included serial murders – made up 8.5 per cent of homicides in 1976, 17.8 per cent in 1981 and 22.5 per cent in 1986. Eighty per cent of all known serial-killing men in the US appeared between 1950 and 1995. Still, while the murder rate in general continued to rise in the US into the early 1990s, serial murders always remained a small percentage of that growing total. There were more of them, but they were still rare in terms of the total number of murders. The FBI quoted an estimate that serial killers made up less than one per cent of all homicides each year. Such scarcity was no doubt another factor in making them a big challenge for investigators.

It was in the 1970s that the term 'serial killer' started to gain currency. It has been attributed to an FBI instructor, Robert Ressler, who, while lecturing at the British police academy in Bramshill in 1974, heard mention of some crimes being in a series. While author John Brophy also used the phrase 'serial murderer' several times in his 1966 book *The Meaning of Murder*, it seems Ressler helped to make it a popular term among the police community. The definition has been open to interpretation, though it is generally accepted that a serial killer murders, most often with premeditation, at least three people over a timescale of more than 30 days. The FBI Crime Classification Manual uses three categories for such killers – organised, disorganised and mixed.

The organised plan their crimes; often stalk their victims; strike up a conversation with them; then frequently capture, kill and dispose of them. They may also have sex with them while they are alive and often use a vehicle. This type can be of attractive appearance, intelligent and employed. They may study police tactics and can be extremely difficult to find.

Disorganised offenders kill spontaneously. They rarely talk to their victims; use a weapon they find at the scene; position the body; and they may perform sex acts with the corpse. They may mutilate the body and use excessive violence. Use of a vehicle does not often feature. They may have been mistreated as youngsters, sexually inhibited and from a chaotic family.

These definitions are vague, but a useful starting point in defining serial killers. They are also not restrictive. Some killers show characteristics of both the organised and disorganised types, though the Nude Killer clearly fits the organised pattern. As for the root causes of psychopathy, science is still wrestling with that question. There is no satisfactory answer to how much it is the product of a damaged upbringing and to what extent it is genetically wired, though recent studies suggest DNA is decisive.

When it comes to what drives the motivation of these murderers, two American criminologists, Ronald Holmes and James De Burger, analysed 400 serial killers and came up with the following broad definitions in 1988. The first is the visionary killer, driven by voices or a vision to attack a category of people. A mission killer has a goal of killing a targeted group. Hedonistic killers commit murder for the thrill or lust of it. The final group identified is the power/control type who enjoy having total control over a victim.

Another tool that has helped investigators to identify and get an insight into the thinking of serial murderers was developed by Canadian psychologist Dr Robert D Hare. It was during the 1960s at the University of British Columbia that his interest in how to classify psychopaths took shape. His Psychopathy Checklist was developed in the 1970s and has helped the police and other professionals to understand psychopathy and how it is linked to serial murder. It is a complex diagnostic tool that assesses the symptoms of a psychopath's personality in two ways. First, it scores them in terms of their emotions – they tend to be glib, egocentric, lack remorse or guilt for their actions, have little or no empathy for others, and they are deceitful and shallow. Second, they can be socially deviant, so the clinician will assess the subject's level of anti-social behaviour, impulsiveness, irresponsibility and their excitement-seeking traits. Which adds up to the view that most people today would have of psychopaths as cold, manipulative and self-serving. While not all psychopaths are serial murderers, they often have many of these characteristics.

The FBI, which utilises much of this research, also tries to ensure its agents do not fall for the myths that have developed alongside the depiction of serial killers in books, films and on TV. These include:

- Serial killers are all dysfunctional loners. In fact, they may be married with children, hold down jobs and be respected in the community.

- They are all white men. They actually come from all racial groups and, though less common, include women.

- They are only motivated by sex. Rage, thrills, money and attention-seeking are among other motivations.

- They travel to kill. Most have a defined geographic area or anchor point, such as their home or place of work (which will be looked at in the next chapter).
- They can't stop killing. Some do cease their campaigns of death, among them the Zodiac Killer, who murdered between six and 37 victims in San Francisco between 1968–69; Dennis Rader, the BTK Killer (bind, torture, kill), who halted his murder spree in 1991, during which he had killed 10 people in Kansas starting in 1974. He was caught in 2005 when he sought media attention; and, of course, the Nude Killer in London.
- They are evil geniuses. Time and again in fictional depictions serial killers are Chianti-quaffing savants like Hannibal Lecter, whereas in fact they are like most other people, ranging in intelligence from borderline to above average levels, and many are very dull.
- They want to be caught. It's more that they become cocky and feel empowered the more crimes they commit; eventually they make mistakes and give themselves away. The Nude Killer certainly did not want to be caught.

Another misleading fictional depiction is that the experts who use training in these psychological tools – criminal profilers as seen on TV shows such as *Cracker* or *Criminal Minds* – can predict exactly what a serial killer will do next, what their favourite colour is and whether they had a mother fixation. Such characters led to an over-inflated view of what profiling could achieve. In addition, the 1992 case of Rachel Nickell, the young mother murdered on Wimbledon Common, dented the image of criminal profiling when the investigation went badly wrong, resulting in the court case against Colin Stagg collapsing and police use of a honey trap to catch him being criticised by the judge. Stagg fitted a profile provided by profiler Paul Britton, who faced a British Psychological Society disciplinary hearing in 2002 for offering advice not backed by accepted scientific practice. The committee heard that the honey trap had been approved by senior Met officers and Britton's work had been checked by an FBI profiling unit. The case against him was eventually dismissed on the grounds that the eight years that had passed made a fair hearing impossible. The actual killer was later found to be Robert Napper, who had been sent to Broadmoor in 1995 for the murder of Samantha Bisset and her four-year-old daughter, Jazmine, in their Plumstead flat.

Some detectives have since voiced disdain for offender profilers, but the profession has improved a lot in the last 25 years. It is now a recognised profession in the UK. The criminal profiler has made way for the behavioural investigative adviser (BIA). Armed with a degree in psychology or criminology, they have a detailed knowledge of behavioural science and take a strictly analytical approach when advising senior investigating officers. The emphasis is on solidly scientific and verifiable profiling techniques. The purpose has been to banish to the past abstract psychological 'insights' or vague, unsupported hunches like those expressed by detectives in 1965, who speculated that the Nude Murders were possibly the 'work of a schizophrenic', driven by sex or a 'mad desire to be vindictive to society'.

BIAs work for the National Crime Agency in London and are not keen to give away their operational techniques to prying criminal eyes. They did confirm to me that homicide and sexual offences were the cases on which they are most often called to assist. Moreover, suspect prioritisation is 'a critical aspect of the work' – and one that the Nude Murders investigation, swamped by an indiscriminate range of potential culprits, was crying out for. BIAs can help to reduce time wasted investigating wholly irrelevant suspects by building a picture of an offender through assessing the crime scene, the offender's level of planning, their amount of aggression and other factors.

A particularly powerful tool for the BIA is geographic profiling, which has a proven record in helping the police to capture elusive serial rapists and killers around the world. The next chapter shows how this relatively new methodology offers an outline of two small areas in west London where detectives could have focused their search for the Nude Killer.

Chapter 18

Is This Where the Killer Lived?

Dr Kim Rossmo is a balding, middle-aged Canadian, a former detective inspector with the Vancouver Police Department. In a TV crime show he would be portrayed by a ruggedly glamorous actor with an intrepid glint in his eye. In the real world, Rossmo's brilliant profiling work is in the less action-packed realm of analysis and research. But it has had spectacular results, helping the police around the globe to catch many terrible serial criminals. When he speaks he is earnest, using words carefully to get his meaning across with precision. No doubt this is a reflection of a sharp intellect, with which he refined an investigative technique called geographic profiling. This tool has enabled investigators to understand the hunting methods of killers, rapists, arsonists, bombers, card fraudsters, burglars and other serial offenders. The analysis is done by a computer algorithm, utilising crime-scene locations and other data to define areas where a serial criminal most likely lives or works. It could have proved vital to Scotland Yard's murder squad in 1964–65.

With Kim Rossmo's assistance and analysis in this chapter, we will be able to see where the Nude Killer most probably had the base from which he started his hunt for victims. Such a profile would have enabled John du Rose and Bill Baldock to direct their searches in two much smaller areas. These were around Hammersmith and a zone where Notting Hill meets Holland Park. The 24-square-mile haystack the two detectives tried to sift would have shrunk dramatically.

After a 21-year police career, Rossmo is today based at Texas State University, where he heads the Centre for Geospatial Intelligence and Investigation. He has used his software, called Rigel, to assist police forces in the USA, Canada, the UK, Mexico, Germany, Italy, Australia, Turkey and elsewhere, sometimes with spectacular success. In addition to geographic profiling, his other area of special interest is analysing where police investigations can go wrong. His insights on the Nude Murders case are thought provoking. About geo-profiling, he has written, 'Because investigative efforts can produce hundreds and even thousands of potential suspects, difficulties with information overload often develop. This is the classic needle-in-the-haystack situation. Information management problems are sometimes the reason an investigation ends up as a cold case.' An assessment that sums up the Nude Murders case pretty well.

This kind of work typifies today's more scientific approach to crime data and its analysis. Where once detectives relied on gut instinct and experience, Rossmo is reluctant to draw conclusions without rigorous analysis to back it up. Consequently, he is dubious about some conclusions of the 1960s murder squad. He is certainly not convinced by the supposition that the killer might have asphyxiated the women while being fellated – 'highly speculative and quite improbable,' he said.

He also questioned police assumptions about the type of clientele the women mixed with, and therefore the possible status of the murderer. The police felt that few of the victims' clients were of 'lower status', as Bill Baldock put it at the time. Rossmo's take on this, 'It is possible this was the situation back in the early 1960s, but it would not be so today. The victims were streetwalkers, with tattoos and missing teeth, which makes me question this conclusion about their client group. Determining how much they charged for sex would help establish the likelihood of any "lower status" customers using their services.' In fact, on several occasions the punters were clearly not high-earning professionals; for example, the self-employed builder Ernest Forrest, who was with Elizabeth Figg on her last night, or one of the unidentified motorists who picked up Frances Brown and her friend, and was said to speak 'roughly'. It was also reported that they charged as little as £1 for sex (roughly £19 in today's money, and that's what Hannah Tailford asked of one punter, a shopkeeper). So, it is clear the killer could have come from a broader social spectrum than detectives thought at the time.

Baldock was also convinced that the killer was 'a person of some standing, either professionally or an established businessman'. Again, Rossmo found that hard to support. 'I don't see any rationale for this conclusion other than the claim [made above] regarding the nature of their clients. Most serial murderers are lower-to-middle class.' Other points put forward at the time that he found speculative were that there was some significance in the victims having missing teeth and that four of them had tattoos. Missing teeth would not be strange if it was common to have them pulled 50 or 60 years ago – and it was. The first Adult Dental Health Survey in 1968 revealed that 37 per cent of people over the age of 16 had full dentures. Given the nature of the victim group (streetwalkers using drugs), Rossmo said that missing teeth and tattoos were probably not out of the ordinary.

The unstinting glare of such analytical reassessment puts into perspective the kind of conclusions and assumptions that were made by detectives five decades ago.

In 1995 Rossmo became the first police officer in Canada to get a doctorate in criminology. It was Crime Pattern Theory that sparked his interest at Simon Fraser University. This stated that crime locations are not random but are connected by the environment of buildings and roads. An insight into these patterns can reveal an offender's probable base. We all have a particular style in how we deal with the geography – the layout – around us, and offenders are no different. Looking at the pattern of their movements can highlight something of their method.

Geographic profiling does not unmask the killer, however. The only way the Nude Murders case, like all other crimes, could have been wrapped up would have been if the police had a confession, a witness or physical evidence. 'You don't solve a case with a profile,' Rossmo said. 'Our role is to support the detective.' But a geo-profile would have been a compass showing Scotland Yard where its overstretched officers could have concentrated its search.

While a doctoral student at Simon Fraser University, Rossmo began to develop his Rigel software, the basis of what is today an incredibly sophisticated geographic-profiling tool used by police forces around the world. He explained to me. 'The Rigel software was developed as a result of my PhD research, which led to the geographic-profiling algorithm. The first system was one I built myself; it had maybe about 500 lines of code. When it became evident that this was something that police forces wanted to adopt, it was obvious that my jalopy-system wasn't going to cut it. With the help primarily of the

Royal Canadian Mounted Police, I got funding and real pro-grammers, and we were able to develop the Rigel system, which now has something like a million lines of code. That gives you some sense of how it has progressed.'

The analogy Rossmo uses to explain the theory behind geographic profiling is a rotating lawn sprinkler. It is hard to predict where the next drop of water will land, but when enough drops have fallen the pattern makes it easy to see where the sprinkler is. We all have a comfort zone where we spend most of our time. Offenders tend to commit their crimes when they find targets within their comfort zones. Many crimes take place close to an offender's home, sometimes no more than a mile away. The further away from his home that you go, the less likely it is he will offend. This is called distance decay. On the other hand, he is unlikely to commit a crime on his doorstep, to protect his identity. So, the area around his residence is known as a buffer zone. The balance between the buffer zone and distance decay is the area where he is often likely to commit his crimes.

This pattern may vary depending on the crime and offender type. For example, robbers typically travel a greater distance from their home than burglars, while adult criminals will travel further than juveniles. Meanwhile, murderers tend to dump their victims further from their home than the places where they encounter them.

To produce a geographic profile using Rossmo's Rigel soft-ware, an analyst would spend a lot of time at the crime scenes and take into account factors such as the weather, nearby bus stops, pubs, types of housing and businesses. Rossmo explains the analyst's goals. 'What's the hunting style of the criminal? How did the offender know about the location? You try to understand the crime from the offender's perspective.'

The analyst enters the crime locations and other data into the software. Rigel places a 40,000-pixel grid over a map of the crimes, and weights each pixel according to the mathematical interplay between the buffer zone and the distance-decay function. The result is a jeopardy surface, a three-dimensional heat map, with the peaks showing the most probable areas of the offender's base, from where he begins his search for crime sites. This location is usually his home or workplace.

The power of geo-profiling is highlighted by Operation Lynx in the UK, a case that Rossmo was called in to help on. This was a huge and complex investigation into a series of five horrific rapes that took place between 1982 and 1995. The rapist forced his way into the car of his first victim in Bradford and drove to a deserted airport car park, where he attacked her. A month later, he raped a woman in the car park of a Leeds hospital (1983), striking again in Leicester (1984), Nottingham (1993) and at a multi-storey car park in Leeds (1995). Involving five different police forces and 180 officers, it became the largest police hunt since the Yorkshire Ripper investigation.

Rossmo was approached by Operation Lynx in 1997. Creating a geographic profile involving three different regions would have been difficult. But there was a lead that had potential. During the second attack the rapist had used a stolen Ford Cortina. The owner's credit card had been left in the car and someone had used it several times in Leeds. If that was the rapist, these locations could also be used in the analysis. Rossmo produced a geographic profile using both the rape sites and the fraudulent credit card purchases. This result highlighted two neighbourhoods in central Leeds – Millgarth and Killingbeck. Using a partial fingerprint from one of the victims' vehicles, a search was made for men aged 35–52 with minor criminal records and presiding in the two central Leeds districts. In 1998, after nearly a thousand hours spent searching 7,000 fingerprint records, a match was made with a man called Clive Barwell. DNA subsequently confirmed he was guilty of the rapes. It turned out that Barwell lived in Killingbeck. His address was in the top three per cent of the geo-profile hit-score percentage. His mother lived in Millgarth. Barwell pleaded guilty and in 1999 he was sentenced to eight life terms in prison.

The value of Rossmo's profile in highlighting the Millgarth and Killingbeck neighbourhoods was important. Operation Lynx had involved 24,000 police actions (inquiries), the testing of 2,177 DNA records and reviewing almost 10,000 suspects. Further names – 33,628 – were entered into the inquiry's database, more than any other case in British history.

All of this demonstrates how important it is to be able to prioritise suspects and addresses in an investigation. The identification of Millgarth and Killingbeck gave the huge Operation Lynx two areas on which to focus their resources, giving detectives the breakthrough they needed.

It is a sad irony of the Nude Murders case that the police were still a few years from being able to use such a technique. A British forensic scientist, Professor Stuart Kind, who died in 2003, had actually been a pioneer of profiling just 15 years after John du Rose's investigation was wound down. This was during the Yorkshire Ripper hunt. In 1980, in typically British-boffin style, he was sent to Yorkshire as part of a review team with four senior detectives – not quite sure what he was supposed to be doing. This was during a five-and-a-half-year reign of horror in which women were hit, usually with a hammer, in ferocious sexual assaults, with 13 of them dying. Kind analysed the locations and times of the attacks, stating, 'I decided to apply the mind of the navigator to see if it would yield any indication of the base of operations of the Yorkshire Ripper on the assumption that, throughout the series, he had used the same starting point.' Further assumptions were that the killer would return home immediately after an attack and that the later an attack had occurred, the more likely it would be closer to his base. Kind made calculations to determine a centre of gravity for the crime scene locations. The findings he gave to the police were that the killer was based in the Manningham/Shipley part of Bradford, an area far removed from where the police had been looking. Less than a month later, in January 1981, Peter Sutcliffe was arrested in Sheffield during a routine police stop. It was found that he lived in Heaton, midway between Manningham and Shipley. Though Kind did not get the credit for the arrest, his approach was inspired.

Today, Kim Rossmo's Rigel system is at the leading edge of the work Kind had embarked on. I discussed the Nude Murders case with Rossmo, knowing that in addition to his police work he had from time to time analysed historic cases. Jack the Ripper in 1888, the Austin Servant Girl Murders case of a few years earlier in 1884–85, the Axeman of New Orleans in 1918–19, and the Zodiac Killer of the late 1960s/early 1970s are among those he has revisited. Based on data supplied by the author, he agreed to run an analysis of the London crime locations, with the caveat that greater access to the police reports of the time and data about the era might have enhanced the analysis.

The result is two peak areas connected to the Nude Murders (see the map in the photograph section). Hot spot 1 to the west stretches from central Hammersmith by the Tube station, up to Boscombe Road, swooping across to Valetta Road, Chiswick, and down to Chiswick High Road. It includes Stamford Brook Tube station, Stamford Brook Common, much of Ravenscourt Park and the mostly residential surrounding streets. The hottest parts of this peak area are between Abinger Road and Stamford Brook Tube, straddling Goldhawk Road north of Dalling Road.

Hot spot 2, to the east of Shepherd's Bush Road, spans Holland Park Avenue. It takes in the southern area of Notting Hill, including part of Portland Road, Lansdowne Road and Ladbroke Grove. South of Holland Park Avenue it includes Campden Hill Road, much of Holland Park itself, and an area around Addison Road. It also includes Holland Park Tube station. Hot spot 2 is surrounded by the kerb-crawling areas of Shepherd's Bush, Notting Hill and Queensway. Here, the hottest parts are around Holland Park, Holland Park Mews and Notting Hill Gate, just east of Notting Hill Tube station.

The top five per cent of these hot spots (seen in the most brightly coloured areas on the map) estimate a 70 per cent degree of confidence that the Nude Killer either lived or worked there. Though less likely, it might also be a recent past residence of the offender or a relative's house if he spent a lot of time there.

As you would expect from the analysis, none of the victims were found within these two hot spots.

The total area of hot spot 1 is approximately 1.6 square miles, while hot spot 2 is a bit over a square mile. Just under three square miles in total for the murder squad to focus on, instead of the mammoth 24-square miles the original investigation attempted with house-to-house inquiries and only half completed. Armed with such a profile Scotland Yard's hunt for the Nude Killer could have been refined to target these areas in more detail. They could have prioritised identified suspects residing or working in them. They could also have zoned in on the addresses of suspect drivers seen kerb-crawling, particularly those in grey Hillman Huskys. They could have sifted police records for local individuals who had been involved with prostitutes previously, as offenders or victims, particularly in instances where there had been violence (rape, assault, robbery, murder). They could have focused media and canvassing campaigns in these two areas; and, finally, they could have checked on locals with a connection to the Heron Trading Estate, where the bodies had been kept.

The police could have given priority to the mass of tips from the public that came in via telephone and letter from the two target areas. When all police officer Stop Books were checked, special attention could have gone to those for F and T divisions, which recorded persons stopped at night in the Hammersmith and Kensington areas.

Rossmo mentioned a further constructive routine he follow. 'If this was an active case, I would meet with detectives to discuss the geographic profile. We would then brainstorm appropriate strategies. This almost always results in new and useful ideas as the investigative team know all the ins and outs of the case.'

Much wasted effort could have been avoided. For example, the house-to-house inquiries in which 17 officers spent five months from March to August 1965 taking dust samples from every shed and garage – in fact, anywhere a body could have been kept really got nowhere. Some 648 streets were visited and an incredible 120,000 people interviewed, before the effort was abandoned. Only half the 24-square mile area had been covered.

Another strategy could have entailed revisiting suspects who had been discounted. During the Heron Estate inquiries the police had found a 39-year-old BBC commissionaire, or uniformed doorman, who behaved oddly when questioned about his movements. He had worked on the estate for several years, first as an employee of Palm Toffee Limited. He became a night watchman for the property when that firm left the building in 1961. The BBC acquired the tenancy in May 1964 and the man took up the job as commissionaire in January 1965. The police wondered about him because he was night watchman of the vacant building for around three years. It was situated on Kendal Avenue, overlooking the unmade road to where Bridie O'Hara was deposited, 50 yards away. He also started his BBC role 19 days before she was found. When the police spoke to this man they were struck by how extremely nervous he was. They decided to interview him on two further occasions, before talking to other employees who knew him. They also looked into his private life, but failed to find anything to strengthen their suspicions about him. However, the man lived in Cardross Street, Hammersmith; a road that features prominently in hot spot 1.

This might have given detectives a good reason to take another look at a man whose nervousness had raised their antennae. Peter Sutcliffe was interviewed and released nine times during the Yorkshire Ripper inquiry. It seems likely that some of those eliminated during the Nude Murders manhunt would have warranted re-investigation had detectives at the time had some kind of geographic focus.

Adjoining Cardross Street is Aldensley Road, where, as seen in chapter 15, child murderer Harold Jones moved in late 1965/1966. Before Aldensley Road, Jones had been living in Fulham until 1962 and Putney until 1965. If he had a connection with the neighbourhood around Aldensley Road before moving there, perhaps a property or work, the killer of two girls would surely have been of interest to murder detectives focused on these peak areas. This is, of course, speculation, but it remains a sobering fact that such a callous killer seems to have passed under the radar of the Nude Murder investigation.

Looking at these profiling tools is not an attempt to say the 1960s murder squad was not competent. Its members were diligent, incredibly hard working and determined to find the man who asphyxiated the seven young prostitutes. Instead, it is a way to gain some perspective on the investigation and understand why, within the confines of the best practice and technology of the period, it failed to expose the guilty man.

With hindsight it can be seen that the dictatorial management of the investigation was going to struggle with the mass of statements, tips and data generated by such a large, unfocused investigation. While they did not directly solve crimes, behavioural and geographic profiling techniques can support and guide investigations. If the techniques had been available in the early 1960s, they might have helped to ferret out the Nude Killer, whose escape mocked the victims and all justice.

'I have no personal hate in my heart for this man… though naturally I should be interested to see exactly what he is,' John du Rose said in May 1965, at a time when the chief superintendent was still confident the investigation would succeed.

This was the biggest police manhunt ever seen at the time. Unfortunately, we will probably never know how close they came to catching the Nude Killer.

Chapter 19

A Killer in Plain Sight

Somebody killed six or seven prostitutes in swinging 1960s London and got away with it. He was probably spotted a couple of times, and was very likely heard while disposing of his last victim, but each time he melted back into the capital's anonymous corners.

It is a crime that taunts us from the past. To this day there has been no justice for the victims – Elizabeth Figg, Hannah Tailford, Irene Lockwood, Helen Barthelemy, Mary Fleming, Frances Brown and Bridie O'Hara. While all media attention at the time was devoted to the police investigation and the lurid lifestyles of London's 'vice girls', the women themselves were largely forgotten. There was also little thought for the victims when the controversy broke out over whether John du Rose had known who the killer was all along. By claiming, on flimsy evidence, that the killer was Mungo Ireland, the Scottish night watchman who committed suicide, du Rose was effectively saying to the victims' families that the case was closed, job done. If the claim was not valid – and there are many reasons to think it was a face-saving exercise by du Rose – then that was a disservice to the dead women's families and descendants.

Some of their children were fostered and they spent the intervening years learning about their mothers and reconnecting with family members. They all deserved an accurate appraisal of the case's status. It is possible that the killer is still alive. Certainly, one of the men under suspicion, the Disgraced Cop described as a 'strong' suspect by Detective Superintendent Bill Baldock, was alive during the researching of this book. This man was interviewed, along with his wife, and investigated in depth in 1965. Despite his 'mental history, knowledge of the area and background' apparently making him a strong contender, the Disgraced Cop could not be charged. No physical evidence or material witnesses could connect him to the victims. Which begs the question: during all the many interviews and inquiries during the entire investigation, did the police ever get close to finding their man?

Time and again suspects were not picked out in an identity parade, their premises were searched and nothing was found, dust samples were taken but no match was established. Time and again Baldock notes there was 'no evidence to hand despite many inquiries', the suspect 'did not possess a car, nor could he drive one', 'no evidence was found', 'again no useful information was obtained', 'no evidence was found to connect him to any of the murdered women'. And so on.

There are two possibilities here. The first is that the murder squad had identified their man but failed to realise it. Baldock mentioned on several occasions that 'time did not permit' them to take certain inquiries further or that 'time or lack staff' did not allow inquiries to be completed. Just as detectives on the Yorkshire Ripper hunt confronted Peter Sutcliffe nine times and let him go, did one of these curtailed inquiries enable the Nude Killer to slip away? Was a vital piece of evidence overlooked allowing a suspect to evade further police scrutiny?

The second possibility is that the guilty man was never even suspected by detectives. Kim Rossmo told me, 'It is definitely possible that the reason they were unable to find sufficient evidence to charge anyone was because they never had the right person... There is nothing about the identified suspects that suggests they should be regarded as anything other than suspects. Dozens, if not hundreds, of people with dodgy pasts and suspicious behaviours come to the attention of the police in major inquiries, especially in serial murder cases. Concluding that a suspect is the offender in the absence of very strong evidence is a mistake.' The suspects described were the men who received the most in-depth police scrutiny, including the Disgraced Cop and night watchman Mungo Ireland. It is easy to assume that the killer was among the group of top suspects. But hundreds, possibly thousands, of other men were also questioned or checked out. As Rossmo makes clear with this hypothetical example, 'If you look at it in just numbers, and I'm looking at 7,000 suspects they interviewed [on the Heron Trading Estate], the probability that he is in the 6,990 who are not top suspects is still higher than the top 10. Just bear in mind that even if you have the top suspects, it could be one of the ones that just didn't come to their [the murder squad's] attention.'

Looked at in these terms and in the light of problems already laid out – a vast investigation spread thinly that could not properly process all the data coming in – it is perhaps not that surprising that a devious, determined murderer could stay in the shadows. One fact should be borne in mind: the officers on this case had never experienced an inquiry of this type or scale before. What had worked on previous cases did not work here. This was a huge challenge for everyone involved.

The Nude Murders hunt was certainly not the first or the last to struggle to catch a serial killer. Jack the Ripper had infamously escaped Scotland Yard's detectives just 77 years before the Nudes Murders case. The Zodiac Killer in the US taunted the authorities in letters to the San Francisco Bay Area press, but he was never caught and the case, dating from the late 1960s, remains open today. And the nature of the apprehension of some serial killers further attests to how difficult they can be to identify, even showing that luck can be the vital ingredient in unmasking them. Ted Bundy confessed to 30 murders in seven US states between 1974 and 1978, though the actual total could have been higher. It was not a brilliant piece of Sherlockian sleuthing that unmasked him but a routine traffic stop by a Utah Highway Patrol officer, Sergeant Bob Hayward. He simply became suspicious of Bundy's VW Beetle passing at 2.30am through the pleasant neighbourhood where Hayward happened to live. It was another diligent patrol officer, Sergeant Robert Ring, accompanied by probationer Robert Hydes, who brought Peter Sutcliffe in for questioning after a routine stop in Sheffield on 2 January 1981. A five-year reign of murder that shocked Britain and rocked West Yorkshire police was brought to an end by uniformed officers on patrol. Thank goodness for no-nonsense sergeants.

The Nude Murders squad never got a break like that. The driver of the suspect grey Hillman Husky blundered when he almost hit Alfred Harrow's Bedford van in Ealing and when he was spotted by the workman in Chiswick. But he rode his luck both times and got away.

So, what kind of man was he?

I believe the killer was an officer, but not the disgraced detective suspected by Bill Baldock. A case against him could not be made and there it must rest. Yet the possibility remains that the real killer was a police officer who was close to the investigation but never struck anyone as suspicious. If he was a man who, in Kim Rossmo's words, 'just didn't come to their attention', then he would have had a fantastic advantage in keeping ahead of the investigation.

Even as the inquiry was winding down, there were suspicions among some officers that the killer had been in their ranks. One, DC Barry Newman, told author Dick Kirby, 'I always thought the murderer was a copper.' The Nude Killer would not be the first police officer to use his job as cover for serial murder. John Reginald Christie was a War Reserve constable during the Blitz, a job that gave him the chance to pry into other people's business, lurk about at night and meet vulnerable young women selling sexual services. He met his first victim, Ruth Fuerst, when she was soliciting on Ladbroke Grove in 1943. Muswell Hill Murderer Dennis Nilsen, currently serving life imprisonment for killing at least 12 young men, had worked as a constable in London before he started killing.

In Angarsk, Russia, Mikhail Popkov used his patrol car to lure 22 women to be raped and murdered between 1992 and 2000. It was the introduction of mandatory DNA testing for all police officers in 2012 that led to the unmasking of 'The Werewolf'. In 2017 he confessed to killing 81 women in total. In the USSR volunteer police officer Gennady Mikhasevich murdered 36 women between 1971 and 1985 and was sometimes assigned to help investigate crimes he had committed. In California, Edmund Kemper, who had already served five years in a unit for the criminally insane for murdering his grandparents as a 15 year old, wanted to join the Highway Patrol. His domineering mother tried to have his juvenile murder record sealed to facilitate this, but in the end he was rejected for being too tall (6 feet 9 inches). He then hung out in bars and cafes with off-duty officers and became friendly with them. One even gave him a trainee's badge and ID card. When he began his next killing spree, during which he killed and mutilated eight women, he used these contacts to get inside details on the investigation. Also in the US, in 1973 Gerard Schaefer was sentenced for two murders committed while he was a sheriff's deputy in Martin County, Florida. He later boasted of having murdered more than 30 females.

There are many such cases. A police badge is the perfect veneer of authority for the type of personality that wants to appear to be a pillar of the community, thereby gaining the trust of unsuspecting, vulnerable victims. If most serial killers are power junkies then what could be more useful than to put on a uniform or carry a warrant card?

Being part of the investigation would have given the Nude Murderer multiple opportunities to facilitate and then hide his crimes.

For starters, all the reasons that Sun journalist Owen Summers gave in his 'Was Maniac Killer a Cop' exposé in 1972 are strong. A police officer who had served around west London would know the alleys and deserted spots where the victims were dumped. He would be able to win the confidence of the women, particularly during the height of the fear experienced by streetwalkers as the body count mounted. In his determination not to leave clues for the forensics teams, he would have been trained to remain calm and determined enough to strip his victims at a secret location. He would be resourceful and able to switch his plans as the murder squad mounted new initiatives. In particular, when the investigation went into overdrive during 1965 with night observations, house-to-house inquiries and WPCs disguised as prostitutes, this was the precise moment he quit. Had he realised he could no longer hunt prostitutes without attracting the attention of a fellow officer sooner or later?

For a rogue officer, his job would have even been valuable in conducting the murder campaign. The killer had a particular type of woman that he preferred – petite prostitutes. On night patrol as a detective, either observing kerb-crawlers or keeping an eye on the pubs and clubs of Notting Hill and Shepherd's Bush, he would have had an excellent vantage point from which to secretly search for and stalk his next victim without attracting suspicion. He could even have got to know them this way – identifying himself and asking if they had seen any dodgy punters would have been part of his job, after all. And, of course, he would never have to avoid the attention of the decoy women officers or the night-observation squads. He was part of the team.

Then there was the chilling incident recounted in chapter 8 that Frances Brown relayed to her friend, Vera Lynch, shortly before she disappeared in October 1964. She had been disturbed by a recent encounter with a man one night. sunnerved by this character, Frances left him in the van on this occasion, but not before he gave her a pound for her trouble, even though there had been no sexual activity.

Vera Lynch can have had little reason to make up or lie to the police about Frances's account. So, if the encounter was genuine and if he really was with CID, what was the officer doing there sitting in a van, chatting with a streetwalker and giving her money? He claimed he was on duty. According to Vera Lynch, Frances had told him 'that he could not nick her as he was on his own and the man said he had his mate up the road and could easily do it'. The man's claim that he was on duty sounds dubious. It is true that 28 officers received authority to use their private motor cars during the night observations to try to spot the killer on the move. But this was not until 23 February 1965, four months after Frances's reported encounter and her death. What is more, Frances apparently said the man's van was 'full of rubbish like clothes' and that it was grey. Both Alfred Harrow in Brentford and the Chiswick decorators described the suspicious van they saw as grey. These are circumstantial details but still flag up the possibility at least that Frances had met her murderer a short time before she disappeared. It would suggest a stalker-killer, a man carefully selecting his victims and using his police credentials – and generosity with cash – to inveigle his way into their acquaintanceship and trust. He even flattered her, saying she had 'a laughing face'. He may have unsettled Frances Brown but he clearly did not want to alienate her.

Frances told Vera that she met this stranger in October. She vanished later the same month. Did she meet him again? If he called her over on a second occasion and said he was interested in business this time, it is easy to imagine her willingly getting into his van again even if he had creeped her out the previous time. She had no doubt met all kinds of strange characters during her career as a prostitute. But, during a year in which four prostitutes had been murdered so far, at least this punter was a cop and free with his money. Senior detectives commented several times on the relative lack of violence displayed in these killings, how often the victims did not manage to put up a struggle. This implies the killer was good at making the women comfortable in his company, lowering their guard for when he assaulted them. As we have seen, modern research suggests this type of organised serial killer is a careful planner who stalks their victims and engages in controlled conversation with them, before capturing, killing and disposing of them at a separate location.

It is a frustrating fact in a case that frustrated Scotland Yard time and again that more is not known of this meeting from October 1964. Frances never gave Vera Lynch a description of the man she met or got the van's number plate. But of course she never expected to become the killer's next victim.

Did the man John du Rose and Bill Baldock were seeking already know what they were looking for and how they might plan to snare him? Baldock mentioned several times that the Nude Killer had left virtually no trace of evidence behind. Not one witness could be found who saw any of the seven victims being picked up in the street. Apart from two of his early crimes – when Hannah Tailford was found in the Thames with her nylons around her ankles and knickers in her mouth and the possible first victim, Elizabeth Figg, who was partially clothed – the killer was completely successful in hiding or destroying all the clothes, dentures and other belongings of his victims. The dust particles were a potential lead but became a long drawn-out dead end. Baldock came to believe as the investigation wound down that the reason the killer had used the Heron Trading Estate as his body store was that he in fact had no connection with the site. The murder squad had pinned great hopes on using the dust and paint particles to establish a link with the killer. Having devoted massive resources and man hours to finding the site and then interviewing 7,000 past and present employees, detectives must have been devastated to uncover no link there to a guilty man. It seems he had been too calculating to be caught through so elementary a mistake. Finally, the epic effort to find the suspicious grey Hillman Husky was abandoned in August 1965. But if the offender really was a murderous detective, what are the chances that he was driving a vehicle registered in his own name, or that he was only using one vehicle?

If the heavy police presence in west London during the spring of 1965 did force a rogue cop to stop the killing, then, as we have seen, it is not unknown for a serial murderer to fade away. The urge, the compulsion, may have dissipated. As former detective Andy Rose pointed out, 'If someone is driven to do this because something is missing in their lives and they find what's missing, then they don't need to do it until that thing gets missed again, and maybe it never will.' Perhaps he felt he could not get away with it forever. Or maybe, as author Peter Vronsky said of multiple killer Edmund Kemper, who gave himself up, a few even suffer burn-out. The 12 months from February 1964 to February 1965 had, after all, been a year of furious activity and near misses for the London slayer.

As has been recounted here, Scotland Yard pitched its best men and extensive resources into catching one of London's most prolific serial killers, but the guilty man escaped. Within the limits of expertise at the time, they gave all they had to finding him. It was not enough. They threw their net too wide and then, with a rather small, autocratic leadership, could not effectively assimilate all the statements and information that came in. We can see that dubious assumptions were made and huge efforts went into chasing futile leads, but we will never know what evidential connections and suspicious characters were overlooked.

It is sobering to think the killer could be alive today – perhaps only in his late 70s. Could he still be exposed for his crimes? It is hard to see how. The investigation is dormant, the original senior investigators have died and all the physical evidence has disappeared. The only way the truth might come out is if the aged killer walks into a police station today with a bag containing the victims' clothing and belongings, and gives a confession, accompanied by photographic/film evidence of the victims in his possession...

The crimes are largely forgotten now, no doubt partly due to a lack of public sympathy for the victims. This has also worked to the killer's advantage. He got away with multiple murders and his crimes have vanished from public attention with the passing decades. Moreover, John du Rose's questionable assertion that the killer committed suicide probably did little to maintain awareness among the public, the authorities and media that the killer could still be out there.

The Nude Murders case was extraordinary. A huge investigation, it rippled through 1960s swinging London, from the 'haute' establishment via the Profumo scandal through to the vice scene on the streets of west London. Having reviewed the case for months and spoken to experts, contemporaries and former detectives, digesting the investigation's almost countless dead ends, curtailed inquiries and false trails, my feeling is that the police never came close to catching the killer. There may have been a crucial link or connection that would have incriminated the perpetrator, but, if there was, it was missed. Perhaps they had the right man without realising it, but compelling evidence that would have exposed him was never found. My suspicion remains that the investigation never latched onto the guilty man. There was never one suspect who rose above circumstantial suspicion, who was tied by a shred of concrete forensic evidence to the victims or the crime scenes. The Nude Killer knew the risks he was running and left little trace of himself for the police. He evaded their searchlight, and yet he was probably in plain sight all along. He was most likely one of them.

Acknowledgements

A huge thank you to the many people who helped me with this book.

Brian Hook and Andy Rose spent many hours with me, generously sharing their expertise as former detectives, their insights and humour. Kim Rossmo was also extremely helpful and forthcoming with his unsurpassed experience in geographic profiling and investigation.

Peter Spindler, Bob Fenton, Albert Patrick, Chris Burke, 'Frank' Chris Gibbings, Goolistan Cooper and Brian Collett were invaluable in either facilitating or doing interviews for the book.

The wonderful team at Mirror Books were terrifically supportive – in particular Melanie Sambells, Fergus McKenna and Paula Scott.

Designer Julie Adams has brought the book alive with her cover and layouts.

I am also particularly indebted to Executive Editor Jo Sollis for her tremendous support and encouragement.

Sources

Murder Was My Business by John du Rose (WH Allen, 1971)
Autobiography of John du Rose

Jack of Jumps by David Seabrook (Granta Books, 2006)
Essential reading on the Nude Murders case because the
author had access to all the police files, but written in a
rambling style that may jar

Who Was Jack the Stripper? The Hammersmith nudes' murders by
Neil Milkins (Rose Heyworth Press, 2011)
Short but painstakingly researched theory proposing Harold
Jones as the killer

Found Naked and Dead: The facts behind the Thames-side murders
by Brian McConnell (New English Library, 1974)
The first, and highly speculative, account of the case

Laid Bare: The nude murders and the hunt for 'Jack the Stripper' by
Dick Kirby (The History Press, 2016)
A look at the case with emphasis on the viewpoint of the
police from all ranks involved

Crime and Corruption at the Yard: Downfall of Scotland Yard
by David I Woodland (Pen and Sword Books, 2015)
Memoir of an officer with 19 years' service in the
Metropolitan Police

Continues

CRIME AND CRIMINOLOGY

Mapping Murder: The secrets of geographical profiling by David Canter (Virgin Books, 2003)
Fascinating look at how geographic profiling can unmask serial criminals by the leading authority on the subject

A History of British Serial Killing: The shocking account of Jack the Ripper, Harold Shipman and beyond by David Wilson (Little, Brown, 2009)

Serial Killers: The method and madness of monsters by Peter Vronsky (Berkley, 2004)

Professionalizing Offender Profiling: Forensic and investigative psychology in practice edited by Laurence Alison and Lee Rainbow (Routledge, 2011)
Overview of how behavioural investigative advisers function as part of criminal investigations

Wicked Beyond Belief: The hunt for the Yorkshire Ripper by Michael Bilton (HarperCollins, 2003)
Powerful, in-depth account of the hunt for Peter Sutcliffe

Yorkshire Ripper: The secret murders by Chris Clark and Tim Tate (John Blake Publishing, 2015)
Thought-provoking look into the possibility that Peter Sutcliffe's killing career began earlier and was more prolific than originally thought

The Survivor: Blue murder, bent cops, vengeance, vendetta in 1960s gangland by Jimmy Evans and Martin Short (Mainstream Publishing, 2002) Gangland memoir

Born Gangster by Jimmy Tippett Jnr with Nicola Stow (John Blake Publishing, 2014)
Memoir about the criminal world

STEPHEN WARD CASE

Stephen Ward Was Innocent, OK: The case for overturning his conviction by Geoffrey Robertson (Biteback Publishing, 2013)
Polemic argued with passion and clarity that Stephen Ward was legally scapegoated by the establishment

The Trial of Stephen Ward by Ludovic Kennedy (Gollancz, 1964)
Fascinating contemporary insight into the trial by a campaigning journalist who was there

LONDON AND CAPITAL SOCIETY

Windrush: The irresistible rise of multi-racial Britain by Mike and Trevor Phillips (HarperCollins, 1998)
Fascinating first-hand accounts of the changing racial landscape of post-war London

Streets of Sin: A dark biography of Notting Hill by Fiona Rule (The History Press, 2015)
Well-researched survey of the area's more notorious episodes since the 18th Century

Murder in Notting Hill by Mark Olden (Zero Books, 2011)
Account of the Kelso Cochrane murder is a riveting background snapshot of Notting Hill in the late fifties/early sixties

Continues

Capital Affairs: London and the making of the permissive society by Frank Mort (Yale University Press, 2010)
Pleasure and danger in London – how British culture was affected by post-war scandals

Common Prostitutes and Ordinary Citizens: Commercial sex in London, 1885–1960 by Julia Laite (Palgrave Macmillan, 2012)
Detailed exploration of commercial sex and its criminalisation in London 1885–1960

Policing Notting Hill: Fifty years of turbulence by Tony Moore (Waterside Press, 2013)
Overview of the area and how it has been policed

Love Now, Pay Later?: Sex and religion in the fifties and sixties by Nigel Yates (SPCK, 2010)
Sex, attitudes and censorship in this post-war period

The Beatles' London by Piet Schreuders, Mark Lewisohn, Adam Smith (St Martin's Press, 1994)
Entertaining compendium, brilliantly illustrated

NEWSPAPERS AND MAGAZINES
UK media: *Daily Mirror, Sunday Mirror, The People, Daily Mail, The Sun, Daily Herald, The Times, News of the World, The Observer, Daily Telegraph*

US publications: *Time* magazine, *Chicago Tribune, Los Angeles Times, The Age, Independent* (Long Beach, California), *Bridgeport Telegram*

FICTION
Bad Penny Blues by Cathi Unsworth (Serpent's Tail, 2009)
Crime novel inspired by the case

The Boy in 7 Billion
Callie Blackwell and Karen Hockney

If you had a chance to save your dying son… wouldn't you take it?

Deryn Blackwell is a walking, talking miracle. At the age of 10, he was diagnosed with Leukaemia. Then 18 months later he developed another rare form of cancer called Langerhan's cell sarcoma. Only five other people in the world have it. He is the youngest of them all and the only person in the world known to be fighting it alongside another cancer, making him one in seven billion. Told there was no hope of survival, after four years of intensive treatment, exhausted by the fight and with just days to live, Deryn planned his own funeral.

But on the point of death – his condition suddenly and dramatically changed. His medical team had deemed this an impossibility, his recovery was nothing short of a miracle. Inexplicable. However, Deryn's desperate mother, Callie, was hiding a secret…

Callie has finally found the strength and courage to reveal the truth about Deryn's battle. The result is a book that everyone should read. It truly is a matter of life and death.

Also by Mirror Books

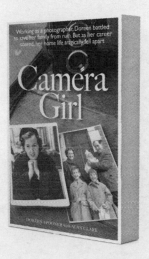

Camera Girl
Doreen Spooner with Alan Clark

The true story of a woman coping with a tragic end to the love of her life, alongside a daily fight to establish herself and support her children.

A moving and inspiring memoir of Doreen Spooner –
a woman ahead of her time. Struggling to hold her head high through the disintegration of the family she loves through alcoholism, she began a career as Fleet Street's first female photographer.

While the passionate affair and family life she'd always dreamed of fell apart, Doreen walked into the frantic world of a national newspaper. Determined to save her family from crippling debt, her work captured the Swinging Sixties through political scandals, glamorous stars and cultural icons, while her homelife spiralled further out of control.

The two sides of this book take you through a touching and emotional love story, coupled with a hugely enjoyable portrait of post-war Britain.

Mirror Books

Also by Mirror Books

1963 - A Slice of Bread and Jam
Tommy Rhattigan

Tommy lives at the heart of a large Irish family in derelict Hulme in Manchester, ruled by an abusive, alcoholic father and a negligent mother. Alongside his siblings he begs (or steals) a few pennies to bring home to avoid a beating, while looking for a little adventure of his own along the way.

His foul-mouthed and chaotic family may be deeply flawed, but amongst the violence, grinding poverty and distinct lack of hygiene and morality lies a strong sense of loyalty and, above all, survival.

During this single year – before his family implodes and his world changes for ever – Tommy almost falls foul of the welfare officers, nuns, police – and Myra Hindley and Ian Brady.

An adventurous, fun, dark and moving true story of the only life young Tommy knew.

The Green Bicycle Mystery
Antony M Brown

The first in a unique collection of books. Each tells the story of an unsolved true crime and then invites the reader to decide on the outcome. Beautifully presented with evidence images and maps – perfect for lovers of puzzles, mysteries and crime stories, this new collection of Cold Case Jury books will not only bring a murder story to life – it will make you part of it.

The series begins with the tragic case of Bella Wright: In a lonely lane running through rural Leicestershire in 1919, a solitary bicycle lies on its side, its metal frame catching the glow of the fading evening light.

Next to the bicycle, lying at an angle across the road, is a young woman. She is partly on her back, partly on her left side, with her right hand almost touching the mudguard of the rear wheel. Her legs rest on the roadside verge, where fronds of white cow parsley and pink rosebay rise above luxuriant summer foliage. On her head sits a wide-brimmed hat, daintily finished with a ribbon and bow. She is dressed in a pastel blouse and long skirt underneath a light raincoat. The blood-flecked coat begins the story...